Spitters, Beanballs, and the Incredible Shrinking Strike Zone

Spitters, Beanballs, and the Incredible Shrinking Strike Zone

The Stories Behind the Rules of Baseball

Revised Edition

by
Glen Waggoner
Kathleen Moloney
Hugh Howard

TRIUMPH
B O O K S
CHICAGO

Library of Congress Cataloging-in-Publication Data

Howard, Hugh, 1952-
    Spitters, beanballs, and the incredible shrinking strike zone/ by Hugh Howard, Kathleen Moloney, Glen Waggoner.
        p.cm.
    Rev. ed of: Baseball by the Rules: pine tar, spitballs, and midgets/ by Glen Waggoner, Kathleen Moloney, and Hugh Howard. c 1990.
    Includes Index.
    ISBN 1-57243-377-9
        1. Baseball—Rules. I. Moloney, Kathleen. II. Waggoner, Glen. Baseball by the rules. III. Title

GV877 .W34 1990
796.357'02'022--cd21

                                                                99-086122

This book is available in quantity at special discounts for your group or organization. For further information, contact:

Triumph Books
601 South LaSalle Street
Chicago, Illinois 60605
(312) 939-3330
Fax: (312) 663-3557

Printed in Canada.

ISBN 1-57243-377-9

Book design by Patricia Frey.

Cover design by Salvatore Concialdi.

Cover photo © Corbis/Bettmann/UPI.

CONTENTS

Acknowledgements

Our thanks go to Mitchell Rogatz, president and publisher of Triumph Books, for launching this venture once again, and to Heidi Hill, editor at Triumph, for helping to reassemble the pieces.

For their research guidance, we would like to express our appreciation to Timothy J. Wiles, Bill Francis, Frank Vito, Amy Essington, and Keri Elberson at the National Baseball Library and Archive. On past visits, others at the National Baseball Hall of Fame Library assisted us in our research, including Tom Heitz, Bill Dean, Joe Fetterman, Pat Kelly, Betty McCarthy, and Jon Blomquist. We also thank Lloyd Johnson of the Society of American Baseball Research.

Thanks, too, go to Sharon McIntosh, Betsy Lawrence, and, in particular, Dominick Abel, our literary agent, for helping to put this book back into play.

The ball, thrown by Yankees pitcher Tino Martinez, is about to hit Cleveland Indians base runner Travis Fryman. That much is obvious. What you don't see is that the Yankees' Chuck Knoblauch, covering on the play, is about to lose his cool and, worse yet, the game. The whole story is told in the Preface.

(AP/Wide World Photos)

"Dugout to dugout, the game happily remains unchanged in our changing world."

—Bill Veeck

Preface

The volume you hold in your hands is actually the third edition of *Spitters, Beanballs, and the Incredible Shrinking Strike Zone*. The first edition was published in 1987, while a second, updated edition appeared in 1990; both were published under the title *Baseball by the Rules*. This revised edition reflects rule changes and events up through much of the 1999 baseball season.

Why three editions? The rules haven't changed all that much. Perhaps the need for this book is expressed better by events, so we'll let a couple of actual occurrences speak for themselves.

In 1998, postseason play was barely underway when lots of folks found themselves referring to their rule books. Among them was Chuck Knoblauch, the Yankees second baseman, who chose a particularly bad time to debate the finer points of Rule 7.09k.

The circumstances were as follows. Game 2 of the American League Championship Series had gone into extra innings. The Yankees and Indians were tied 1–1 in the twelfth. With Indian Enrique Wilson on second, the batter laid down a sacrifice bunt and the Yankee pitcher fielded the ball. Knoblauch hustled over from his second-base position (so far, so good) to cover first. The throw never reached him, however, as it struck the runner on the back.

Knoblauch immediately made the call: he adjudged the runner to have been out of the base line and thus, he indicated to the umpire, the runner was obviously out. Unfortunately for the Yankees, Knoblauch forgot all about Rule 5.02, which says that the ball is alive until an umpire calls time. While Knoblauch was fervently making his case to the umpire, the ball rolled away from him. Meanwhile, Wilson raced around the bases and scored the winning run.

The Book doesn't play such an obvious and dramatic role in every game, but a knowledge of its intricacies is essential for the game's participants and a pleasure for those of us in the stands. Didn't most people have an opinion about that drive Mark McGwire stroked in Milwaukee for what would have been his sixty-sixth homer if it hadn't been ruled a ground-rule double? Or about Roberto Alomar's spitting incident? Or whether the tar on George Brett's bat should have negated his homer?

You'll find those stories here, as well as many others, new and old, that offer a sense of the game that is wonderfully alive today, yet steeped in the past. Baseball is a game that rewards attention to detail. Its fans are absorbed by box scores and such minutiae as lineup cards, double switches, ERAs, and the rest. The niche in the marketplace that this book has found attests to the intensity and diligence of baseball fans. They want to understand the nuances, and this book seeks to help them accomplish that.

So let's play ball!

G. W., K. M., and H. H.

Note to the Reader

pitters, Beanballs, and the Incredible Shrinking Strike Zone and the *Official Rules of Baseball* are not one and the same book. *Official Rules of Baseball* (which, for convenience, we have referred to in these pages as "The Book") is issued by the Commissioner of Baseball. It is a legalistic document, full of the dos and don'ts of the game of baseball. It isn't rich in character or indicative of the history and fun of baseball.

Spitters, Beanballs, and the Incredible Shrinking Strike Zone is intended to explicate The Book, to take each of the dry-as-toast rules and illuminate them with real-life stories. In short, *Spitters, Beanballs, and the Incredible Shrinking Strike Zone* is intended to do for the *Official Rules of Baseball* what being at the ballpark does for hot dogs.

In these pages we've tried to put the rules into the context of the game and to show how they work in real-life situations. And because we think that a knowledge of the evolution of the game enhances an understanding of it, we've included rule-change chronologies at the close of most chapters. At the end of the book there's also a compendious listing of all the major league rule changes in chronological order.

The organization of *Spitters, Beanballs, and the Incredible Shrinking Strike Zone* is the same as that of The Book—ten chapters—but within each chapter we have taken some small liberties with the organization in order to make this book more readable. There is a fair amount of repetition in The Book, particularly in Chapters 3, 4, and 5, and we've tried to keep it to a minimum while maintaining the substance of all the rules. We've also taken a few liberties with spelling; when The Book and Webster don't agree, we went with Webster.

When a rule is quoted or summarized, we cite The Book's rule number in The Book; this should make it easier if you decide to take a look at The Book yourself—something we strongly suggest. (Copies of the *Official Rules of Baseball* can be purchased in bookstores, most sporting goods stores, or from Triumph Books directly, for $9.95. The *Official Rules of Baseball* we used was the most recent version available when this volume went to press, the 1999 edition.)

"Popcorn, peanuts, souvenir programs . . ."

Introduction
The Rules of the Game

The hitter swung from his heels. He made contact with the ball, but it dribbled along the first base line in foul territory. Undaunted, the batter hustled toward first.

The catcher took off after the ball as if possessed. When he caught up with it, he cocked his arm to throw it to the first baseman, but then he reconsidered. He moved menacingly toward the base runner.

The runner commenced to take evasive action. He took a stride toward second and leaped back. Then he zigzagged in the general direction of first, moving in and out of the base line.

The catcher still made no attempt to throw to first base, which wasn't really a base at all but a wooden stake about four feet high. He instead ran straight for the base runner. When he got about six feet away from him, the catcher took aim, fired the ball, and hit the runner square on the backside. The player was out.

You're confused, right? What's all this about running on a foul ball? Since when is a runner allowed to leave the base line? And isn't it illegal to throw at a runner, let alone hit him? What happens in a situation like this?

That was one play we saw during an exhibition game in Cooperstown, New York, while we were doing research for this book. It was a baseball game, all right, but it was the "Massachusetts Association Game"—played under the rules codified by the Massachusetts Association of Base-Ball Players in 1858. The game was arranged by Thomas R. Heitz, the head librarian at the National Baseball Hall of Fame (and the umpire in that game), and Lloyd Johnson, executive director of SABR, the Society for American Baseball Research (and the above-mentioned catcher).

The game was great fun to watch, but it wasn't anything like baseball as we know it today. Much simpler than the game with which we're familiar, the Massachusetts game had only twenty-one rules. And the parlance was different then, too; there were "knocks" instead of hits, "strikers" instead of hitters, and "throwers" instead of pitchers. The force-out didn't exist, a runner was out when he was

1

hit by the ball (softer than today's "hardball"), and for all intents and purposes there were no such things as base lines. Needless to say, we didn't see the designated hitter that summer evening.

Seeing the Massachusetts game was a diverting exercise in time travel, but it did more than give us a few laughs and remind us of how far we've come since Alexander Cartwright and Abner Doubleday. (It also pointed out yet again how important are the rules of the game. If you think there are a lot of disputes at a baseball game today, try attending one in which the rules haven't benefited from a century of debate.)

Since those regulations were first put on paper, the rules of baseball have burgeoned from two short pages to the one hundred-plus pages of the *Official Rules of Baseball.* And that volume doesn't include the *Instructions to Umpires* (another eighty-odd pages), the *Baseball Blue Book* (a doorstop-sized guide to the business of baseball), or the many other rules-related communications regularly dispensed by the league presidents and the baseball commissioner.

Much has been written about baseball's resemblance to law. Some of the comparisons may seem a bit forced, but the overall observation is legitimate. Baseball's rules have evolved in much the same way society's have. Just as in the face of life's increasing complexities statutes are developed and the constitution is amended to address and redress life's cruelties and injustices, so the rules of baseball must change when it becomes necessary. Think about it: the infield fly, the ground-rule double, and the phantom double play were not invented out of whim. They developed out of a logical and well-meaning desire to maintain the spirit of the game. (Rule changes are made by the Official Baseball Playing Rules Committee, which consists of representatives from each league, the commissioner's office, and the owners, but, strangely enough, no players or umpires.)

One key to understanding baseball—and, for that matter, its rules—is appreciating how neatly bundled together are baseball's past and present. Its history is every bit as important as today's roster changes or next week's phenom. The people who play the game of baseball are unique, but everyone is governed by one thing: the rules. It is those rules that inform the players—and the fans—of the game's possibilities. There are surprises, of course, but the game of baseball is played within the realm of certainty. As football is a game of mayhem, baseball is a game of law.

Several months after we sat on that Cooperstown elementary school playing field and watched the Massachusetts game, we saw another important baseball game together—a Mets-Astros playoff game in Shea Stadium. By then we'd been immersed in the baseball rules for months, and we had visions of rule changes dancing in our heads. That night we were a long way from "strikers" and wooden stakes, but we found ourselves talking about not how much the game had changed but how little.

Certainly the nineteenth century was filled with revolutionary alterations to the game, but except for a few banner years—1920 and 1968, to name two—this century has been a model of traditionalism. The game we saw that night (2–1 Houston) was not very different, all things considered, from the games played at the turn of the century.

And like Bill Veeck, we think that's just fine.

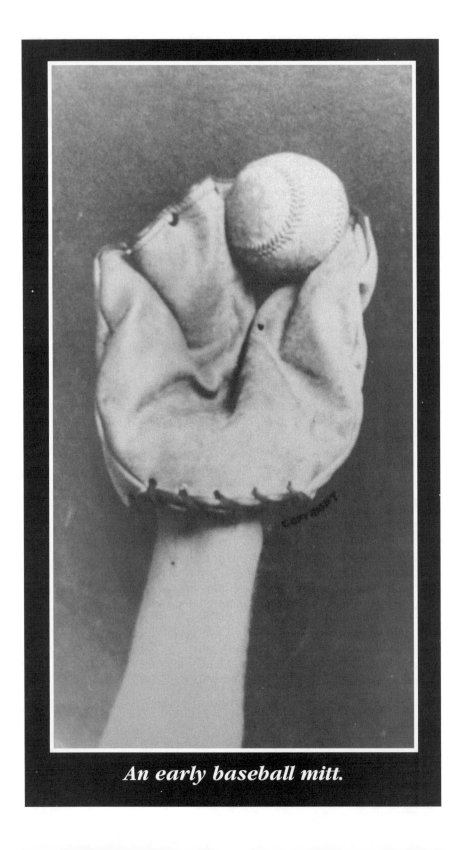

An early baseball mitt.

"Win or lose, we eat pizza."
—Robert E. Hood, The Gashouse Gang

Chapter 1
Objectives of the Game

Depending on whom you believe, baseball is "a game of inches" (Branch Rickey), a "religion" (Hall of Fame umpire Bill Klem), or "A kid's game that grown-ups only tend to screw up" (Bob Lemon).

If you go by The Book, however, baseball is a game "between two teams of nine players each, under the direction of a manager, played on an enclosed field in accordance with these rules, under the jurisdiction of one or more umpires." Sounds simple enough, right? Well, even the simplest things can get confused. Not so many years ago, Angels center fielder Devon White was making a phone call in the clubhouse as the game got underway. The first pitch was thrown before right fielder Chili Davis was able to draw the umpires' attention to the fact that the Angels were fielding an eight-man defense. Davis blamed it on the umpires: "They're not only blind," Davis observed. "They're deaf, too." [1.01]

The Book next tells us the objective is to score more runs than your opponent and that the winner shall be the team with more runs at the game's conclusion. [1.02 and 1.03]

These rules are obvious enough even to a baseball novice. And for the purposes of the opening section of The Book, it's the whole story as far as the objectives of the game are concerned. The framers of the rules apparently decided that in The Book, the detailed discussion of the intricacies of playing the game should follow the specifications for its implements and the environs in which the game is to be played. Thus it is with the field and the equipment that this chapter is primarily concerned. So let us take you out to the ballpark.

The Playing Field

Talk of the field involves numbers and geometric precision. First comes 90 feet, the length of the sides of the infield square, along with 127 feet, 3 3/8 inches, the distance across the field from home to second and from first to third. The catcher's box, batter's box, and the "next batter's box" (colloquially, the on-deck circle), and the base lines must all be of a prescribed size and configuration. The Book also insists that the base lines and home plate be level (see diagrams 1 and 2). [1.04]

The Fences. While the infield specifications are non-negotiable, the rules regarding fence distances are more flexible. All fences must be a minimum of 250 feet from home plate, but it is said to be "preferable" for the foul lines and center field fences to be at a distance of at least 320 feet and 400 feet, respectively.

There is a legal concept known as the "grandfather clause"—an exception that allows for circumstances that existed before the passage

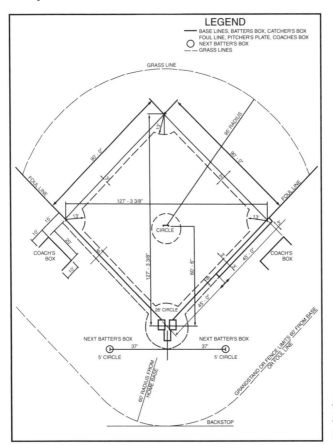

*Playing Field
Dimensions
(Diagram 1)*

*Playing Field
Dimensions
(Diagram 2)*

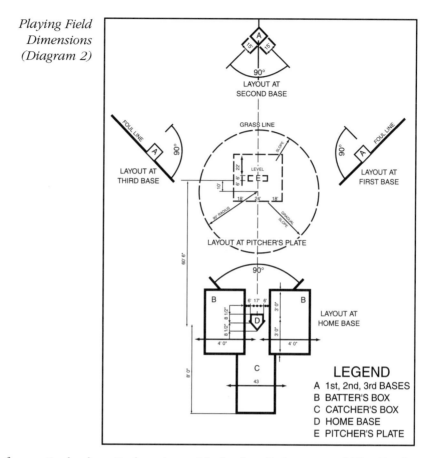

LAYOUT AT
SECOND BASE

LAYOUT AT
THIRD BASE

LAYOUT AT
FIRST BASE

GRASS LINE

LAYOUT AT PITCHER'S PLATE

LAYOUT AT
HOME BASE

LEGEND

A 1st, 2nd, 3rd BASES
B BATTER'S BOX
C CATCHER'S BOX
D HOME BASE
E PITCHER'S PLATE

of a particular law. In keeping with the legalistic tenor of The Book, we'll see some grandfathering here and there.

Grandfathering is a fine thing in the case of fences, since it has allowed for some older exceptions, one of them being Boston's beloved Fenway Park. Its right field line was a mere 302 feet. (The Green Monster in left that supposedly loomed so close was 315 feet away.) All parks built or remodeled after 1958 are obliged to have at least 325 feet down the lines and 400 feet in center. In practice, this has meant that as the antique fields are demolished one by one and new parks replace them, more and more fields are meeting the preferred specs.

Rules are rules, but there's always room for change when the game's gray heads convene. With a multi-year trend of improved pitching and decreased hitting at its peak, a number of moves were made in the late sixties to give the batter an edge. One was the innovation of the designated hitter (we'll see more about the DH in

Chapter 6). Another was a short-lived minor league experiment in 1970 to angle the foul lines outward from the first- and third-base bags. The lines flared out an extra three degrees, a change that added roughly three percent to fair territory. Used in the Gulf Coast Rookie League, it didn't catch on, so today we still have the same geometry that Alexander Cartwright laid out in 1845, when he codified his rules for the Knickerbocker Club of New York.

One adjustment—not to the rules but *within* the rules—that has made it to the majors numerous times over the years is the old move-the-fences trick. It was put to use wholesale in 1969. Oakland Athletics owner Charlie Finley (he of the mule mascot, "Charlie O") moved his fences that year, as did the White Sox, Braves, Dodgers, and Phillies. Years earlier, when Bill Veeck was chief showman at Cleveland, he was said to have had his fenceposts located in sockets in the ground so that he could move them from game to game.

The prototypical fence-mender was Frank Lane, general manager of the White Sox in 1949. The previous year, the White Sox as a team hit a mere 55 homers, while pennant-winning Cleveland led the league with 155. Lane decided he had seen enough (that is, *not* enough), so he brought in the left and right field fences twenty-two feet.

Then in early June the Senators came to town. They'd hit a pathetic thirty-one as a team the previous year, but by the end of the three-game series with the Sox, fourteen round-trippers had been hit. The fences moved back, but legend has it that it wasn't the opposition's home-run output that led Lane to end his experiment. It was his own Floyd Baker, a man described in the press as a "notorious banjo hitter." Contrary to his billing, Baker hit one out that weekend—the only homer of his career. Lane reportedly screamed upon seeing Baker's ball leave the field, "Take [the fence] down! Throw the thing into Lake Michigan." That year Lane's White Sox hit forty-three homers, the least in the league. One upshot of Lane's move is that today a team may not move its fences or otherwise alter the playing field during the season.

Major League Ballparks

American League

Location/ Team Name	Park Name	Opening Year	Surface	Dimensions (LF/CF/RF)
Anaheim Angels	Edison International Field	1966	Grass	330/406/330

Location/Team Name	Park Name	Opening Year	Surface	Dimensions (LF/CF/RF)
Baltimore Orioles	Oriole Park at Camden Yards	1992	Grass	333/400/318
Boston Red Sox	Fenway Park	1912	Grass	310/390/302
Chicago White Sox	Comiskey Park	1991	Grass	347/400/347
Cleveland Indians	Jacobs Field	1994	Grass	325/405/325
Detroit Tigers	Comerica Park	2000	Grass	345/420/335
Kansas City Royals	Kaufman Stadium	1973	Grass	320/400/320
Minnesota Twins	Hubert H. Humphrey Metrodome	1982	Carpet	343/408/327
New York Yankees	Yankee Stadium	1923	Grass	318/408/314
Oakland Athletics	Oakland-Alameda County Coliseum	1968	Grass	330/400/330
Seattle Mariners	Safeco Field	1999	Grass	331/407/327
Tampa Bay Devil Rays	Tropicana Field	1998	Carpet	322/407/322
Texas Rangers	Ballpark at Arlington	1994	Grass	334/400/325
Toronto Blue Jays	Skydome	1989	Carpet	328/400/328

National League

Location/Team Name	Park Name	Opening Year	Surface	Dimensions (LF/CF/RF)
Arizona Diamondbacks	Bank One Ballpark	1998	Grass	330/407/334
Atlanta Braves	Turner Field	1997	Grass	335/401/330
Chicago Cubs	Wrigley Field	1914	Grass	355/400/353
Cincinnati Reds	Cinergy Field	1970	Carpet	330/404/330
Colorado Rockies	Coors Field	1995	Grass	347/415/350
Florida Marlins	Pro Player Stadium	1987	Grass	330/410/345
Houston Astros	Enron Field	2000	Grass	315/433/325

Los Angeles Dodgers	Dodger Stadium	1962	Grass	330/395/330
Milwaukee Brewers	Miller Park	2001	Grass	342/400/356
Montreal Expos	Stade Olympique	1977	Carpet	325/404/325
New York Mets	Shea Stadium	1964	Grass	338/410/338
Philadelphia Phillies	Veterans Stadium	1971	Carpet	330/408/330
Pittsburgh Pirates	Three Rivers Stadium	1970	Carpet	335/400/335
St. Louis Cardinals	Busch Stadium	1966	Grass	330/402/330
San Diego Padres	Qualcomm Stadium	1967	Grass	329/405/329
San Francisco Giants	Pacific Bell Park	2000	Grass	335/404/307

Moving fences seems to have become something of a tradition at real estate-rich Comiskey Park. In 1981 the White Sox returned from spring training to a center field shortened from 445 to only 402 feet, and the center field distance at Comiskey has been changed in at least sixteen different seasons. In 1991 the White Sox ownership went their predecessors one better: they moved the club into an all-new Comiskey Park.

The Book also specifies that the imaginary line from home to second should be on an east-northeast axis, and that the lines on the field should be of "wet, unslaked lime" or of another suitable white material. [1.04]

The Plate and the Bases. Home plate and the base bags must fit certain specs, too. Home plate is beveled, and of the dimensions specified in Diagram 2. The bags must be fifteen inches square and three to five inches thick, made of canvas, and filled with soft material. All four bases must be in fair territory. [1.05 and 1.06]

The bases didn't start out being the bags they are today; originally they were wooden stakes, but largely because so many players were injured, they were substituted with other, less pointed objects. Flat stones were used for a while, and in 1840 sand-filled sacks came into existence in some areas. It was in 1877 that today's fifteen-inch-square, canvas-covered bases became the standard.

Home plate, too, was subject to certain changes over the years. For one, under Massachusetts rules, the batter's box (then called the "striker's box") was located midway between first base and the "fourth" base the runner crossed to score. In 1885 and 1886, home plate was allowed to be marble as well as "whitened rubber." For some years, it was a twelve-inch square, and it wasn't until 1900 that the present five-sided design was adopted.

Grass vs. Carpet

Given all these careful specifications, it is a little surprising that there is one not-so-small aspect of playing field design that isn't specified in The Book: namely, the material of which the "grass" is to be made.

Natural grass sufficed nicely for more than a century. Then, after the grass planted in the Astrodome for its grand opening in 1965 died, artificial nylon baseball turf made its debut. (The deceased natural grass was Tifway 419 Bermuda, for any horticulturalists out there.) The result was baseball on so-called "carpet." (More trivia? The first game played on Astroturf was played on April 8, 1966. And, yes, it is possible for rain to postpone even an indoor game: on June 15, 1976, an Astros game was rained out because of flooding—on the streets of Houston.)

Grass vs. carpet is a debate that rages among sports fans, players, and management alike. Does it cause injury? Probably, given that there is concrete beneath the carpet's underpadding, though artificial turf-related injuries seem less prevalent in baseball than in the National Football League. One study conducted after the Cincinnati Reds' arrival in carpeted Riverfront Stadium in 1970 reported an increase in abrasion and burn injuries, particularly to the palms and knees, but no notable change in the frequency of other injuries. No one believed it then—especially the guys with all kinds of leg problems caused, at least in part, by patrolling rock-hard outfields and sliding on the unforgiving surface. In the decades since, the superiority of grass has virtually been conceded. Consider the fact that of the new parks opened between 1990 and 1998, *eight* have grass surfaces, and only one has carpet.

Artificial turf has had an undeniable effect on the speed of the game. The ball gets through the infield faster, which has led the interior defenses to play deeper. If it gets through, an extra-base hit seems more likely on turf than on grass. As Tom Seaver said a few years ago, "Even hitters like Mike Schmidt of Philadelphia have begun to put turf to work, swinging for the gaps when they get a pitch that's unsuited to pulling for a possible home run. The current style of compact, golf-style swinging, taught by Charlie Lau and epitomized by George Brett of the Royals, is perfectly suited to artificial turf."

The Pitcher's Plate. The pitcher's mound is to be ten inches higher than home plate and the base lines, and is to have a pitch of one inch per foot for the first six feet from the point six inches from the rubber toward the plate.

The familiar pitcher's mound didn't get that way overnight. For much of the nineteenth century, pitchers were required to pitch from a "box," a rectangular space marked on the field. The box changed in size a number of times (at its largest, it was 4 by 12 feet, and it gradually shrank to 4 by 5 1/2 feet in 1866 and 1887, respectively). It didn't have the familiar pitcher's rubber until 1890, and

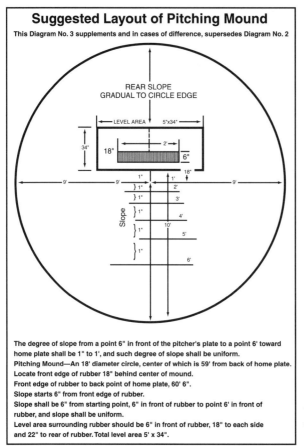

Pitcher's Mound Dimensions (Diagram 3)

even after the rubber was added, the "box" remained until 1893. In 1895, the rubber, which had been twelve by four inches, was enlarged to its present size of twenty-four by six inches. [1.07]

The distance of the mound from home also changed, moving from forty-five feet to fifty and eventually to the present sixty feet, six inches. That distance is measured from the front edge of the rubber to the facing side of the plate.

History has it that the pitching speed of one Amos Wilson Rusie (alias "The Hoosier Thunderbolt") led to the rubber being moved back 10 1/2 feet to its present distance for the 1894 season (it was moved from 45 to 50 in 1881). Apparently, the Thunderbolt (who won 243 games in a mere ten seasons and was named to the Hall of Fame) came by his nickname honestly. Connie Mack said he was the fastest pitcher he had ever seen.

The change to sixty feet, six inches didn't have much effect on Rusie, since he went 36–13 in 1894 and had a number of successful seasons thereafter. His career finally ended after the Giants traded him to Cincinnati (for one Christopher Matthewson) and he hurt his arm. He sustained his injury while experimenting with a pickoff move to first—without moving his feet.

The Bench. There are requirements for team benches, too. They have to be at least twenty-five feet from the base lines, and they're required to have roofs and walls at the back and ends. While The Book doesn't specifically prohibit it, there aren't supposed to be campfires in them, either. But Dizzy Dean and Pepper Martin once built a fire in front of their bench on a 110-degree day in St. Louis. They donned blankets and sat Indian-style before the fire. The public loved it. The umpire's reaction went unrecorded. [1.08]

The Ball

The baseball is to be spherical. It must be composed of a small cork core, followed by a layer of rubber, woolen, and cotton yarn, and covered with two strips of horsehide or cowhide tightly stitched together at the seams. Its weight is to be between 5 and 5 1/4 ounces avoirdupois; the circumference must be 9 to 9 1/4 inches. [1.09]

Baseball's first half-century saw many changes in the ball. In 1845, it weighed three ounces. That was increased to a range of 5 1/2 to 6 1/2 ounces for the 1854 season. The present specs for weight and circumference were established in 1872.

A meeting of the Mad Scientists' Club? No, this particular un-American activity features the league presidents (William Harridge of the AL, right, and Warren Giles of the NL) flanking Commissioner Judge Keneshaw Mountain Landis and an aide. In this 1943 photo, they are deciding that "reclaimed" cork and rubber can be used in manufacturing wartime baseballs. (AP/Wide World Photos)

The Lively Ball. Officially, the ball hasn't changed very much since 1872. So how come Mark McGwire hit seventy homers and Sammy Sosa sixty-six during the 1998 season? The fact is the manufacture of the ball probably isn't the answer.

On the other hand, earlier changes did have an impact. In 1910 the rubber center was replaced with cork, and in 1926 the cork was cushioned. And in both instances, there was, quite legitimately, much talk of a livelier "rabbit ball," as the home run gradually came to be a commonplace event in that period (before that, league leaders had hit somewhere between eight and a dozen home runs).

But since then the only significant changes have been that during World War II synthetic rubber had to be used; in 1973 the place of manufacture was relocated to Haiti (the 108 stitches must be done by hand, and labor is cheaper there); and in 1974 cowhide (as well as horsehide) was authorized for use, since there wasn't enough horsehide available for the quarter-million-plus baseballs the majors require each year. The most meaningful impact of these last changes was that the cowhide ball seemed to explode more often, which led to a bulletin to the umpires from the league office. The umps were told that in the event a ball broke into more than one part during a play, the largest part of the core was to be used to complete the play.

Yet the baseball has been seen as a vehicle for change in the game, even though its changes, especially in recent years, do not explain the radical fluctuations in the delicate pitcher-hitter balance that are attributed to it. Several reported rebirths of the "lively ball," which was widely discussed in the seventies, are instructive.

Consider the opinion of Ted Williams, then manager of the Washington Senators, when he said in 1970, "I know the ball is souped up. [But] I asked [American League president] Joe Cronin about it and he said, 'Oh, no, the ball's the same.' " The skeptical Williams added, "Yeah, *sure* it's the same."

Asked what he thought, Charlie Lau, then coaching at Oakland, said, "I think we're using two balls." Then, blindfolded, he correctly identified which was the 1969 ball and which was the 1970 ball.

Another change seems to have taken place when the manufacturer changed. Albert Goodwill Spalding was a major league pitcher, manager, and very successful businessman. His namesake company, A. G. Spalding, of Chicopee, Massachusetts, was the exclusive supplier of major league baseballs for a century, beginning in 1877 with the National League and in 1901 for the junior league. (Though the American League ball carried the A. J. Reach Company name, Reach was a subsidiary of Spalding.) Then, in 1976, the Spalding company withdrew because it said it could no longer make the ball profitably. Into the breach stepped the Rawlings Sporting Goods Company of St. Louis, to supply the big leagues with the hundreds of thousands of balls it needs each season.

Come opening day, controversy ensued. Much as Williams and the rest had asserted a few years before, in 1977 the talk again was of a livelier ball. Scientific tests conducted by the University of Missouri revealed that the "coefficient of restitution" of the balls was up only 1.3 percent from 1976 (*translation: "The ball's about the same, boys"*). It was also true that Rawlings had been making balls for Spalding under contract off and on for half a dozen years. Still, lots of managers and pitchers complained about the "new" rabbit ball. It took philosopher George "The Boomer" Scott to put it all in perspective: "All the talk about the ball is a lot of bleep." (Credit the quote—and the expurgation—to the *Boston Herald*.)

As succinct and to the point as Scott's observation was, it doesn't quite explain why, by season's end, the American League home run total had soared to 2,013 from 1,122 the previous year. Even the addition of two expansion teams (Toronto and Seattle) couldn't account for that.

The (apparent) enlivening of the ball seems to be a cyclical thing, like the phases of the moon and managerial hirings and firings. In 1980 announcer Tony Kubek and others brought the subject up again, just as it has come and gone dozens of times over the years. While it is usually so much talk, talk, talk by sportswriters and ballplayers alike, we certainly have seen a number of happy-hitter seasons lately. In 1987, there were record numbers of homers hit, and in 1996, veteran manager Sparky Anderson took to calling an apparent rebirth of the lively-ball phenomenon "nitro ball." And talk of the lively ball grew loud again in 1998 with the record-breaking race between Sosa and McGwire.

Only once, however, did a rule directly affecting the ball truly change the game. That was in advance of the 1920 season, and the lively ball era was the result—the very era, in fact, that characterizes the brand of baseball played ever since. That 1920 rule change didn't change the ball itself, just the way it was used. It partially banned the spitter (there was a grandfather clause for active spitballers), and it banned the emery ball. Most important of all, however, it required that a clean ball be kept in play. We'll see more of that ruling and of Carl Mays (whose spitter killed a man in 1919) in Chapter 8.

Lively ball or no, certain rule changes have improved batting averages. For example, the lowering of the mound in 1969 did deliver improved hitting statistics, and there have been other changes that contributed to baseball's cyclical shifts. The pitchers seem to dominate for a few years, then the hitters seem to come

To the Victor Go the Spoils

In 1872, The Book declared that the winning team was to be awarded the game ball.

In 1887, the rule was amended to read that the winning team was to get the last ball used in the game.

It isn't a formal part of the rules, but today balls involved with the most meaningful events end up in Cooperstown at the Baseball Hall of Fame—or in the hands of collectors.

Waste Not, Want Not

Most modern clubs require dozens of balls per game. That's what made June 29, 1929, a GM's dream come true: the Cubs and Reds played a nine-inning game and used only one baseball.

back to life. Or at least there are statisticians who make a case for such ebb and flow. Until McGwire's heroics, it usually seemed that reports of the births and deaths of lively-ball eras were greatly exaggerated.

The Orange Ball. If Charlie Finley had had his way a decade or so ago, we really would be in another age—the "Orange Ball Era." The ever-imaginative Oakland owner very much wanted to use an orange baseball. But even Bill Veeck, who loved to experiment, scoffed at the idea: "Back in the 1920s, when my dad was head of the Chicago Cubs, we thought of an orange baseball . . . in those days the male fans all wore white shirts and made a bad background for the hitters. So we came up with the orange baseball idea . . . But how many men these days wear white shirts?"

All of this is not to say that every ball that emerges from the Haitian heat is absolutely identical. In fact, everyone seems to agree that they aren't, though the degree of variation is hotly disputed. Further, the conditions in which they are shipped and stored do affect them. How much effect humidity and temperature have on a baseball is suggested by a story Paul Richards told of his days as manager of the Orioles in the early sixties.

"We had a pregame home-run-hitting contest against the Yankees," recounted Richards. "Luman Harris [a Baltimore coach] heated up one batch of balls and froze another. Mickey Mantle didn't know it, but he had to swing at the frozen ones. He hit nothing but pop-ups. Then up comes Gus Triandos for us and he gets the hot balls. He hit them out of sight."

The bottom line was drawn nicely by Dodgers pitching great Don Newcombe, who commented, "It was alive when I threw it but dead when I hit."

The Historic Ball. This is, forgive us, a whole different ballgame, having nothing to do with the way the game is played. But let it be duly noted here that balls hit for legendary home runs do have at least an economic life after baseball. Two examples? The ball Babe Ruth stroked out the park for the first home run hit at

Yankee Stadium was discovered by a nine-year-old New Jersey boy in his great-grammy's attic a few years ago. It sold for $126,500 at auction. And that's mere pin money compared to the *$3,005,000* paid for McGwire's Number 70. Go figure.

The Bat

The Book dictates maximums. Each bat is to "be a smooth, round stick not more than 2 3/4 inches in diameter at the thickest part and not more than 42 inches in length. The bat shall be one piece of solid wood." [1.10]

Like those of the ball, standards for the bat have remained largely unchanged in this century, but the nineteenth century saw several versions. In 1862 the first restriction was introduced, as the bat was to be not more than 2 1/2 inches in diameter. In 1895, the present maximum of 2 3/4 inches was established. The length was limited in 1868 to 42 inches, as it is today.

Big Bats, Little Bats. No weight requirements for bats have ever been specified, and it's probably a good thing, since fashions seem to change when it comes to bat weights. Babe Ruth used a fifty-two-ounce bat. "It's not only heavy but long," Ruth told *Baseball* magazine. "Most bats weigh under forty [ounces]. My theory is the bigger the bat, the faster the ball will travel. It's really the weight of the bat that drives the ball, and I like the heavy bat. I have strength enough to swing it, and when I meet the ball, I want to feel that I have something in my hands that will make it travel." It wasn't until about thirty years later

It's Not the Bat, It's the Motion

The smallest bat on record? Wee Willie Keeler, at 5 feet, 4 1/2 inches and 140 pounds, used a 30 1/2-inch bat.

They may have laughed at his bat, but it seems unlikely that many people made fun of Keeler's results: The Wee One batted a not-so-small .432 in 1897 (the third highest batting average in baseball history), and he had eight 200-hit seasons.

Even by today's standards, Keeler's was a Little League-sized bat, but in those days, big sticks were the rule. As Stan Hack recalled, "My thirty-four-ounce bat was the lightest on the champion 1935 Cubs. The other fellows used to ask, 'How can you hit with that matchstick?'"

that "bat speed" became the key term in bat-chat.

Another believer in the heavy bat was Hack Miller. In 1923, he hit a then-impressive twenty home runs using what he claimed was a sixty-five-ounce bat. Though he played in portions of others, that was his only full major league season. Perhaps he was just plain tuckered out after a year of swinging that giant club.

By the 1950s, lighter bats had come into favor. Mickey Mantle used a bat in the range of thirty-two to thirty-four ounces; Willie Mays liked a thirty-three or thirty-four. As a spokesman for Spalding said then, "Our normal assortment of a dozen bats used to range from thirty-six to forty-two ounces [but] we can't even give away the big bats anymore." The trend has continued as Mark McGwire, who designed his own bat in 1987 and hasn't switched since, uses a bat that's 34 1/2 inches long and weighs thirty-three ounces (that's 1 1/2 inches shorter than Roger Maris's and nine ounces lighter than Babe Ruth's). Its label says "BIG STICK," which McGwire can get away with, even though his bat is close to the average size of thirty-four inches, thirty-two ounces.

If you like to get technical, talk about bats with Al Campanis, he of blacks-can't-be-managers fame. Here's what he has to say: "It has been proven that energy or force is equal to mass times velocity squared. In applying this formula to batting, the significant factor is velocity, since it is squared.

Bat Superstitions

Ballplayers are known as a superstitious lot, and that's particularly true when it comes to bats. Many players have had favorites over the years, not least of all Babe Ruth, one of whose cracked Louisville Sluggers resides in the Hillerich and Bradsby Museum. It has twenty-one notches cut into the wood around its trademark, one for each of the twenty-one homers he hit with it in 1927—that is, twenty-one of the sixty he hit that year.

Orlando Cepeda had a theory that every bat had one hit in it, so every hit meant a new bat. Wade Boggs feels somewhat the same way. He discards a bat when he feels he has exhausted its supply of hits.

Then there's the pragmatic Ted Williams. He wasn't notably superstitious, but he had an uncanny sense of weight and balance. He could detect even tiny variations in the weight or length of a bat. He once returned a shipment of bats for being five-thousandths of an inch off.

"In other words," Campanis continued, "the faster swing you can make with the lighter bat more than compensates for the reduced weight." If Einstein had spent more time at Ebbets Field and less at Princeton University, he might have come up with $E=mc^2$ a little sooner.

Bat-Making. Major league bats are made by either the Hillerich and Bradsby Company of Jeffersonville, Indiana (across the river from Louisville, Kentucky, where the company began and from which it took its famous product name, "Louisville Slugger"); the Adirondack Bat Company (owned by Rawlings) in Dolgeville, New York; or Worth (manufacturers of the "Tennessee Thumper"), of Tullahoma, Tennessee.

White ash has long been the preferred wood (*Fraxinus americana*, if you're interested). Most of it comes from New York and Pennsylvania, and the most suitable ash trees are sixty- to seventy-five years old and roughly twelve to fourteen inches in diameter. The best part of the log is the butt, or base, of the trunk. The bats you buy at the sporting goods store are made by automatic lathes, but pro bats are shaped on hand lathes.

Colored Bats. The dark bats you see have a so-called "Hickory Finish"; the tan ones have a light brown stain, named the "Hornsby Finish," after Rogers, whose lifetime .358 batting average suggests he knew a thing or two about bats. The two-tone bats date from a visit that Harry "The Hat" Walker made to the Hillerich and Bradsby plant. The only bat they had in stock that day that fit his needs was being used to stir stain. He took it anyway and got four hits that evening. The two-tone bat became his trademark, and to this day, it is known as having a "Walker Finish." More recently, there was the (George) "Foster Finish," for the black beauties he used. Tony Gwynn's favorite design has a black barrel with a white handle, while Andy Van Slyke chose a rose-colored barrel with a natural handle. These natural shades are allowed, but Rule 1.10d prohibits "colored" bats.

Metal Bats. Professional baseball has for years been the last bastion of the wooden bat: Metals bats are not allowed in the majors but aluminum accounts for some ninety percent of bat sales. Since 1974 metal bats have been legal in college play and it has long ceased to be news when a team signs up a prospect who has never used a wooden bat. Not so many years ago, *Sports Illustrated* decreed the wooden bat on the verge of obsolescence.

The tide may be turning, however, as the NCAA passed new regulations in 1998. Bat makers were required to make their bats heavier and with a smaller barrel, to slow bat speed and reduce the velocity of the ball flying off the bat. Injuries—especially to pitchers—is the primary explanation, but cost is a factor, too. (Some aluminum bats cost $300 or more.)

Illegal Bats. The sharp "pinging" sound a metal bat makes when it comes in contact with a ball is a dead giveaway, so it simply isn't possible to get away with using a metal bat in the majors. But a number of other illegal bats do get put into play.

The flattened bat is one variety. Bobby Bonds recalled, "When I was a rookie, I spent four hours flattening one side of the bat where I made contact . . . In my first at-bat it broke. I never doctored a bat again. But a lot of guys use cork and other things."

To doctor a bat with cork requires only a little woodworking skill. The end of a regulation bat is sawed off, and a hole roughly six to ten

The umpires take possession of the evidence, Albert Belle's corked bat. That's first-base umpire Joe Brinkman on the left, and home-plate umpire Dave Phillips on the right. Little did they know that this incriminating bat would shortly "disappear" from the umpires' locker room. (AP/Mark Morency)

inches long and about an inch in diameter is drilled and packed with cork. The end is glued back on and, presto, *The Natural's* magic bat comes to life. (Wonderboy, the bat Roy Hobbs used in the Malamud novel, wasn't corked, but it was made from a tree split by lightning.)

Some say that corking adds as much as fifty feet to a long ball and gives a grounder added zip to carry it through the infield. It isn't the cork that adds the oomph, by the way. It's probably more a matter of bat speed. The cork (or rubber or whatever is used) merely deadens the sound the bat makes on contact, since a hollowed out bat will make more of a *boom!* than a *crack!*

Just ask Albert Belle about corked bats. He knows more than most of us, and the confiscation of one of his corked bats resulted in one of the more intriguing now-you-see-it, now-you-don't events of recent baseball history.

On Friday evening, July 5, 1994, the White Sox and Indians were playing at the new Comiskey Park. A rumor was making the rounds that Belle's bat had been corked. Pale Hose manager Gene Lamont strode to home plate and challenged the bat's legality. Umpire crew chief Dave Phillips promptly confiscated the bat and locked it in his dressing room for later inspection.

Along with other members of the Indians, Jason Grimsley knew that Belle's bat was illegal and, worse yet, that an illegal bat meant an almost certain suspension for Belle, the team's best hitter. The White Sox and Indians were in a tight playoff race and Grimsley recognized that they needed any edge they could get. He took matters into his own hands.

While the game was going on, Grimsley headed back to the dressing area, removed a ceiling tile in his manager's office, and clambered on top of an eighteen-inch wide cinder block wall. Guided by a flashlight and with a legal bat in tow, he made his way in secret to the umpires' locker room, where he switched the bats.

Grimsley's escapade quickly became no more than a footnote to history. The umpires knew immediately upon examining the bat in their locker room that it had been switched. It bore the name of Belle's teammate Paul Sorrento. (Every one of Belle's bats was corked, so Grimsley had been hard pressed to find a legitimate one, choosing Sorrento's by default.) The enraged umpires made various threats and there was even talk of calling in the FBI. On Sunday, after immunity had been promised for the culprit who'd purloined the corked bat, the Indians handed it over. An X-ray subsequently showed it had indeed been "treated with cork." Just to be sure, the bat was sawed in half, revealing that a hole had been drilled in its end, a cork plug inserted, and the end plugged, sanded, and stained. Grimsley's role remained unacknowledged until April of 1999, when he came clean. *The New York Times* ran the story on page one.

It isn't only cork that makes its way into the barrel of illegal bats. There's a story of a minor leaguer who managed to insert a tube of mercury inside his bat, believing that its shifting weight provided him a power boost. (See Chapter 6 for more on illegal bats.)

Rule 1.10 rules out some other bats, too. Laminated bats or other "experimental" bats are forbidden, except when the manufacturer has received official Rules Committee approval. On the other hand, cupped bats are acceptable. (A cupped bat has a curved indentation at its end up to an inch deep.) Also called a "teacup" bat, it has been used by, among others, Keith Hernandez. When George Foster was mired in one of the slumps that characterized his career with the Mets, he borrowed a teacup bat from Hernandez and got four hits in a game.

Toby Harrah had his bat confiscated in 1982—he'd sawed off the handle and then refastened it with glue and a wooden peg. However, American League president Lee MacPhail declined to take further action against Harrah, apparently believing Harrah's explanation that he hadn't doctored his bat to produce more power; he had simply shortened it because a new shipment of size thirty-fours hadn't arrived.

The Book also explicitly prohibits "loaded" or "freak" bats that will produce "a substantially greater reaction or distance factor than one-piece solid bats."

The Pine-Tar Incident. When talk turns to bats, the brouhaha over George Brett's pine-tar bat invariably comes up. And so it must be in this book, too, because it was a dramatic and revealing moment.

The event in question occurred on July 24, 1983. Brett came to the plate in the visitor's half of the ninth inning at Yankee Stadium. He and his Royals teammates were down 4–3, and there were two down and a man on. Brett, with the simple efficiency of a man who was arguably the best hitter in baseball at that moment, hit the ball out of the park.

Billy Martin, then in his umpteenth (but not his last) tour of duty with the Yankees, emerged from the Yankees dugout and played the card he had been saving for just such an occasion: he complained to the umpire that Brett had used an illegal bat.

Graig Nettles had observed two weeks earlier that Brett's bat was practically awash in pine tar. Brett, you see, was one of the last players in the majors to hit barehanded rather than using batting gloves. "I like the feel of raw hands on raw wood," Brett said. Apparently, word got around the Yankees dugout. "I had known about the tar," said Rich Gossage, the Yankees relief pitcher who gave up Brett's homer. "But when I watched that ball, all I could think of was a two-run homer."

But more conniving minds prevailed, at least that day. Martin made his case to the umpires: the pine tar was too far up on the bat. He referred to Rule 1.10c, which then specified, "The bat handle, for not more than 18 inches from its end, may be covered or treated with any material (including pine tar) to improve the grip. Any such material, pine tar included, which extends past the 18-inch limitation, in the umpire's judgment, shall cause the bat to be removed from the game."

Then there's Rule 6.06d: "He [who] uses or attempts to use a bat that . . . has been altered or tampered with in such a way to improve the distance factor . . . [shall be] called out [and] the player shall be ejected from the game."

Ergo, concluded Martin, there's no home run, and Brett is outta here.

After some discussion, the bat was duly examined. Home plate umpire Tim McClelland, lacking another suitable measuring device, laid the bat on the plate, which is seventeen inches across. The tar extended quite a bit more than another inch.

"I was laughing at the umpires when they were deciding what to do," Brett said later. His smile disappeared when, after the umpires huddled, he was declared out. The Yankees were the winners, 4–3.

Brett went berserk. He actually made contact with the umpires and, in his words, told them "everything my father used to tell me when I brought home my report card." He ended up with his head locked under the arm of umpire-in-chief Joe Brinkman.

That's not the end of the story, of course. The Royals filed a formal protest with American League President Lee MacPhail. Even they probably didn't think much of their chances, given that in MacPhail's ten years in office he had never upheld a protest.

Five days later he did the unexpected and reversed the umps' decision.

"It is the position of this office that the umpires' interpretation, while technically defensible, is not in accord with the intent or spirit of the rules and that the rules do not provide that a hitter be called out for excessive use of pine tar. The rules provide instead that the bat be removed from the game. The protest of the Kansas City club is therefore upheld, and the home run by Brett is permitted to stand. The score of the game becomes 5–4 Kansas City with Kansas City at bat and two out in the top of the ninth inning." Thus, Brett's homer was restored and the game was completed (final score: 5–4). Today, minor word changes have been made in The Book.

The Uniforms

A team's uniforms are supposed to be . . . uniform. Besides having the same "color, trim, and style," each should have its owner's number in six-inch numerals on its back. [1.11a] The consistency extends to sleeves as well—same length for the entire club and no ragged or slit sleeves, please. [1.11c]

There are other specifications, including the following:

◯ Each team is to have home and away uniforms.

◯ No tape or other material of a different color from the uniform may be added.

◯ No portion of the uniform is allowed to resemble a baseball.

◯ No glass buttons or polished metal may be used.

◯ Spikes are limited to the "ordinary shoe plate and toe plate."

◯ No commercial patches or designs may be added. [1.11d through 1.11h]

It is up to each league to determine whether players may adorn team uniforms or not, and any name other than a player's last name must be approved by the league. [1.11i]

It was Bill Veeck who put names on uniforms in the first place, back in 1960, but it was Ted Turner who tried to out-Veeck Veeck by using nicknames. In the mid-seventies, Turner's Atlanta Braves had such names on their uniforms as "Nort" (Darrel Chaney, named after Art Carney's "Honeymooners" character Norton), "Gallo"

(Rogelio Moret), and "Jay Bird" (Jerry Royster, for reasons unknown even to him).

The rules regarding today's uniforms followed a predictably varied evolution. The first baseball uniform, which was worn by the 1849 New York Knickerbockers, included straw hats. Curiously, so-called knickerbocker pants had to wait seventeen years for their introduction—by the Cincinnati Red Stockings.

In 1876, the year the National League was organized, the name A. G. Spalding crops up again. Spalding was managing the Chicago White Sox, and everybody on his team was dressed in a cap of a different color. (In those days it was the socks rather than the uniform or hat that distinguished members of one team from another. Most of the socks were wool, though the White Sox wore silk.)

In 1882, stocking colors were standardized geographically: Boston clubs wore red; Chicago, white; Buffalo, gray; Worcester (Massachusetts), blue; Detroit, old gold; Troy (New York), green; and so on. Color must have been on everybody's mind that year, as cap and shirt colors were assigned, too. (In this case, however, colors were assigned according to a player's fielding position. All first basemen wore scarlet and white, second basemen orange and black, and onward around the color wheel. That experiment lasted a year.)

If there is one thing the diehard Yankees fan likes to do, it's wax poetic about those beloved pinstripes. Well, we've got bad news: the Bronx Bombers weren't the first to wear them. The Giants wore pinstripes for at least four years before the Yanks adopted them in 1915.

Numbers didn't appear on uniforms until 1916 (in Cleveland) and were not mandatory until 1931 and 1933 for, respectively, the American and National leagues.

For decades, baseball tradition required that teams wear white at home and gray on the road. It was Charlie Finley who broke the color barrier when he had his Kansas City Athletics don new uniforms in 1962 (the colors have been recorded as "wedding white, kelly green, and Fort Knox gold"). Their opposition that first game (the Yankees, dressed in the aforementioned pinstripes) got such a kick out of the new uniforms that they were heard to call from their dugout, *"Yoooo-hoooo, boys!"* to the Athletics—and were also seen blowing kisses at any Athletics player foolish enough to look their way.

In 1976, the Chicago White Sox tried out knee-length shorts. They weren't the first, though; a number of minor league teams experimented with them around 1950. In the late fifties, the Cincinnati Reds introduced their vest-style uniforms, reportedly because of muscular Ted Kluszewski's habit of chopping off his sleeves to reveal his biceps.

Mitts and Gloves

One July day in Baltimore in 1969, the umpires were faced with a problem. Clay Dalrymple was to catch for Baltimore that evening, but he emerged from the dugout with both a catcher's mitt (on his hand) and a fielder's glove (in his back pocket).

"I asked him about it," reported home-plate umpire John Rice. "And he told me he was going to switch to the fielder's glove if he had a play at the plate."

The umpires huddled, and though they couldn't think of a rule that specifically forbade the use of the second glove, they exacted

Baltimore Oriole catcher Gus Triandos with the catcher's mitt that his manager, Paul Richards, devised for catching knuckleballer Hoyt Wilhelm.

27

a promise from Dalrymple that he wouldn't use the glove until a ruling was made by the league office.

Oriole manager Earl Weaver argued, of course. "If nothing covers it in the rules," offered Earl, "then why rule *against* the glove? Why not *for?*"

When it comes to catcher's mitts, Rule 1.12 ought to be called "The Oriole Rule." There are two reasons for that. The first is because now The Book allows the catcher to wear only "a leather mitt," while prior to the Dalrymple debate, the catcher could wear "a leather glove or mitt." (Mitt is short for mitten, so mitts by definition have two sections: one for the thumb, the other for the rest of the hand.)

The second reason for linking the Orioles to this subsection involves Oriole manager Paul Richards, and it happened in the late fifties. The rule in its entirety in those days read, "The catcher may wear a leather glove or mitt of any size, shape, or weight." That made it possible for Richards to put his imaginative baseball mind to work. His stopper out of the bullpen was Hoyt Wilhelm, a knuckleballer who accumulated a then remarkable 227 career saves. Unfortunately, Wilhelm's elusive knuckleball was often as difficult to catch as it was to hit.

Richards came up with a solution. When Wilhelm came in, Richards' catcher, Gus Triandos, would don an oversized catcher's mitt, one with a circumference of forty-five inches. It helped reduce wild pitches and passed balls. Over the next few years, however, enough bellyaches were heard from the opposition that finally, in 1965, the rule was changed to prohibit gloves with a circumference of more than thirty-eight inches.

(Apparently, the mitt didn't help Charlie Lau when he tried catching Wilhelm's knuckleball. In a game in 1962, he allowed four passed balls, three of them in one inning.)

Other Catcher's Equipment. Although the rules don't offer any specifications for the catcher's mask or chest protectors, both are essential equipment. The first mask, put to use in 1875, was a modified fencing mask. It was invented by Fred W. Thayer and used by James Tyng of Harvard. Ten years later, the chest protector was introduced, and in 1908 Roger Bresnahan of the New York Nationals introduced shin guards.

Fielder's Gloves. The fielders of baseball's earliest generations actually played barehanded. It should come as no surprise to anyone that it was the first basemen and catchers who started the move to handwear. Fingerless gloves that just fit the palm came first. Charles Waite is thought to have been the first to use one, and when he took the field with a flesh-colored glove in 1875, the fans literally called him "sissy."

Reenter Albert G. Spalding. In 1877, he switched from pitching to playing first and decided to wear a black kid glove. Though it did contain some padding, Spalding's glove bore a considerable resemblance to today's golf gloves. As Spalding was one of the game's better-known and respected personages, he gave the glove legitimacy. Needless to say, in the years to come entrepreneur Spalding also turned it into profit, selling his "Spalding's model" for $2.50.

The Catcher's Mitt. The catchers were the first to put gloves with fingers to use in the 1880s. In fact, in those years catchers used gloves on both hands, though the glove on the throwing hand remained fingerless. The pillow-type mitt came next, and it was first

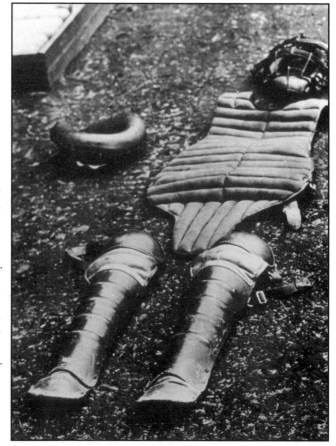

Old catchers never die; they just become invisible. Here's a 1940 photograph of the "tools of Ignorance": a catcher's mitt, mask, chest protector, and shin guards. Today, of course, there would be a catcher's helmet, too.

used in 1888 by Buck Ewing, the New York Giants catcher. The Book, however, didn't acknowledge the presence of gloves or mitts of any kind (though it didn't preclude them, either) until 1895. The pillow-design catcher's mitt, though different in many details, is essentially the configuration that remains in use today.

Unlike the catcher, the first baseman today "may wear a leather glove or mitt." (Fielders are not permitted to use mitts, just gloves.) Like the catcher, however, the first baseman has a variety of limitations on his glove's or mitt's specifications. It may not be more than twelve inches long or in excess of eight inches from the base of the thumb to the outer edge of the mitt. Other dimensions are specified, too, but the glove "may be of any weight." [1.13]

The baseball glove has evolved considerably from those Spalding and Waite used. Bill Doak was one important innovator. A spitball pitcher for the Cardinals, Doak devised a multi-thong web in 1919. Another glove designer, Harry Latina, came up with a variety of innovations while working for Rawlings, including the Deep-Well Pocket (1940), the Snugger Wrist Adjustment (1942), and the TRAP-EZE six-finger glove (1959). Ozzie "The Wizard" Smith, the perennial Gold Glove winner at short for the Cardinals in the 1980s (he won it all ten years!), swore by the TRAP-EZE design. In fact, since he liked them hard and stiff, Smith broke in a new glove every six weeks during the season. Today, the glove is such a part of the game that as one commentator wrote earlier in the century, "The fielders have become so inseparably attached to their gloves that if you jerked one off a man's hand, you'd almost expect to see him bleed to death."

The specifications for the fielder's glove are that it must be leather, though the webbing may be leather thongs or panels, and the panels may not be wound or wrapped "to make a net type of trap." [1.14]

Pitcher's Gloves. Pitchers were the last players to put on their gloves. For some reason, there was a notion prevalent for years that a pitcher would be rendered ineffective if he muffled either hand. A minor leaguer named McVicker is said to have been the first pitcher to wear a glove.

In recent decades there have been some rule changes regarding pitcher's gloves. Today, they must be uniform in color and cannot be white or gray. The pitcher's glove must not have "any foreign material" of a different color attached to it. [1.15]

Batting Helmets. Batting helmets and attached ear flaps are relatively new as equipment goes, and they became mandatory only in recent years. All players today are required to wear batting helmets, and all but the handful of 1982 major leaguers who objected to the single-ear flap helmet must have the flap, too. [1.16]

Catcher's Helmets. A recent addition to The Book concerns helmets for catchers and bat/ball boys or girls. All are now required to wear a "protective helmet" while performing their appointed tasks. [1.16]

Other Equipment. The last rule in this section is a catchall for bases, bats, balls, the plate, uniforms, catcher's mitts, and everything else to do with the game. It says that no "undue commercialization" of any equipment will be allowed. [1.17]

Playing Field and Equipment Rule Changes: The Highlights

c. 1845 While there are no restrictions on bat size or shape at the game's inception, the ball is required to weigh three ounces. The pitching distance is to be forty-five feet.

1849 The New York Knickerbockers introduced the first uniforms, blue and white cricket outfits.

1854 The ball increases in weight to 5 1/2 to 6 1/2 ounces and is required to be 2 3/4 to 3 1/2 inches in diameter.

1859 The first limitation on bat size is introduced: bats are to be no more than 2 1/2 inches in diameter (previously a bat like that used in cricket with a 4-inch-wide flat face had been commonplace).

1860 Whitewash is used for the first time to mark the foul lines.

1863 All bats are required to be round and of wood, but the dimensions remain unchanged. Length is still not restricted.

1865 The pitcher's box is introduced, replacing a twelve-foot line. The box is to be a three-by-twelve-foot space.

1866 Another change for the pitcher's box: it is enlarged to a four-by-twelve-foot rectangle.

1868 The experimentation continues as the pitcher's box shrinks to a four-by-six-foot box. The batter, too, faces a new restriction, as the bat finally has a length limit established: no more than forty-two inches long. The Cincinnati Red Stockings introduce knickerbocker trousers.

1869 The pitcher's box changes again, this time to a six-foot square.

1872 The weight standards of the ball are refined (it is required to weigh not less than 5 or more than 5 1/4 ounces) and its circumference specified (not less than 9 or more than 9 1/4 inches).

1875 The glove (unpadded) is introduced, by Charles G. Waite.

1877 The bases must be canvas covered. The required size of a base is fifteen inches square, which it is to this day. Home plate is relocated to what we now know as its final resting place, just within the diamond at the intersection of the first- and third-base lines.

1881 The pitchers are moved back to fifty feet from the plate.

1882 The three-foot base line is adopted.

1885 Home base specifications permit it to be made of marble or whitened rubber. The bat may have one flattened side. (This change lasts a year.)

1886 The pitcher's box shrinks to four by seven feet. First and third bases are moved within the foul lines.

1887 Home plate now can be made only of rubber; it's not yet the shape we recognize, but a twelve-inch square. Yet another new size is specified for the pitcher's box: 4 by 5 1/2 feet.

1893 The pitcher's plate (to be made of rubber) is introduced and the "box" abandoned; the rubber is twelve by four inches. Pitching distance, too, is changed, increased to sixty feet, six inches, where it has remained.

1895 The pitcher's rubber is enlarged to twenty-four by six inches, where it is to stay. Bat maximum diameter changes for the last time, increasing to 2 3/4 inches.

1900 The familiar five-sided, seventeen-inch-wide plate replaces the twelve-inch square.

1904 The height of the pitcher's mound is limited to fifteen inches above the base lines.

1910 The cork-center ball is adopted for regular use (it had been used in the previous year for occasional play).

1920 Enter the "lively ball." One explanation is a change in the yarn used. Australian yarn is put to use in this year, and it is said to be stronger than its American equivalent. Because the balls are wound tighter, their bounce and hardness are increased.

1926 The cushioned cork-center baseball is introduced.

1934 For the first time, both major leagues are required to adopt the same brand of baseball.

1950 The pitcher's mound is required to be a standard height: fifteen inches above the level of the base lines.

1954 For the first time, the bat is allowed to be made of two or more pieces of wood laminated together.

1959 Minimum fence distances are established for new ballpark construction (325 feet down the lines and 400 feet in center field).

1962 Oversize gloves are banned for use by pitchers, infielders, and outfielders. Players are allowed to apply any grip-improving substance to their bats, though not for more than the first eighteen inches of its length beginning at the handle.

1968 The pitcher's mound is lowered to ten inches.

1971 Protective helmets are required for batters.

1975 The baseball may be covered with cowhide; before this, only horsehide had been allowed. Cupped bats are allowed.

1988 Protective helmets are mandatory for catchers.

The way we were. South Side Ball Park, Chicago, 1905.

"Baseball is almost the only orderly thing in a very unorderly world. If you get three strikes, even the best lawyer in the world can't get you off."

—Bill Veeck

Chapter 2
Definition of Terms

hapter 2 of The Book is unlike the nine other chapters in that it's the only one that doesn't list and explain rules. Instead, it consists of an alphabetized list of the most commonly used terms in baseball and their definitions. It's there that you find out exactly what is meant by Adjudged, Battery, Force Play, Pivot Foot, Squeeze Play, and a few dozen other baseball terms. In short, although it is anything but comprehensive, Chapter 2 is a glossary.

At the end of *this* book (starting on page 233) we've included all the terms in the Glossary, but here we'd like to focus, however briefly, on only five commonly used baseball terms, since we think they need more than simple defining and they aren't discussed sufficiently elsewhere. The terms are Catch, Double Play, Fair and Foul Territory, Infield Fly, and Strike Zone.

Catch

According to The Book, a player makes a legal catch when he gets secure possession of the ball in his hand or glove (no fair using his cap or any other props). In addition to possessing it securely he must also hold onto the ball long enough to prove that he has control of it.

In the process of catching a ball a fielder may not perform any extraordinary feats of gymnastics. For instance, he may not jump over a fence, a railing, or a rope that marks the limits of the playing field, and he's not permitted to run into the stands. On the other hand, he may reach over a fence, railing, or rope, and he may *reach into* the stands (although he does so at his own risk). If he falls into

Brooklyn Dodgers outfielder Andy Pafko gives an impressive demonstration of a fair catch in a 1952 game against the Yankees. The guy who was robbed: outfielder Gene Woodling. (UPI)

Birds Gotta Swim, Fish Gotta Fly

One day in 1947 when the St. Louis Browns were playing in Fenway, Browns pitcher Ellis Kinder was interrupted by a foul smelt. A seagull—undoubtedly a Sox fan—dropped his catch onto the mound between pitches, where it missed Kinder by a gill. Undaunted, Kinder pitched the Browns to a 4–2 victory.

uncharted territory as a result of his momentum after making a catch, that too is legal provided he's able to hold on to the ball.

A player may step into or reach into the dugout of either team in order to chase down a ball. However, if the fielder or catcher, after having made a legal catch, falls into the stands or dugout or among spectators, the ball is dead and the runners advance a base.

It is not a legal catch if a fielder touches a fly ball that then hits a member of the offensive team or an umpire and is caught by another defensive player. (Rule of thumb: if you're going to play volleyball out there, play it with your own team.)

Finally, if simultaneously or immediately following his contact with the ball a fielder collides with another player or with the wall and drops the ball, it is not a legal catch. The crucial words here are, of course, "immediately following." What exactly is meant by them is up to the umpire.

On September 26, 1982, the umpire's judgment about these matters cost the Atlanta Braves a run in a deciding game against the San Diego Padres. For want of a run the game was lost, and for want of a game the chance to tie the Dodgers for the lead in the Western Division of the National League also was lost.

It was the third inning in Atlanta, and the Braves were winning 1–0. Padres outfielder Gene Richards stepped to the plate with no one on base and two out. He made solid contact and sent the ball high along the left-field line. Third-base ump Ed Vargo hightailed it to the outfield to watch Braves left fielder Terry Harper chase the fly and make a running catch just as he crossed the foul line. Vargo gave the signal for a fair ball.

But Harper wasn't quite finished running. His momentum carried him into foul territory toward the bullpen railing. He grabbed the railing to keep from flying over it, but while he was at it, he dropped the ball. By the time Harper had collected himself Gene Richards was rounding third, with the umpire's complete approval. Richards ended up with an inside-the-park homer, and the Padres won the game 3–2.

According to Ed Vargo, Harper didn't hold onto the ball long enough to demonstrate that he had control over it. To make matters even worse (at least temporarily) for Harper, the official scorer charged him with a four-base error. However, the error was eventually overruled by the League office; the run counted, but it was scored as a hit.

Double Play

What we're concerned with here is not so much the textbook definition of the double play (DP)—The Book says it's a play by the defense in which two offensive players are put out as a result of continuous action, with no errors between putouts—but rather the awarding of the "automatic double play," also referred to as the "phantom double play."

When you first start watching baseball games, the scene definitely takes some getting used to. You know how the game is played, and the rules say that in a double play a fielder must touch the bag for the force-out and then throw to the preceding base to get the second force-out. Yet you've been watching really carefully, and you're sure that the fielder didn't even come close to touching second before releasing the ball to first. The umpire called the runner out, and no one is complaining, let alone throwing vegetables. What gives?

What gives is an unofficial rule—a fielder may be excused from actually tagging a base if in doing so he's likely to be injured by a base runner. No one is too crazy about this "rule," but it's very much a part of the game. As long as there are base runners whose job it

Apocryphal-Sounding Story # 1

In May of 1910 a game was in progress in Harrison, New Jersey. It seems that the park, which was situated near a train station, had some fairly unusual ground rules, since the outfield backed onto the railroad tracks. The bases were loaded, and a big hitter had just come to the plate. True to his reputation, the batter hit one high and hard into left field. The fielder gave chase, but the ball went over his head and into the smokestack of a passing locomotive. Four runs scored. The ump's ruling? The runs counted, since the smokestack was in fair territory.

is to break up double plays by interfering with the fielder's throw—and possibly with his motor skills—the automatic DP will be with us. The alternative is a playing field littered with the bodies of infielders and/or base runners.

Some critics of the phantom DP say that calling interference (called on a base runner who goes out of his allotted space during a play—about which there's much more in Chapter 7) would go a long way toward reestablishing a double play that's executed by the book, but the fact is that interference is rarely called. Some umpires, veterans of twenty or more years of service, have literally never made the interference call.

Fair and Foul Territory

Hall of Fame pitcher Early Wynn used to say: "The space between the white lines—that's my office. That's where I conduct my business."

No, it's not a crap game. It's a close call by umpires Ed Vargo and Sam Crawford (kneeling). The umps eventually saw the ball—hit by Pittsburgh center fielder Matty Alou in a 1966 game against Atlanta—roll foul. (AP/Wide World Photos)

Apocryphal-Sounding Story # 2

It was the fifth inning of a minor league game between San Francisco and Sacramento one summer day in 1947. San Francisco was winning, but Sacramento had runners on base and a chance to get back in the game. The eager batter swung away and hit a foul ball so high that some spectators swore they thought it would never land. But land it did, in the tuba of a member of the band. Unfortunately for Sacramento, the band had seats not in the bleachers but in the box seats behind the plate. Foul ball.

That's as succinct a definition of fair territory as we've come across, but naturally, there's a little more to it than that.

Officially, fair territory is the area of the playing field from home plate within and including the first-base and third-base lines to the bottom of the playing field fence and perpendicularly upward. A fair ball is:

⚾ A batted ball that lands on fair territory

⚾ A batted ball that flies over fair territory past first or third on its way to the outfield or out of the park

⚾ A batted ball that touches first, second, or third base

⚾ A batted ball that hits a player or an umpire in fair territory

Foul territory is the part of the playing field outside the first- and third-base lines extended to the fence and perpendicularly upward. A foul ball is:

⚾ A batted ball that lands on foul territory between home and first or home and third

⚾ A batted ball that passes over foul territory before passing first or third base on its way into the outfield or out of the park

⚾ A batted ball that hits a player, an umpire, or any "foreign object" in foul territory

If a fair fly ball is deflected into the stands in fair territory, it is a home run. (The Red Sox were victimized by this twice in 1986 postseason play.) If a fair ground ball is deflected into the stands in fair territory, it's a ground-rule double.

In most team sports—football, basketball, tennis, and soccer, to name a few—lines and poles are considered out of bounds, but in baseball the foul lines and foul poles are fair territory. Over the years many people have crusaded for a change in terminology; they say that we should start calling them "fair lines" and "fair poles."

The Infield Fly

It's probably safe to say that the infield fly is the only rule in The Book that has been or ever will be the subject of a legal tract—to wit, "The Common Law Origins of the Infield Fly Rule," which appeared in volume 123, number 6, of the *University of Pennsylvania Law Review* in June of 1975.

Scintillating the paper is not (sample sentence: "As a preliminary matter, it is necessary to emphasize that baseball is a game of English origin, rooted in the same soil which grew Anglo-American law and justice."), but despite its highfalutin language and its forty-eight footnotes, it's a *tour de force* with a legitimate point. The most important part of that point is that the infield fly rule was a logical reaction to play, established in order to eliminate activity not in the spirit of the game.

The infield fly rule has been in effect since the 1890s, and The Book's definition is quite clear: an infield fly is a fair fly ball (not a line drive or an attempted bunt) that can be caught by an infielder with ordinary effort when first and second or first, second, and third bases are occupied before there are two outs. Runners are to regard the ball as they would any fly ball; they must tag up before proceeding to the next base.

Technically the word "infielder" usually excludes the pitcher and catcher, but for the purposes of the infield fly rule they and any outfielder in the infield are considered infielders as well.

An infield fly must be called by an umpire—most umps point to the sky and holler, *"infield fly"*—and much is said in the umpires' general instructions about avoiding undue haste in making the call. If an umpire is not certain whether an apparent infield fly will stay in fair territory, he may point to the sky and holler this tongue twister: *"Infield fly, if fair."* If the ball goes foul, it's treated like any other foul ball.

The Strike Zone

"Pitchers control the game, and the strike zone controls the pitchers—that's a cardinal rule of baseball. You can change the game by what you do with the strike zone." Joe Morgan (wearing his commentator's hat, not the cap he sported when he played second base for the Astros and the Reds, among other teams) wrote those words in the Spring of 1999, because the all-important strike zone was once again in the news.

Why the fuss? Not because the strike zone was being changed—officially it was the same as it had been since 1995—but because word had come down from on high: it was time for the guys calling balls and strikes to abide by The Book.

What, you say? You mean they don't? Anybody who watched any baseball at all in the '90s can tell you that the answer is no.

The strike zone had gotten fatter (three inches off the black is a strike) and shorter (anything above the belt is a ball), so the Commissioner's Office decided to do something. Sandy Alderson, executive vice president of Major League Baseball, sent a memo to teams and umpires in the Spring of 1999: "This is to inform you that The Strike Zone, as defined in the official rules, will be more strictly

Eddie Gaedel shows off his famous strike zone, all 1 1/2 inches of it. (UPI)

enforced." Then, fatefully, he went on: "The upper limit of the strike zone will extend two inches above the uniform pants."

Huh? According to that, unless a batter wears his britches pulled up under his pecs, the pitcher is still not going to be given the high strike as defined in The Book. Maybe the deep thinkers in the Commissioner's Office feared panic and chaos if the game's rules were strictly enforced, so they settled for *more* strictly enforced.

It looks as though the strike zone will continue to be something of a moving target for a while longer. As it finds its way back to the official definition in The Book, we close this discussion with the wisdom of Joe Morgan: "You hear a lot of umpires grumble, 'My strike zone has been like this for twenty years.' Well, I say, it's not your strike zone, it's baseball's strike zone. The strike zone is what the rule book says it is. Period."

To think that so few words could produce so many arguments! Some of the bickering comes as a result of the umpire's judgment, but most stems from the second part of the description, about the batter's natural stance and where, by extension, his strike zone actually falls.

Once upon a time the batter had some say in deciding *where* in the strike zone a pitcher had to throw the ball. From 1870 to 1887 the batter was actually allowed to call for a high ball, a low ball, or a fair ball. (High was between the shoulders and the waist; low was between the waist and the knees; fair meant anywhere between the shoulders and knees.) When he came up to take his turn at bat, the batter placed his order with the umpire, and the umpire passed the word on to the pitcher. After the first pitch, the batter was not permitted to change his mind during that time at bat.

As of 1887, the strike zone went from the top of the batter's shoulder to the bottom of his knee, and there it stayed until 1950, when it got a bit smaller—the area from the batter's armpits to the top of his knee. In 1963 it grew—back to the top of his shoulder to the bottom of his knee again—but in 1969 it changed to the armpits to the top of the knee. Today it extends from the midpoint between the top of the shoulder and the top of the pants to the top of the knee.

The popular wisdom (not popular among umps, however) is that despite the clear definition of the strike zone, umpires don't often call strikes above the belt line; the debate is a perennial subject for sports columnists and wounded pitchers. Umpires counter with their own perennial comebacks: (a) a batter's natural stance is determined by the umpire when he sees the batter take a swing at the ball, and when a batter is swinging, sometimes his armpits aren't much higher than his belt line, and (b) they call 'em like they see 'em.

Those are garden-variety strike zone grumblings, but in June of 1986 the disagreements about the strike zone grew into a confrontation of a more substantial nature.

Umpire Jim McKean started it all when he told *Sports Illustrated* magazine that American League umpires were calling a larger strike zone on Yankees outfielder Rickey Henderson, whose usual stance is a crouch. That was all that Yankees owner (and notorious civil libertarian) George Steinbrenner had to hear. He fired off his reply: "I will not allow Rickey Henderson to be selectively prosecuted."

Baseball commissioner Peter Ueberroth was not amused by any of this, and he wasted no time in firing off a pointed directive to the umpires of both leagues: "The strike zone is the same for all players."

Well, yes and no. Joe DiMaggio, Willie Mays, and Ted Williams had notably big strike zones. Rickey Henderson's and Oscar Gamble's were small. Pete Rose's strike zone used to change right before your eyes; he'd crouch while he waited for a pitch and then straighten up when the ball was halfway to the plate.

The game's most famous strike zone is unquestionably that of Eddie Gaedel, a twenty-six-year-old, 3-foot-7 Chicago stuntman

The Baseball Fan

"Baseball fans are junkies, and their heroin is the statistic."

—Robert S. Wieder
In Praise of the Second Season

"A baseball fan has the digestive apparatus of a billy goat. He can—and does—devour any set of diamond statistics with insatiable appetite and then nuzzle hungrily for more."

—Arthur Dailey, sportswriter

"I began soaking up records like a sea sponge before I even knew what they meant. I like the way you could read around baseball without ever getting to the game at all."

—Wilfrid Sheed

Hey, this game is fun! The best ballplayer of his generation—some say the best ever to play the game— Ken Griffey Jr., plays baseball with the exuberance and pure joy of a kid. (Ric Fogel/Sportfolio)

who pinch hit for Bill Veeck's last-place St. Louis Browns against the Detroit Tigers in the second game of a doubleheader on August 19, 1951. His strike zone was a minuscule 1 1/2 inches. In his first (and last) appearance in the major leagues Gaedel walked on four straight pitches from Bob Cain, who had trouble keeping a straight face on the mound.

The Browns lost. And by the way, Bill Veeck wasn't the first manager to send a midget to the plate. Red Sox manager Joe Cronin sent his mascot, 3-foot-6 Donald Davidson, to bat in an exhibition game in 1938.

The strike-zone directive from the Commissioner in 1999 was intended to be an equalizer. Time will tell if his plan worked.

Fogged out. (UPI)

"There are surprisingly few real students of the game in baseball, partly because everybody, my eighty-three-year-old mother included, thinks they learned all there was to know about it at puberty. Baseball is very beguiling that way."

—Alvin Dark

Chapter 3
Game Preliminaries

In the late 1940s, the collective genius of baseball decided that The Book needed to be revised. The Professional Baseball Official Playing Rules Committee proceeded to recodify and amend the rules, and on December 21, 1949, in New York City, the results were announced to the world.

It wasn't that the old rules had been bad, mind you; it's just that they were assembled in a more or less random order. The recodified rules were divided into the ten chapters that also constitute the organization of this book.

For the most part, the new arrangement makes eminently good sense. It's reasonable to give the batter, runner, pitcher, umpire, and official scorer their own chapters (Chapters 5 through 10). It also makes sense to put the implements of the game together (Chapter 1) and even to have one easy-to-find location for the definitions of the most crucial terms in the game (Chapter 2).

There, however, the logic of the recodified rules founders. Yes, the titles given to the remaining three divisions of the code sound reasonable enough (Chapter 3: "Game Preliminaries;" Chapter 4: "Starting and Ending the Game;" and Chapter 5: "Putting the Ball in Play"). But in practice, there's a lot of overlap.

All of this is to say that as you read this chapter and the two that follow, you may feel a little as if you're going in circles. Rest assured, though, that you really aren't. Red Barber once said: "Yessuh, baseball is more than a little bit like life." We take that to mean that it's a lot more complicated than it seems at first.

Preparing the Ball

When an umpire makes an unpopular call, thousands of angry fans will caterwaul. At that moment, the ump is perhaps the most exposed—and hated—man on earth.

At such moments we are acutely aware of the umpire's presence, but most of the time the umpire goes essentially unnoticed. He goes about his job, attending to the hundreds of little things that either we take for granted or of which we are entirely ignorant. Many of these tasks are completed before the call of "Play!" is heard; others are performed after the first pitch is thrown.

Probably the ump's easiest job is the one he and the rest of his crew do before taking the field. Provided by the home team with fresh baseballs, each still sealed in its package and bearing the signature of the league president, the umpires perform, as part of the pregame ritual, an inspection of each ball. As The Book tells them to do, they remove "the gloss" from each ball.

The preferred method is to rub them with mud from the banks of the Delaware River, which is not your average mud, as it removes the gloss but doesn't change the color. Five dozen balls is the usual ration for a game, eight dozen for a doubleheader. When the plate umpire takes the field and the game begins, he must have three balls in his possession. The first he will put into play; the other two will be held as alternates. [3.01c and 3.01d]

Mud pies, anyone? An umpire removes the gloss from the new balls before a game.

The ball in play can be replaced when it is batted out of the playing field, when it becomes discolored, or when the pitcher requests an alternate ball be put into play. It cannot be replaced, however, until the previous play has ended.

Some pitchers are very choosy about the balls they throw. To judge from one story told about Sal "The Barber" Maglie, he was very picky indeed. (For those of you born yesterday, he got his nickname because he never shaved on game day. He felt his shadowy growth made him look menacing. It did. Maglie enhanced his reputation for toughness by employing the brushback pitch. If he felt an opposing hitter was getting a little too comfortable in the batter's box or was encroaching on the strike zone, Maglie would fire his fastball high and inside.)

Umpire Tom Gorman once told of the time Maglie called for a new ball. "I gave him a new one, but he threw it back," remembered Gorman. "Didn't suit him. I gave him a second ball. Didn't like that one, either. Finally I gave him a third ball. He still wasn't satisfied."

Gorman had a half-dozen more balls in his uniform pockets, so he cradled them on his forearm and walked to the mound. "Here, Sal, be my guest. Pick one yourself."

Warren Giles, then president of the National League, fined Gorman the next day for "making a travesty of the game."

(It's a good thing that Maglie wasn't playing baseball before 1886. Until that year, even the apparent loss of a ball wasn't enough of a reason to break out a new one. Players were given five minutes to find the old one before a new one was issued.)

The home-plate umpire is responsible for policing the pitchers' and other players' abuse of the ball, as it is forbidden to "discolor or damage the ball by rubbing it with soil, rosin, paraffin, licorice, sandpaper, emery paper or other foreign substance."

Before a 1920 rule change mandated that a clean ball be used, the arrival of a new ball into a game usually called for sending it on a trip around the infield, during which fielders would squirt a little tobacco juice onto the shiny white ball. Some would rub on a little dirt or even touch the ball up with some special substance they just happened to have with them. Not any more. These days, if an infielder or catcher does any of these things, he is subject to ejection. If the pitcher delivers a "discolored or damaged ball" (whether he did the defacing or not), he's subject to ejection and a ten-day suspension. [3.02] (See Chapter 8 for more about the pitcher.)

The umpires must monitor not only the ball but also the players' equipment to be sure all of it is within the rules. The ump is also responsible for making sure every batter wears a helmet (and that most in the American League and all in the National League have the regulation ear flap). All equipment, including batting gloves, uniforms, and bats, is subject to his inspection, and he may order any illegal goods to be taken out of the game. [3.01a]

The Playing Field

Before a game can get underway, the umpire must also establish that the playing lines (the base and foul lines and the lines that delineate the batter's, catcher's, and coaches' boxes) are "easily distinguishable." [3.013] But it is the manager of the home club who has the principal responsibility of deciding whether a game should or should not get underway because of weather conditions or "the unfit condition of the field." He gives the go-ahead to the umpire.

There is a caveat to this rule, however; the responsibility of deciding to play or not to play may be shifted to the league president "during the closing weeks of [the league's] championship season in order to assure that the championship is decided each year on its merits."

We haven't been able to come up with any instances in which this kind of intervention was necessary, but we can think of a fiction-based-on-fact circumstance in which it might have become an issue.

In 1986, the Mets clinched their division championship at Shea Stadium. A tumultuous celebration ensued the moment Dwight Gooden induced Chicago Cub Chico Walker to bounce a ground ball to Wally Backman at second. Backman fielded the ball cleanly and threw to Keith Hernandez at first base for the last out.

Fans and players alike celebrated. The players did so with the traditional champagne, but the fans followed another, less honorable tradition, established after their successful 1969 and 1973 seasons. They tore up the field, removing great gobs of sod and rendering the field unplayable.

As soon as the police managed to herd the destructive celebrants out the center field gates, the grounds crew went to work. They spent most of the night replacing sod and patching up the damage as best they could so that the Mets and Cubs could play the game that was scheduled for the following afternoon. When Mets manager Davey Johnson saw it the next day, he observed, "Oh, man, the field is terrible."

"Hey, Gary, isn't this Howard Cosell's toupee?" Pitchers Tom Seaver and Gary Gentry view the damage done to Shea Stadium by the fans after the Mets' 1969 World Series victory. (UPI)

The teams played, but as New York Times writer George Vecsey put it, they were forced to "tiptoe their way through a 5–0 Met victory the way soldiers would patrol a mine field." It was a meaningless game, one of seventeen insignificant contests the Mets had to play before getting to the business of the playoffs, and the damaged field was little more than a temporary inconvenience (though there were some strange infield hops in the World Series a month later).

But consider this theoretical situation. What if the Western Division race had still been close? (In fact, the Houston Astros had a ten-game lead and clinched it a few days later.) What if one of the teams remaining in contention in the Western Division—rather than the Cubs—had been the Mets' opponent that Thursday afternoon? Those are rather large "what ifs," but nonetheless, it is conceivable that a couple of bad-hop grounders could have a direct impact on the outcome of a game or two. That sort of situation is the reason why The Book allows any team to appeal to the president to "assume the authority" to make the to-play-or-not-to-play decisions when a championship hangs in the balance.

In the event a field is deemed unplayable, the visiting team becomes the winner by virtue of the home team's forfeit. To wax

51

hypothetical once again, how would you feel if your team lost a division title by a single game and the team that beat you "won" by virtue of a forfeiture? That would be more than reason enough to write to your congressman.

In the case of the second game of a doubleheader or of a suspended game, resolution of the to-play-or-not-to-play question shifts to the umpires. In one case not unlike that at Shea in 1986, the field at Comiskey Park was damaged by fan "enthusiasm," and the Tigers won the second game of a doubleheader by forfeit because the fans tore up the field between games on "Disco Demolition Night," a promotion that, needless to say, hasn't been repeated. Fortunately the division race wasn't at stake. [3.10b and 3.11]

Ground Rules

Ground rules, those regulations peculiar to a certain ballpark or to conditions on that park, are established before the beginning of the game. The home-team manager is obliged to present to the umpire the rules governing such issues as spectators in the playing area, unusual aspects of the field, and other special contingencies. Should the visiting manager object to any of the proposed ground rules, the umpire is charged with establishing which rules will be in effect for the game to be played. [3.13]

Ground rules may be specified to cover any number of idiosyncrasies. For instance, a rolled-up tarpaulin may be termed out of play; or if the bullpens are on the playing surface, some portions may be designated as being (or not being) in the field of play.

Sometimes ground rules are created to address hypothetical situations. During the 1989 World Series, Game 3 was postponed just minutes before the scheduled start because of a devastating earthquake. (This was an all-Bay Area Series, pitting the Oakland Athletics against the San Francisco Giants). Ten days later, the game was (finally) about to get underway, and umpires Rich Garcia and Al Clark convened the ritual pregame meeting to brief the opposing managers, Tony La Russa for the A's and Roger Craig for the Giants, on the ground rules. Their conversation was recorded by Major League Baseball Productions and included in that year's official World Series video.

Garcia began. "I just want to bring one thing up. It was brought up by the commissioner's office. If we get a situation where we get a tremor, whatever happens, happens. Everything's in play."

They may look like they're practicing a dance routine, but these Houston Colts outfielders (Rusty Staub, right, and Carl Warwick) are chasing down a ball that Cub Ron Santo hit into the ivy at Wrigley Field. They found it and held Santo to a triple. (AP/Wide World Photos)

Clark emphasized the point. "The ball's not dead when the tremor occurs. It just keeps on going until the play is over."

Garcia offered a little elaboration. "Just like a bad hop. It would be like a ground-ball bad hop."

There followed a respectful silence, during which you could almost hear the managers' brains whirring. Then Craig deadpanned, "Does it count if we have a jackhammer on top of their dugout once the game starts?"

It's refreshing, isn't it, when people bring a sense of humor to things? On second thought, maybe Craig didn't take matters seriously enough: his team was swept in four games.

All parks have their peculiarities. The adornment of Wrigley Field's outfield walls with ivy vines is a classic example (we think of it as being crucial to Wrigley's character, but the fact is, the park was built nearly twenty-five years before the ivy was planted—by the groundskeepers and Bill Veeck himself—in 1937).

The ivy is in play, as Cubs outfielder Andy Pafko learned in the 1945 World Series when he lost a Tigers hit in it. Once Roberto Clemente had the same problem. When he did find the ball, he tried to make one of his rifle throws to the plate, only to discover that the flash of white he had thought was the ball was actually an empty Coca-Cola cup. In his Cubs days Bill Buckner was glad for the vines: he got a homer out of a ball he hit that bounced into the vines and disappeared.

Indoor stadiums usually require some special ground rules. Just ask Mike Schmidt. He once hit a towering "home run" in the Astrodome; it struck a speaker 117 feet up and 329 feet from home. It probably would have traveled more than 500 feet (and been out of almost any other park), but at the Astrodome it fell into center field. All he got for his clout was a single.

At least he got credit for a hit. Dave Kingman hit what surely would have been a home run in the Seattle Kingdome, but the ball hit a roof support wire and was caught by the left fielder for an out. Another time, Kingman hit a towering pop-up in the Hubert H. Humphrey Metrodome that went right through a hole in the canvas roof. Although the Twins infielders waited patiently for it to come back down, it didn't. Kingman was credited with a ground-rule double.

Teams playing at Dodger Stadium the first year after its construction had to deal with an unusual ground rule. Contrary to the usual custom—and The Book—the "foul poles" there were in foul territory. For the 1962 season, the Dodgers played their home games with a special dispensation from the National League that declared that their foul-foul poles were, officially, fair. (During the following off-season, the poles were moved to fair territory.)

One unusual situation that wasn't covered at the pregame ground rule discussion at home plate occurred shortly after the turn of the century during a Baltimore Orioles game. The Orioles were playing in the Eastern League in those days, and their home field was old American League park. One of its unusual aspects was that there was a shack for the ground crew sitting in one corner of the outfield.

That day a member of the crew was watching the game from his distant vantage and saw a visiting hitter smash a hit straight at the shack. When the ball approached, the crewman simply stepped inside, allowed the ball to roll into the shack, then slammed the door on the surprised outfielder pursuing the ball.

When the Twins were the Senators and Washington, D.C., was their home, they played in Griffith Stadium. In center field was "the Dog House," a small box that was used to store the flag. According to Griffith's ground rules, the Dog House was in play. Once a

Senators player slugged a long drive over the head of Philadelphia Athletic Socks Seybold. Seybold gave chase, only to see the ball disappear into the Dog House, its small door having been left accidentally ajar. He went in after it but proceeded to get his shoulders stuck. His teammates were able to extricate the embarrassed Socks from the doorway, but by the time they did, the hitter had long since scored on one of the oddest inside-the-park homers ever.

Once ground rules are established, they shouldn't be a subject for debate—they exist to help avoid arguments later. Yet sometimes they call for judgments that themselves can lead to debate.

In his book *How to Umpire,* old-time umpire Billy Evans recalled an incident that took place in the 1909 World Series. It was at Pittsburgh's Forbes Field, and the Pirates' opponent was Detroit. Two of the ground rules established for the game were (1) a hit that bounded into the outfield stands in foul territory was to be a ground-rule double, and (2) if the ball bounced into the stands in fair ground, it was a home run. (It was not until 1931 that The Book established that if a ball bounced over the fence or into the stands it was a double.)

In the middle of what was shaping up to be a big inning (one run in, a man on third), a long drive was hit down the right-field line. It touched down just inside the line, then bounced out of sight.

Neither Evans nor Bill Klem, who was umpiring the base paths, had seen the hop clearly, so neither was confident about the call. Meanwhile, the Pirates cleared the bases, assuming it was a home run. Evans recounts the story this way.

"I rushed out into right field . . . 'Was that ball fair or foul?' I asked.

"There was none but Pittsburgh rooters in that section . . . and in an instant a hundred voices yelled, 'It was fair by a foot.'

"It was then up to me to learn into which stand the ball bounded after striking the ground. The fans did not know a ground rule had been agreed upon.

" 'Well, if it was fair, where did it bounce?' I called back.

" 'It bounced into this stand,' yelled back the fans. 'Yes, and I have the ball and I am going to keep it,' said one spectator, as he exhibited a brand new ball.

"Since the stand was in foul territory, the ball was ruled a ground-rule double, and given the homegrown source of the testimony, the

Pirates had little room for argument." (The Pirates lost the game 7–2 but won the Series in seven.)

Substitutions

A substitute may be sent in for another player when the ball is dead (in Chapter 5, we'll talk at length about how to tell a dead ball from a live one). The Book also decrees that a substitute shall bat in the same position in the batting order as his predecessor, and that the replaced player is no longer eligible to play (although if the replaced player is a player-manager, he may go to a coach's box).

When two players come in as substitutes, the manager is responsible for telling the umpire-in-chief where in the lineup they will bat before they take their positions in the field. If the manager doesn't tell the ump, the latter himself may designate their places in the batting order. [3.03] This is what the announcers are talking about when they say a National League manager is making a "double switch": he's setting up the lineup so that a new pitcher brought into the game won't be required to hit until after the other substitute comes to the plate.

The Book specifies at what point a substitute is regarded as having officially entered the game if, inadvertently, his arrival is not announced. For a pitcher or batter, it is the moment he takes his position in the pitcher's or batter's box. When a fielder reaches his position and play commences, he is officially in the game. A pinch runner is on the record the moment he takes the place of his predecessor. [3.08]

Those directives seem straightforward enough, but at times there are still problems. One came up when a rookie umpire named Joe Lansalata was working a Yankees–Red Sox series in Boston in the early sixties. A pinch hitter came to the plate, and Lansalata put him into the game. Yankees manager Ralph Houk later protested, saying he hadn't sent in the pinch hitter. American League president Joe Cronin happened to be in the stands that day and saw the whole thing. He upheld the protest.

Despite his record of twenty-six years as a manager without a pennant, Gene Mauch was known as a master strategist. But even he was known to get confused when it came to player substitutions. When he was managing the Phillies in 1968, one of his chief offensive weapons was Richie Allen. Usually in the outfield, Allen was occasionally asked by Mauch to play third, but after the Phillies had taken a 6–3 lead over the Cardinals in the fifth, Mauch decided for defensive reasons to move Allen to left. That also meant he would move his left fielder to center, shift the second baseman to third, and bring Gary Sutherland into the game to play second.

It was a little complicated, and Mauch managed to confuse even himself. "I was thinking Sutherland," said Mauch later, "but I told Lock to go in."

Mauch then walked to the plate and told plate umpire Ed Sudol about the shifting of his players and that he was substituting Sutherland. Meanwhile, Don Lock took the field, and the other players switched positions as instructed.

It only took a moment for Mauch to realize what he had done, and he signaled Lock out of the game. But Sudol informed him that, according to the rules, Lock was officially in the game since he had reached his position.

Mauch argued briefly, asserting that his notification of the umpires should take precedence over the field appearance of a player. The umpires disagreed, and Mauch announced that the game was being played under protest.

Who won? We'll never know. The case was never adjudicated, as they say in lawyer-land, because the Phillies won and Mauch withdrew his protest. (If we were to decide, we'd rule for Mauch.)

Speaking of substitutes, it's about time for a Billy Martin story. We just happen to have one about substitutes in which Alfred Manuel Martin figures.

In July of 1976, he was managing the Yankees in a game against the Kansas City Royals. Martin's opposite number, Whitey Herzog, inserted Hal McRae, his designated hitter, into the defensive lineup in left field. Before the inning began, McRae exchanged five warm-up throws with center fielder Al Cowens.

Since the game was not ready to resume, McRae prepared to take a sixth throw, but umpire Lou Di Muro called upon him to cease and desist. Lou is the kind of guy who's not satisfied with knowing The Book backward and forward; evidently he feels the need to have the league regulations down pat, too. He knew that there's an obscure American League rule that limits a designated hitter who comes in to play defense to five warm-up throws.

It turns out that Lou wasn't the only guy at the park that day who knew about the rule. So did Martin, and as McRae blithely pegged the ball a sixth, seventh, and eighth time to Cowens, the Yankees manager rushed onto the field to demand McRae's ejection. A "discussion" ensued but quickly came to an end. Martin lost the argument, but promptly announced the game was being played under protest.

If you have followed Yankees history during the Steinbrenner era, the next act will sound familiar. The first thing the next morning, Yankees owner Steinbrenner was on the phone to the American League office, insisting that the game be replayed or at least that the Yankees be given three more outs. The protest was not upheld. (For the record, McRae made no defensive play of any sort during his time in the game.)

Close textual analysis of The Book is a venerable managerial tradition, and every manager is looking to provide his team with an edge. Almost a century ago, one of baseball's first real superstars, King Kelly, tried to pull a fast one with a rather broad interpretation of the substitution rule.

A handsome Irishman with a drooping mustache, Michael Joseph Kelly was idolized by his fans. They followed him around on the streets and presented him with a glistening white horse and a carriage in which to ride to and from the ballpark. His popularity was such that management, too, had to acknowledge his value—one of his nicknames was the "Ten Thousand Dollar Beauty," a reference to his purchase price. He was an outfielder of great skill and an accomplished batsman (one year he batted .388), but it was his quick thinking rather than his feats with a bat or glove that earned him a place in these pages.

This story concerns Kelly's days as captain of the Boston Beaneaters. Because of a hand injury, he was sitting out a game during the 1889 season. In the ninth inning his club was up by a run, but the opposition had a man on second and only one down. The batter then hit a high foul pop in the direction of the Boston bench. Kelly realized that his catcher, Charlie Ganzel, wasn't going to be able to cover the ground needed to make the catch. Kelly also realized that he, as captain of the team, was empowered to substitute one player for another. While the pop was still flying high, his mind whirred.

Before the ball came down, he made his decision. Leaping from the bench, he declared, "Kelly now catching for Boston," got under the pop, and made the catch. Although the umpires disallowed the putout, the story and Kelly have outlasted other memories of that game.

Substitute Pitchers. The Book commands that the starting pitcher named in the batting order must pitch to the first batter unless he is injured or falls ill. A relief pitcher, too, must pitch to the batter he is brought in to face unless he is deemed too hurt or sick to continue. If an "improper substitution" is made for a pitcher (that is, if a reliever is brought in before the pitcher previously in the line-up has pitched to anyone, assuming the first pitcher is physically able to pitch), the umpire is charged with ordering the first pitcher to return. On the other hand, if no one notices, it becomes history as soon as the second pitcher (the "improper pitcher," according to The Book) becomes the "proper pitcher." [3.05]

When a manager elects to call in a reliever, he must notify the umpire of where the reliever will appear in his team's batting order. (This is another case in which a manager will often do a double switch—he'll bring in another substitute as well as a pitcher, particularly if the pitcher is scheduled to come up in the next inning.) In turn, the umpire shall have the substitute announced. [3.06 and 3.07]

No discussion of the vagaries of baseball's rules would be complete without a mention or two of Eddie Stanky. Though he had another nickname ("Muggsy"), it is as "The Brat" that he is better known.

He earned the nickname, too. One story told about him took place when he was managing the Cardinals. A couple of close calls went against him, and he went out to the mound to talk to his pitcher.

The umpire gave him a moment to consult with his players. Then, in the umpire's words, when he felt that Stanky was "dillydallying," he went out to the mound. Stanky promptly waved to the bullpen. While the jeep was fetching the relief pitcher, the umpire asked Stanky who was coming in. He didn't answer. The ump asked him a second time, "Who's coming in?"

This time Stanky replied, "Houdini."

The ump had had enough. "Okay, Eddie," he said to the Brat, "I'll tell you something. If Houdini doesn't get out of that jeep, you're done for the night." The relief pitcher was Al Brazle, who had a pretty good curve but couldn't always get out of an inning, let alone a straightjacket in a tankful of water. Stanky was out.

Buried in The Book's fine print is a sentence that says, "A pitcher may change to another position only once during the same inning." [3.03] How often does that come up, you ask? Well, New Yorkers seem to have a talent for getting into debates about substitutions.

This time it's the Mets we're concerned with, during their pennant-winning 1986 season.

On Tuesday, July 22, the Mets were playing in Cincinnati, and the game had gone into extra innings. The Mets were shorthanded because of ejections for fighting earlier in the game.

Manager Davey Johnson brought in Jesse Orosco to pitch the tenth. He had managed to get two men out when Johnson emerged from the dugout and announced that Orosco was moving to right field and that another relief pitcher, Roger McDowell, was coming in to pitch. McDowell got the last out of the inning, and the two-pitcher Mets returned to their dugout.

When they came out for the eleventh, both Orosco and McDowell were still in the game. McDowell started the inning, and Orosco finished up. Orosco pitched the twelfth, and McDowell the thirteenth and fourteenth, moving back and forth from the mound to right field. Johnson also flopped his outfielder/pitcher from left to right, depending on the batter, to "protect" Orosco or McDowell.

Cincinnati protested the game, objecting to the fact that every time the Mets "changed" pitchers, Orosco or McDowell took eight warm-up throws.

The upshot? The protest was denied, because Johnson had stayed within the letter of the law. Our only lingering question is, Why don't more managers use the strategy, especially when they're shorthanded?

Pinch Hitting. When you talk about substitutions, the first situation that comes to mind is probably pinch hitting. There's ample potential for confusion there, too.

One name that will be associated with pinch hitting as long as hot-stove leagues flourish is that of Forrest "Smokey" Burgess. He began his career as a catcher, but it is as a pinch hitter that he and his left-handed stroke are remembered. In 1965, all but two of his plate appearances for the White Sox were as a pinch hitter, and he stroked twenty hits in sixty-five chances, with a remarkable twenty-four runs batted in. As Joe Garagiola once said of him, "Smokey Burgess could wake up at six A.M. on a cold January day, go outside in his pajamas, and hit a line drive."

Other notably successful pinch hitters include Dave Philley (his average in the pinch role was .299) and Manny Mota, who in his career had 150 pinch hits. Tommy Davis prolonged his tenure in the majors as a pinch-hitter, with a career pinch-hitting average of .320. However, it isn't these notable gentlemen but a hitter (designated and otherwise) named Cliff Johnson who managed to get himself most interestingly crossed up by the rule book.

His entry would have been "Most Pinch Hits in an Inning: 2." But it wasn't meant to be.

Johnson's big chance came in June of 1975, when he was with the Astros. Brought in as a pinch hitter, he cracked a double. Other bats on his Houston team must suddenly have taken fire, because they got so hot the club batted around. So up comes Johnson for a second at-bat, and he hit it outta there. Two pinch hits, right?

Nope. Seven months later the Records Committee arrived at a new and broader definition of "pinch hitter." That august body agreed that only on the first at-bat in an inning is the hitter considered a pinch hitter.

Pinch Runners. The Book prohibits "courtesy" runners (you remember the courtesy runner—the boy who ran for the kid with the cast on his leg during pick-up games when you were a player or two short?), but pinch runners are acceptable. No player in the batting order may run for another player. A pinch runner is considered a substitute, and the player for whom the runner substitutes is no longer eligible to play. [3.04]

Interference

The next several rules are intended not for the players but for other people, including umpires and managers, officers of the law,

The Designated Runner

In 1975, the Class A Midwest League became the first circuit in professional baseball to have a "designated runner" for a full season.

The rule ran as follows: The DR was to be named by the manager on his lineup card. He was not to be used more than three times in one game as a pinch runner for any base runner and not more than once in an inning, except as a substitute for the same player. The DR was prohibited from batting or playing defensively. The player(s) for whom the DR "substituted" remained in the game. If injured, the DR could be substituted for.

Apparently, the results of the experiment weren't encouraging. To date, the DH is the only designatee allowed for in The Book.

watchmen, news photographers, and employees of the home team who, "authorized by the home team," may happen to be on the field of play—not to mention the whole host of uninvited characters who might be there.

One rule addresses those nonplayers who are allowed on the field: if they are struck with a ball while it is in play, whether it is hit or thrown, the ball remains live unless their "interference" was intentional. Thus, if a photographer on the field is struck with a batted ball, the defensive team still must field the ball, since it is still in play. On the other hand, if a ball strikes an usher and he kicks it, the ball is declared dead. [3.15]

Spectators can't touch the ball at all; it is officially dead the moment the ball is interfered with. The rule goes even further: if a spectator interferes with a fielder on the field trying to catch a fly ball, the batter is declared out. On the other hand, it is specifically not interference when a fan affects a play when the fielder is reaching over a fence. That's a trespass-at-your-own-risk situation. [3.16]

Despite the precise instructions given in the rule book, the umpires don't always make the right call. In the opening game of the 1996 American League Championship Series, the Orioles were leading the Yankees in the eighth inning. Yankees shortstop Derek Jeter hit a deep fly, and Orioles outfielder Tony Tarasco drifted back to make the catch. But another glove grabbed the ball first; the soon-to-be-famous Jeffrey Maier, a twelve-year-old kid from Jersey, leaned over the fence, plucked the ball out of the air, and pulled it into the stands.

Having seen the photographic evidence, we easily make the call: Just read The Book, which states with admirable clarity, " . . . should a spectator reach out on the playing field . . . and plainly prevent the fielder from the catching the ball, then the batsman should be called out for the spectator's interference."

Back in real time, however, Jeter and the Yankees got an early Christmas present. Umpire Rich Garcia ruled it a homer. In a New York minute the game was tied. The Yanks went on to win on Bernie Williams's homer in the eleventh but not before Orioles manager Davey Johnson got the heave-ho for vehemently protesting the call. Maier got his fifteen minutes of fame (he was a hero in New York, demonized in Baltimore). After reviewing NBC's video replays, even Garcia allowed as how he "probably should have called fan interference."

Two years later, an interference call went the other way, and it cost Mark McGwire what would have been the sixty-sixth home run of his record-setting season. In Milwaukee's County Stadium, he stroked a deep one in the fifth. Umpire Bob Davidson ruled that a fan leaned over the left-center railing and touched the ball *before* it cleared the fence. He ruled it a ground-rule double, but later replays showed the fan hadn't reached beyond the yellow line demarking the field of play. Sorry, Mark.

It's a good thing former Dodger Frank Howard is a gentle giant, because one day at Wrigley he had a good reason to go after the fans in right field. (Listed at 6 feet, 7 inches, Howard was thought by many to be even heftier than the 255 pounds usually given as his playing weight.) On that particular afternoon, he was in pursuit of a fly ball when he was showered with peanuts by the Cubs fans. He missed the fly ball coming his way, and it was ruled a single.

Interference calls invariably lead to arguments. One took place on July 4, 1986, when the White Sox nipped the Yankees 2–1. The winning run scored on a disputed call.

The photographic evidence is clear: young Jeffrey Maier did indeed reach into the field of play. Judge for yourself. (AP/Wide World Photos)

It was all even at 1–1 in the eighth inning at Comiskey Park when Pale Hose lead-off hitter John Cangelosi knocked one into the right-field corner. According to one New York newspaper account the next day, a fan leaned out of the stands and "appeared to touch the ball" as he tumbled onto the field. Yankees right fielder Claudell Washington, anticipating the interference call, took his time fielding the ball. Meanwhile, Cangelosi, who that season tied an American League rookie record for steals, was hustling around the bases. He made it easily to third.

The Yankees appealed to the umpires. "I clearly saw him [the fan] touch the ball," recounted Washington afterward. "He altered the course of the ball." First-base umpire Mike Reilly said, "When a fan hits the ball, it usually changes directions. This one never did . . . [And] a fan falling onto the field is not interference unless it interrupts the flow of the play."

The triple stood. On the next pitch Ozzie Guillen hit a sacrifice fly, and Cangelosi scored. Game to the White Sox.

Players, too, can be guilty of interference if they are not legitimately involved in play. One outrageous incident that took place in the minors years ago stands as an example of how this can happen. [3.17]

Jay Kirke was famous for his inability to hit a curve ball; in fact, his promising major league career (he spent parts of seven seasons in the majors before World War I) was abbreviated by his chronic weakness. At one point he was sent down—along with his plummeting batting average—to minor league Chattanooga, only to meet with a constant diet of curveballs.

Then in one game, his team got a man to second base. With Kirke on deck, the next hitter singled and the man on second started for home. Kirke watched the play unfold as the outfielder picked up the ball and gunned it toward home. Well, it wasn't exactly toward home; the throw was off the mark and soared directly at Kirke.

Kirke, no doubt thrilled at finally seeing something besides a breaking pitch, swung away and knocked it all the way to the fence. Needless to say, his "hit" did nothing for his batting average. It was ruled interference, the previous hitter was credited with a single, and the runner was allowed to score because the umpire judged he would have made it home anyway. However, though The Book today allows for ejection, Kirke was allowed to remain in the game. He went to the plate to take his rips—and promptly struck out. No doubt on a curve.

The home team is responsible for maintaining order in the ball-park. If the home fans interfere with the game, the visiting team may refuse to play; if after a reasonable time the field is still not cleared, the umpire may declare a forfeit. The visitors win, 9–0. [3.isi]

Back in 1974, Cleveland had "10-cent Beer Night." (You read it right, ten cents . . . that was a long time ago!) The fans took advantage of the cheap brew: an estimated 60,000 cups of beer were consumed by about 25,000 patrons, with riotous results.

The trouble started with a father-and-son team who mooned the crowd from center field. Streakers were next; one naked woman even kissed an umpire. Fans started running onto the field between innings, then between pitches. With the score tied 5–5, more fans ran onto the field, and one of them threw a punch at Texas right fielder Jeff Burroughs. When Burroughs punched back, he was instantly surrounded by Indians fans. In the melee that ensued, fans fought with one another and the police as well as with the players. Umpire Nestor Chylak was conked on the head with a chair and promptly did what The Book demands, called a forfeit and gave the Rangers a 9–0 win.

The forfeit rule has come into play more recently, too. On August 10, 1995, the Dodgers lost a ballgame by forfeit thanks to their fans, who tossed souvenir baseballs onto the field. On another night, the umpires didn't rule a forfeit. Instead, they delayed a demonstration game to be played in Folsom Prison. A group of players who spent their winters in California had gotten together to play a team of convicts, but two inmates had seen it as more than an opportunity to test their mettle against the pros. They figured that the game would provide a perfect diversion for an escape.

They gave it a try, but before the two convicts managed to rediscover their freedom, the siren went off and the guards gave chase. The game was held up until the men-on-the-run could be apprehended.

Two and a half hours later, play resumed. The attempted escapees were the only members of the prison population not in attendance at the game.

Leftovers

It appears that while they were reordering The Book, the diligent members of the Professional Baseball Official Playing Rules Committee ended up with a handful of extra bits. (Perhaps it was like model-making, when you end up with a couple of unused and unidentified pieces to that '57 Chevy.) The Committee still had to put the extra rules somewhere, so they threw them in here.

One leftover rule is that players in uniform are forbidden to "address or mingle" with the spectators, whether it is before, during, or after the game. The rule is rarely enforced. [3.09]

Not that communication with the fans is unheard of. Just ask Gary "Sarge" Matthews about his days of leading bleacher cheers at Wrigley Field or Reggie Jackson about his memories of kibbitzing with right-field patrons at Yankee Stadium. More often, however, it is one-way communication—the other way, as boos come from the stands or bottles are thrown. But sometimes the players return the favor.

During the last month of the 1986 season, Boston Strongboy Jim Rice felt compelled to do more than "address" a couple of fans at Yankee Stadium. While he may have violated the rules, he wasn't punished for his transgression.

Although the Red Sox held a commanding lead over the Yankees in their divisional race, they were losing to the Yankees 11–6 on that particular September day. In the eighth inning, a Yankees hitter lofted a pop to left. Rice and shortstop Spike Owen both moved in to make the catch. Neither realized that the other was still in hot pursuit of the ball, and they collided near the seats on the foul line. Rice managed to catch the ball, but Owen was shaken up on the play.

Boston manager John McNamara and several other Boston coaches and players took the trip to short left to check on Owen's condition. It was decided he would leave the game, but as he did so and the gathering of Red Sox players adjacent to the stands started to break up, a fan grabbed Rice's hat from the ground and ran up the aisle with it. Rice took off after him—with McNamara and the rest of the Boston team and coaching staff right behind him.

"Evidently the guy grabbed the hat and Jimmy asked for it back, and the guy gave him some obscenities about him and the ballclub," McNamara reported later.

Rice got his hat back, and three people were arrested. One was the hat-taker, another a fan who had tried to tackle Rice in the stands, and the third a fan who had fallen out of the stands during the fracas. The game continued.

Players and coaches are also not supposed to fraternize with players on opposing teams while in uniform. If you make it to the ballpark early enough to see batting practice, you know that this is a rule that generally goes entirely unenforced. [3.09]

Another miscellaneous rule in this section that made its appearance in The Book relatively late in the game is the one that requires all members of the offensive team to take their gloves and other equipment off the field with them when they return to their bench. As The Book says, "No equipment shall be left lying on the field, either in fair or foul territory." [3.14]

If you've ever seen vintage film footage of baseball in the first half of this century, perhaps you've noticed an infielder make an inning-ending play, only to top it off by throwing his glove into the outfield before going back to the dugout.

It wasn't until 1954 that players were required to take their gloves with them when the defensive team returned to the bench. When the rule book was written, gloves were not the key pieces of equipment that we consider them today, so the rule book ignored them. It was commonplace for outfielders on their way back to the bench just to drop them at the fence or the foul line, out of the way of the other team's fielders.

Game Preliminaries Rule Changes: The Highlights

1872 The rules specify that an "injured" ball is to be replaced—but only in even innings and upon request of the captain of either team.

1880 The umpire is empowered to call for a new ball whenever he sees fit.

1886 If a ball is lost, a new ball is to be put into play immediately by the umpire. (Previously players had been required, upon the umpire's instruction, to search for five minutes to find the lost ball.) Another new rule requires the umpire to have two baseballs at his disposal at all times, as it does to this date.

1891 Free substitutions are allowed for the first time; once a player is substituted for, he may not return.

1897 Intentionally discoloring or injuring the ball is punishable by a five dollar fine. The ball is to be replaced.

1920 The umpires are required to remove the gloss from the balls before the game.

1954 Offensive players are required to "carry all gloves and other equipment off the field . . . while their team is at bat."

Game called on account of snow.
The Polo Grounds.

"Now there's three things you can do in a baseball game. You can win, or you can lose, or it can rain."

—Casey Stengel

Chapter 4
Starting and Ending the Game

To the unsuspecting spectator a baseball game seems to get underway when the last off-key strains of our national anthem have faded from the air and the umpire hollers, *"Play!"* And even though baseball is a game in which things often are not what they appear to be, this is one of those rare occasions in which that unsuspecting spectator would be absolutely right. The game does begin with the umpire's signal (usually *"Play Ball!"* although The Book specifies *"Play!"*). But before that happens, there is a certain amount of business to conduct. [4.01]

Before the Game

Before starting the game the umpire-in-chief and his staff of field umpires (see Chapter 9 for a rundown on the hierarchy of the various umpires) are responsible for seeing that the field is fit for play. If the field isn't ready, the umpire has the authority to get the ground crew working to clean it up or fix whatever is wrong. If there are special ground rules for the park, it is the umpire's job to announce them before play begins.

Until five minutes before a game, the home team has the option of postponing a game on account of weather or delaying the start of a game, but after that the umpire is the sole arbiter. As of five minutes before game time, the umpire is completely in charge of the field and the game. He decides when a game is over, when there will be a time-out, when the lights should be turned on, and when a game is to be called, suspended, or forfeited.

Lineup Cards. Umpires have many responsibilities before a game begins—among other things, they get the game balls ready (see more about this in Chapter 3), but probably the ump's most important pregame chore is to go onto the playing field five minutes before the game starts to meet the managers of both teams (or their appointed stand-ins) and officially receive their lineup cards. Both the home team manager and the visiting manager must hand over two copies of the batting order to the umpire-in-chief. The umpire then checks to see that the two copies are identical (they should be, since lineup cards come with carbons) and calls any discrepancies he notices to the managers' attention. This is the only chance that the umpire has to correct errors in the lineup.

Once he's satisfied that each manager has prepared the list properly—with the right number of players, and only one man per position, for instance—he keeps a copy and gives the other to the opposing manager. And so it comes to pass that the batting order is engraved in stone, or at least in duplicate. From then on unless a player is substituted for another, the batting order must be followed. (Batting out of turn is covered extensively in Chapter 6.)

Getting into Position

Once the lineups have been exchanged and the managers have returned to their dugouts, it's time for the defensive players to take

The Boudreau Shift, the Cleveland Indians' answer to the powerful bat of Ted Williams. Fenway Park, July 14, 1946.

the field, the pitcher to ascend the mound, the batter to take his place, and the umpire to call, "Play!" The game begins. [4.02]

When the game is in progress, the rules dictate that all fielders except the catcher must be in fair territory, but only the pitcher and catcher have specific spots where they must stand. Ever since 1901 the catcher has had to stand directly behind the plate, with both feet within the lines of the catcher's box, until the ball leaves the pitcher's hand. (Before that date the catcher was permitted to catch the first two strikes on the bounce.) And of course, the pitcher must be on the mound (see Chapter 6 for more about where and how the pitcher must comport himself). If any player but the catcher is in foul territory or if any player is out of position, the penalty is a balk. [4.03]

The other fielders may position themselves anywhere they like, provided it's somewhere in fair territory. Many a first baseman opts to keep his left foot outside the foul line when holding a man on the bag—certainly Mets first baseman Keith Hernandez always did—but the rule violation is almost never called. Once in a great while, though, an umpire plays hard ball about rule 4.03. For example, in a Detroit-Boston game on May 1, 1984, Red Sox second baseman Jerry Remy caused a balk to be called on pitcher Bruce Hurst when he stepped into foul territory while the ball was in play.

For obvious reasons, most fielders tend to stand in the same general area, but naturally, they make adjustments to allow for the tendencies of individual batters. One of the best examples of the "personalized" approach to fielding has to do with Ernie Lombardi, who played with Cincinnati and New York in the thirties and forties. When Lombardi would come up to bat, the opposing infielders usually played the hard-hitting but slow catcher on the outfield grass. When asked how he felt about it, Lombardi was quoted as saying, "I was in the majors for four years before I realized that Pee Wee Reese was an infielder."

The "Boudreau Shift"—playing slugger Ted Williams about twenty-five degrees to the right—is part of baseball legend, but perhaps the most creative, and most eloquent, fielding strategy of all came during a 1947 Red Sox exhibition game in Dallas. When Ted Williams came to bat for the first time, everyone on the Dallas team except the catcher and the pitcher climbed into the stands and sat down.

Coaches

The offensive team may have two base coaches—and no more than two—on the field during its time at bat, one stationed near first base and one near third. The coach has only two basic things to remember: he must wear a uniform, and he must remain within the coach's box at all times. While the regulation about the uniform is unbreakable, umpires tend to be very lax in their enforcement of the second rule. [4.04]

Chicago Cubs third-base coach George Myatt throws himself into his work as he instructs outfielder Jim Bolger to slide. It worked: Bolger was safe. Note that Myatt obeyed the rules; he stayed in the coaching box.

When they're signaling a runner to slide or to return to a base, many coaches step out of the box, and umpires usually let them get away with it unless the other team complains. (The opposition complains only at its own risk. Once an umpire is asked to enforce the rule, he enforces it strictly, and for everyone.) Because they're given so much leeway, many coaches leave one foot—or a lot more—outside the box unless there's a runner on third. Mets third-base coach Bud Harrelson was so far out of the box during the 1986 World Series, it's a wonder he didn't miss some of the action.

Dos and Don'ts for All Personnel

Coaches aren't the only ones who have to follow orders, of course. The following rules apply to base coaches, managers, players, substitutes, trainers, even batboys and girls:

⚾ They may not incite the spectators to misbehave (as if spectators need inciting). [4.06a1]

◯ They may not use language that reflects badly on players, umpires, or spectators. Or if they do, they had better do it quietly. Someone very wise once told umpire Billy Evans, "An umpire's success is in a large measure determined by his ability to hear only the things he should hear and see only the things he should see." [4.06a2]

◯ While the ball is in play, they may not do anything to distract the pitcher from his appointed rounds. [4.06a3]

For instance, they're not supposed to do what Minnesota Twins infielder Jerry Terrell got away with on May 29, 1974. That was the day Terrell helped his team beat the Red Sox by employing one of the oldest tricks in the book.

The score was tied in the top of the thirteenth inning with one out, Terrell was at the plate, and there were runners on first and third. Just as Diego Segui, the Red Sox pitcher, was starting to pitch, Terrell reached down in the batter's box for some dirt. Segui balked, and unfortunately that's exactly what the ump (mistakenly) called it. The Twins won.

◯ They may not touch the umpire. If you've watched Earl Weaver, Billy Martin, and others, you know that they may come perilously close. [4.06a4]

◯ Fielders may not distract batters or move into their line of vision. The Minnesota Twins tried this tactic once against the Boston Red Sox in order to try to slow down a Wade Boggs hitting streak. When the "Chicken Man" (it's his favorite food) came to the plate, Twins shortstop Greg Gagne and second baseman Steve Lombardozzi tried changing positions just as the pitcher released the ball. But plate umpire Joe Brinkman wasn't having any of it—he ruled that the players were illegally distracting the batter, and he told them that if they didn't stand still when their pitcher delivered the ball, he'd throw them out of the game. What was even more frustrating for the Twins is that in that three-game series Boggs went nine for fourteen. [4.06b]

Ejections

When players, coaches, or managers don't behave as they're supposed to on the playing field, the punishment that fits the crime is usually ejection from the game. The overall rule is simple and to the point: the umpire may eject anyone on the playing field for any violation of the rules. When a manager, player, coach, or trainer is ejected from the game for any reason, he has to leave the playing field immediately. He may not station himself anywhere near the dugout or the bullpen, and he may not take any further part in the game. [4.07]

In a sense, this rule has the fewest "teeth" of any in The Book, at least as it is applied to managers. It works for players, for obvious reasons, but as any student of the game knows, ejected managers don't always do as they're told. They usually duck out of sight and continue to communicate with their players through the coaches (California Angels manager Gene Mauch didn't make much of a secret of this during the 1986 Angels–Red Sox playoffs). Sometimes their behavior is even more flagrantly rebellious than that.

In a 1951 game between the Cardinals and the Dodgers in Ebbets Field, Brooklyn manager Chuck Dressen was given the thumb for mouthing off to the umpire. Following orders, Dressen immediately left the dugout and changed out of his uniform, but minutes later he reappeared in street clothes in a box seat next to the dugout. Clearly he was doing more than cheering his team on to victory, but there wasn't much that anyone could do about it. Cardinals manager Marty Marion protested the game, but he didn't get any real satisfaction. Dressen was fined for his behavior, but the results of the game remained the same.

Not Valentine's Day

On June 9, 1999, in the twelfth inning of a fourteen-inning game against the Blue Jays in Toronto, New York Mets manager Bobby Valentine had a little disagreement with the umpire and was summarily ejected from the game. According to rule 4.07 of The Book, any manager, coach, player, or trainer who is ejected must leave the field instantly and remain in the clubhouse until the game is over, but perhaps Valentine's copy of the rules is missing that crucial page. Instead of staying in the clubhouse, the manager donned sunglasses, a black baseball cap, and a fake mustache and took a seat in the stands near the dugout, where he was soon spotted by reporters. For flouting the rules Valentine was fined five thousand dollars by the National League and suspended for two games.

When the players on the bench are too obstreperous in their criticism of an umpire's decision—or perhaps part of the umpire's sensory apparatus—the umpire must first warn them to knock it off; then he can start tossing players out of the game. If the ump isn't absolutely sure who the offender is, he can take a guess. [4.08]

Plate umpire Red Jones had a little problem with this on July 19, 1946. It was the White Sox against the Red Sox. The White Sox pitcher threw what umpire Jones thought was a beanball at Ted Williams, so the ump gave the pitcher a warning. That's when the complaints started coming from the dugout—or at least Jones thought they were coming from the dugout. Jones issued a stern warning to the bench. Soon he heard the voice again, loud and distinctive. Jones didn't recognize it, but he *thought* that it sounded like outfielder Ralph Hodgin. So he threw him out.

Even with Hodgin gone, the voice could still be heard, loud and insistent in its heartfelt criticism of Jones. The umpire threw out three more players. The wisecracks continued, so another White Sox player bit the dust. By this time the players on the bench were in hysterics, and the mysterious critic had been suddenly joined by a virtual chorus. Incensed, Jones threw out the whole bench—players, coaches, everyone.

With the White Sox dugout empty, Jones relaxed a little and instructed the pitcher to resume play. A few minutes later, however, the same voice was heard across the land: *"Hey, Meathead! Let's see some hustle before the home folks."* White Sox fan 1, umpire 0.

Ending the Game

It's over when it's over, and whoever scores the most runs wins. It all seems so simple. But neither scoring nor winning is quite that simple. Every time a runner legally touches all the bases before three men are out, a run scores—*almost*. The exception occurs when the runner goes home on a play in which the third out is made either by the batter-runner before he reaches first or by the force-out of any preceding runner. No run scores in such instances. [4.09]

A baseball game ends when the last run of a complete game scores—*almost*. If the game ends with a home run, the game isn't over until the batter-runner crosses the plate (even if his isn't officially the winning run). If the winning run scores in the bottom of the ninth or the bottom of any extra inning and the run is made because of a base on balls, a hit batsman, a balk, or any other play

It Ain't Over 'til You-Know-When

Boston Red Sox outfielder Gary Geiger once went from a hero to a goat in a matter of seconds. It happened in Fenway Park in 1961 in the eleventh inning of a game against the Angels. Geiger hit what he thought was a game-winning triple, so he left the base line and headed happily for the dugout to tell reporters how it felt to win the game. Alas, his actions were premature. The three-bagger had simply tied the game. He was tagged out.

that forces a run home, they have to go through the motions as well; the batter has to touch first, and the runner has to cross home plate. However, if the fans run onto the field and make it impossible for the runner to score, the umpire won't stand on ceremony. (See Chapter 7 for more base-running rules.)

A Matter of Time

Herb Caen, a famous San Francisco journalist, once said, "The clock doesn't matter in baseball. Time stands still or moves backward. Theoretically, one game could go on forever. Some seem to." He was not the first pundit to intimate that the game of baseball does not proceed at a breakneck pace, and he won't be the last. Furthermore, studies show that baseball games are taking longer these days than they used to. No one is sure why, but here are several good guesses:

 Managers are more aggressive now and depend more on specialization—putting in a specific hitter or pitcher for every situation. Substitutions, particularly pitching changes, take time.

 More runners are trying to steal bases. When you consider the look over to first, the pick-off attempt, the pitchout, and so forth, you realize that no maneuver in baseball is more time-consuming than base stealing. (If you don't agree, check out how long a pitcher takes when Rickey Henderson is on base.)

 Hitters are getting pickier every day. As the strike zone shrinks, batters are taking more pitches than they did in the olden days. This too uses up time. (For more about the strike zone, see Chapter 2.)

 According to some experts, more and more pitchers, especially those in the American League, are becoming afraid to throw fastballs down the middle; they'd rather nibble even if it means throwing more pitches—and using up more time.

◯ Individual players slow down the game. If you doubt it, get your hands on some footage of the plate performances of Lee Mazzilli, George Foster, Mike Hargrove, Cliff Johnson, and Carlton Fisk or check out Jim Bibby and Charlie Lea on the mound.

◯ Time is money, at least when it comes to showing games on television. Unless the eleven o'clock news is about to come on, the networks are not in a hurry to get the game over with.

In late July of 1995 three regulations were added for the purpose of speeding up the game. However, as anyone who has ever watched a baseball game knows very well, these rules are not always strictly enforced.

◯ One, the break between half-innings in nontelevised games was reduced from two minutes, thirty seconds to two minutes, five seconds.

◯ Two, it was declared that batters may not wander more than three feet out of the batter's box during an at-bat.

◯ Three, managers and coaches are asked to signal a pitching change as they leave the dugout, not when they reach the mound.

Baseball's Longest Game

Granted, baseball games can be a little (how shall we put this?) long sometimes, but this one was off the charts. The longest game in professional baseball history, between the Pawtucket Red Sox and the Rochester Red Wings, began on April 19, 1981. According to reports, 1,740 fans were in attendance when the umpire hollered, "Play ball!" Some thirty-two innings and eight hours, twenty-five minutes later—when exhausted umpires finally suspended the game—nineteen diehards were still there. (It was 4:07 A.M., and they say the sun was just beginning to come up.) When play resumed, in June, a bases-loaded single ended the game in the bottom of the thirty-third inning. The Red Sox won it, 3–2. Let's play two!

The word is that everyone is trying to speed up the game—in their "general instructions" umpires are explicitly told to keep things moving (see Chapter 9), and managers are instructed to ride herd on their players. Pitchers are encouraged to observe the twenty-second rule (that's how long a pitcher is allowed between pitches when the bases are empty). Even announcers in many ballparks have been ordered to call the next batter's name as soon as a player is finished with his turn at bat. But they can (and should) do only so much. After all, as Bill Veeck said, "This is a game to be savored, not gulped."

Regulation Games

The platonic ideal of a baseball game is nine innings, twenty-seven outs per side, but there are many exceptions to the ideal. According to The Book, a regulation game has nine innings unless it's *extended* because of a tie score (in which case the game continues until the tie is broken) or *shortened*, for one of two reasons: (1) because the home team is leading as the teams go into the bottom of the ninth, or (2) because the umpire calls the game. [4.10a]

When an umpire does decide to call a game, there are no warnings; the game is over immediately. [4.11d]

A called game is considered a regulation game if five innings have been completed; if the home team has scored more runs in four or four and a fraction innings than the visiting team has scored in five; or if the home team scored one or more runs in its half of the fifth inning to tie the score. [4.10c]

As if those rule refinements were not enough to bring on a mild migraine, here are a few more conditions pertaining to called games:

⚾ If each team has the same number of runs when the game is called, it is a tie. There aren't many ties these days, but back in Brooklyn on August 13, 1910, there was a real beaut— between the Dodgers and the Pittsburgh Pirates. Each team had eight runs, twenty-eight at-bats, thirteen hits, twelve assists, two errors, ten players, two pitchers, five strikeouts, three walks, and one passed ball. Now *that* was a tie. [4.10d]

⚾ If the ump calls a game while an inning is in progress and before it's completed, the game is deemed "suspended" if the visiting team has scored one or more runs to tie the score and the home team hasn't scored; or if the visiting team has scored one or more runs to take the lead and the home team has not tied the score or retaken the lead. [4.11d]

⊘ If a game is called before it has become a regulation game, the umpire declares it, imaginatively enough, "No Game." [4.10e]

Rainouts

Nobody likes a rainout. Even if your team wins, you end up feeling robbed, not to mention soggy. Actually it's not just calling the game that annoys people; it's the rule about what constitutes a complete game. In the case of inclement weather five innings constitute an official game if the home team is trailing, or four and a half innings if the home team is ahead. Any regulation game called on account of the weather with the score tied must be played over in its entirety. [4.12a]

And that's where the problem starts. When the skies get cloudy and rain appears imminent, there are inevitable problems with teams who, despite the rules, try to speed up the game or slow it down. In a Brewers-Tigers game on August 1, 1972, it was a toss-up as to which team behaved worse. When the rain started in the fourth, Detroit (who was trailing) tried, naturally, to slow the game down. At one point, an outfielder went so far as to refuse to catch a fly ball, and the Tigers' pitcher repeatedly threw to first base, despite the fact that the runner had taken virtually no lead off the bag. On the other hand, the Brewers made no secret of the fact that they wanted to get the game over with. In a shameful display their base runners begged to be tagged out, but the Tigers wouldn't oblige them.

The game was eventually called after six innings, by which time the umpire-in-chief was completely appalled by the tactics of both managers—Del Crandall of the Brewers and Billy Martin of the Tigers. He recommended that the managers be fined one thousand dollars apiece.

Even if both teams behave like perfect gentlemen, rainouts tend to have extremely unsatisfying, "Who-knows-what-might-have-been?" results. Here's a typical rainout story about a Kansas City–Baltimore game in May of 1972. The Royals scored five runs in the bottom of the fifth, making the score 5–0. In the top of the sixth, however, the Orioles started to come back. They scored three runs, and with a runner on second with two out, they still had a chance. But then the rains came, and play was halted. After waiting for an hour, the umpires finally called the game. The outcome: 5–3 Kansas City.

These sorts of inequities probably even out over time, but that doesn't make them any easier to take when they happen. If many sports columnists have their way, some changes will be made to the rule. The change most often suggested is that all rain-halted games, officially complete or not, would be suspended—and picked up where they left off. The statisticians are understandably opposed to this idea, since they can't complete their stats until a game is officially over, but justice would probably be better served.

Of course, there's rain and there's *rain*. It's a wonder that umpires aren't required to hold advanced degrees in meteorology, since they're routinely called upon to decide whether precipitation is going to cease or keep coming down. One of the controversial aspects of the rainout rule is the length of time that an umpire must wait before calling a game.

On May 8, 1977, there was a dispute over just this question. In the top of the seventh in the second game of a Giants-Mets doubleheader, the Giants were ahead 10–0 with one out. The game was called on account of rain, and the final score remained 10–0 Giants. Because the umpires had not waited the requisite amount of time before calling the game (the minimum is an hour and fifteen minutes in the National League), the Mets protested. The National League president upheld the protest and said that the game must go on. Perhaps not eager to pick up the rout where it left off, the Mets withdrew their protest and let the 10–0 Giants victory go on the books.

For an entirely different reason, rain delays became a particularly controversial issue for the duration of World War II. During the war years sportscasters were forbidden to talk about the weather; the fear was that enemy spies might use the information in planning bomber attacks. Always incorrigible, Dizzy Dean was on the air one day when a Cincinnati Reds–St. Louis Cardinals game was delayed by rain and eventually called. Here's what Dean, a true patriot, told the people: "Before we go off the air, I can't tell you folks why this here game has been stopped by the umpires, but if y'all will be kind enough to stick your heads outta your windows, you kin see for yerselves. And you better hold an umbrella over yer head when you do."

Raindrops Kept Falling on Their Heads

The 1911 World Series—between the Philadelphia Athletics and the New York Giants—gave new meaning to the words rain delay, when Games 3 and 4 were interrupted by a full week of precipitation. With Philly up 2–1, the first drops fell on October 17, and the umbrellas didn't get put away until October 24. In the end the Athletics enjoyed a soggy victory, four games to two.

Suspended Games

Suspended games are regulation games that have to be completed at a later date. A game is suspended if it's called because of legal curfew, league time limits, a malfunction of the home team's equipment, darkness, and, sometimes, inclement weather (see Rainouts, above). [4.12]

Once in a great while a game is suspended because a key player is unable to continue the game. The umpires made the call on June 13, 1999, when Houston Astros manager Larry Dierker suffered a grand mal seizure and collapsed in the dugout in the eighth inning of a game against the San Diego Padres. With the Astros up 4–1 (thanks to a Derek Bell grand slam) the game was suspended.

The rules are quite specific about when a suspended game must be completed or played over: before the next regularly scheduled game between the two teams on the same field or before the next doubleheader if no single game remains on the schedule. If the suspended game was the last one scheduled between the two teams in that city, then the game must be played before the next scheduled game (or doubleheader, if necessary) in the opposition's home town.

When a suspended game is resumed, the game is picked up where it left off with the same batting order and the same rules regarding substitutions. The pitcher of record in the suspended game does not have to start the new game, but if he doesn't start, a substitute must be officially sent in for him.

If it's impossible to resume or replay a suspended game, it becomes a called game.

Game Called on Account of Pooch

In an extra-innings matchup between a couple of minor league teams—Olean, New York, and Bradford, Pennsylvania—a hard-hit ball sent to the left-field foul line was fielded by a player not listed on the lineup card, a black and white spaniel. The Bradford outfield gave chase but had no luck in getting the ball back from man's best friend. When the infield joined the hunt, they too came up empty. The enterprising dog ended up racing out of the park with the ball still clamped in his mouth. Since it was the only ball the teams had that day, the game was officially over.

Doubleheaders

Rule 4.13 says, logically enough, that you have to finish one game of a doubleheader before you can start the next one. It also makes sure that the players don't dawdle between games. Unless the umpire allows a few extra minutes (no more than ten), the second game of a doubleheader has to start twenty minutes after the first one is over. On special occasions—Bat Day or Small Appliance Day or whatever other gimmick the home team happens to have cooked up—the league president may extend the time between games. (Sometimes this practice gets a little out of hand, to say the least. Banner Day at Shea Stadium sounds pleasant enough—fans show off their colorful banners between games of a doubleheader—but the ninety-minute delay is a pain for the umpires, the players, and the fans.)

There's nothing in The Book about tripleheaders, because like the triple feature at the Bijou, the tripleheader has become extinct. Only one tripleheader has been played in the major leagues in the 1900s, on October 2, 1920, the last week of the season. The Pirates and the Reds played three that day to decide a close race in the National League.

The Brooklyn Robins were leading the league, the Giants were second, and the Cincinnati Reds were third. Then came the Pirates in fourth, three and a half games behind the defending world champion Reds. The Reds were in Pittsburgh for a three-game series, which was to be followed by single games between the Pirates-Cubs and the Reds-Cardinals. The Pirates had only a small chance of ending up in third place, but in those days finishing third meant collecting cash, while the fourth place team came up empty. Those last few games were crucial for the Pirates.

Friday's game was rained out, and there were no makeup dates available. The only thing the teams could do about it was what Pirates owner Barney Dreyfuss suggested they do: play three on Saturday. The Reds won the first game 13–4 and the second 7–3. When the third game was called on account of darkness in the sixth, the Pirates were up 6-0. The Pirates didn't capture third place, but the fans certainly got their money's worth.

Forfeits

It seems amazing that a subject as dull as forfeits could take up four separate rules in the rule book, but it's true: Rules 4.15 through 4.18 are devoted to a discussion of when and how a game is forfeited. Only the umpire-in-chief may declare a forfeit, and only under these conditions:

⚾ If a team doesn't show up at all or refuses to start playing within five minutes of when the umpire calls "Play"—unless there are extenuating circumstances acceptable to the umpire.

⚾ If a team fields fewer than nine players.

⚾ If a team employs tactics designed to delay or shorten the game. (They could have—and probably should have—declared a forfeit in that Brewers-Tigers rain delay travesty, but it would have been hard to decide *who* should forfeit to *whom*.)

⚾ If a team refuses to continue to play once the game begins or fails to resume play after a suspension within a minute after the umpire says "Play."

⚾ If a team "willfully and persistently" violates any rule of the game after being warned by the umpire.

⚾ If a team fails to remove a player after being ordered to do so.

⚾ If a team is late for the second game of a doubleheader.

⚾ If the grounds are not properly prepared. (When this happens, the home team forfeits the game to the visitors.)

Dire threats from ballpark announcers notwithstanding ("Ladies and gentlemen, boys and girls, throwing things on the field may result in a forfeit for the home team . . ."), forfeits are quite rare. But one occurred in Philadelphia on August 21, 1949, when the Phillies went up against the Giants. A decision by umpire George Barr was unpopular with the fans—he said that a line drive to center fielder Richie Ashburn had been trapped, not caught—and they were apparently not content to bombard the ump with catcalls. This time they threw bottles, cans, papers, even vegetables. The umpires put up with the barrage for fifteen minutes, but they finally ran out of patience. The umpire-in-chief announced a forfeit.

The official score of a forfeited game is 9–0. When there is a forfeit, the umpire has his usual forms to fill out; he must send a written report to the league president within twenty-four hours.

Protests

According to The Book, a manager may not argue with an umpire about his judgment, but he may embark on a general discussion of jurisprudence with him. That is, a manager may not protest a judgment call, but he may make a protest when he thinks that a decision that an umpire has made violates the rules of the game. [4.19]

Sometimes you have to wonder why a manager even bothers. First of all, overrules are very uncommon; and second, even if a protesting manager is considered technically correct, the decision of the umpire usually stands. And then on those rare occasions in which a protest is upheld, the game isn't played over (which is the best that a team can hope for) unless the league president thinks that the bad call significantly altered the game. The league president's decision is final.

Imagine, for instance, the frustration of the Detroit Tigers back in September of 1979. They protested a 3–1 loss to the Yankees because when Yankees first baseman Chris Chambliss left the field

---

Divorce Court

Philadelphia Phillies third baseman Willie "Puddin-head" Jones once got quite a bit more than he bargained for when he obliged the hometown fans by turning out for Old Timers' Day. While the game was in progress, Jones was served a bench warrant sworn out by his estranged wife, to whom he allegedly owed more than fifteen thousand dollars in child support. He was permitted to finish the game, but then he was taken off to jail.

to have an injury looked at (or his "equipment adjusted," as one report had it), Lou Piniella went on the field to keep the infielders warmed up. When his injuries had been tended to, the first baseman came back on the field. Detroit manager Sparky Anderson complained, saying, quite correctly, that substitution is substitution. When Player B takes the place of Player A, Player B is officially in the game, and Player A is out. The league president's ruling agreed with Sparky's, but he saw no reason to play the game over on account of a technicality. The Tigers won the protest but lost the game.

Should he want to take his chances with a protest, however, the manager has to do it correctly. He must tell the umpire that he's protesting a call before the next pitch is thrown or a batter is retired. If the play he's protesting ends a game, he has until noon the next day to make his protest official.

The most famous protest in recent memory is certainly The Pine Tar Incident, the gory details of which are explored in detail in Chapter 1. But there are a couple more worth mentioning here.

In August of 1979, in a game between the Reds and the Pirates, there was a heated argument that led to an even more heated protest. In the bottom of the fourth inning the Reds were winning 4–3. The Pirates had runners at the corners, with two out. Outfielder Omar Moreno was at the plate facing a 3–1 count, and Cincinnati's Fred Norman was pitching. As Norman delivered the next pitch, the runner, Lee Lacy, broke from first. Catcher Johnny Bench fired the ball ("instinctively," he said later) to Davey Concepcion at second, and Lacy was called out.

What Lacy didn't know was that the pitch to Moreno had been out of the strike zone; the ump had called it ball four. Lacy started his walk to the dugout, but suddenly he noticed that Moreno was taking his base. Turning on his heel, Lacy raced back to second, but he was too late. Concepcion tagged him, and Lacy was out, this time for keeps.

Pirates manager Chuck Tanner screamed that they'd been robbed, and a half-hour argument ensued. Along the way the home-plate umpire, Dick Stello, conceded that a mistake had been made, but he stuck to his ruling. Tanner lodged an official protest, but it was disallowed by National League president Chub Feeney. In Feeney's judgment, (a) there had been no misinterpretation of the rules, and (b) Lacy should have been paying closer attention anyhow. Case closed.

One of the most unusual protests was one that Bill Veeck simply threatened to make. After a sixteen-inning game that the White Sox lost to the Rangers 6–5 in June of 1976, Veeck said he was planning to protest the game. Why? Because the Rangers had used an ineligible player, pitcher Bill Singer.

Singer, who started the game for the Rangers and pitched until he was taken out in the sixth, was traded that day—part of a six-player deal in which the Rangers got Bert Blyleven and Danny Thompson from the Minnesota Twins and Texas gave up Roy Smalley. News releases announcing the trade were distributed during the game, so Veeck concluded that Singer had not had any business pitching that day. When reporters questioned the league

Some ejections are more dramatic than others, and no one appreciated drama more than New York Giants manager Casey Stengel. Here Casey gets a police escort from a 1920s game.

president about Veeck's "unofficial" protest, Lee MacPhail responded, equally unofficially, that it was understood that the trade would take effect after the game.

If a manager is looking for instructions on how *not* to lodge a protest, he need only check out Leo Durocher's behavior during a 1973 Atlanta Braves–Houston Astros game at the Astrodome. On an attempted double play umpire Bruce Froemming called Braves base runner Dave Johnson safe at second base—a close call. To make matters even worse, the Astros' first baseman had been so sure that Johnson was out, he tossed the ball to the umpire and walked to the dugout. That was when Dusty Baker bolted from third and scored. The fans went crazy.

Durocher expressed himself, too. Not content with the traditional shouting match this time, he resorted to other measures. A few minutes later, after play resumed, the scoreboard lit up like a proverbial Christmas tree. The message: *"Manager Durocher has announced the game is being played under protest. Umpires Froemming and Donatelli have blown decisions two of the last three days."*

Durocher got in serious trouble, and even the general manager of the Astros, Spec Richardson, was harshly criticized for his behavior—and fined three hundred dollars. Even so, some people, among them sports columnist Dick Young, said that the Astros got off easy.

Outraged that umpires should be treated thus, Young also reminded his readers of some recent Reds-Astros business and wondered rhetorically how Spec Richardson would have felt if the umpires had taken charge of the scoreboard and sent their own message: *"What a lousy trade the Astros made for Joe Morgan!"*

Baseball in Boston, circa 1890.

"Since baseball time is measured only in outs, all you have to do is succeed utterly; keep hitting, keep the rally alive, and you have defeated time. You remain forever young."

—Roger Angel

Chapter 5
Putting the Ball in Play

To the track athlete, the report of the starter's gun signals the race is underway; to a basketball player, a whistle announces the ball is in play. In baseball, the umpire—his voice like a foghorn—roars, *"Play!"*

Actually, the umpire may have a small voice, and his announcement may even be unnecessary if all the players and coaches are paying attention. But The Book says it is the umpire who, "at the time set for beginning the game," announces the ball is in play. [5.01]

Much of this chapter concerns the circumstances under which the ball is deemed to be "in play" and when it is "dead." But there are also a number of rules in this chapter that probably could have been located as well in the opening section of the rule book ("Objectives of the Game"), so let's take them first.

More Objectives of the Game

When the ball is in play, the batter hits and runners advance. Outs are made and runs are scored while the ball is alive. As The Book has it, it is the pitcher's job to "deliver the pitch to the batter"; the batter may swing or not, "as he chooses." [5.03]

When the ball is dead, however, none of these things can happen except in those cases in which, as a result of something that occurred while the ball was still live, the runner can advance. A home run is one example: the ball is dead the moment it leaves the field of play, but any runners on base can come around to score. [5.02]

This surely comes as no surprise to you, but the offensive team's purpose is "to have its batter become a runner, and its runners advance." In turn, the objective of the defensive team is to prevent runners from getting on base and then, should they fail at that, to "prevent their advance around the bases." [5.04 and 5.05]

Finally, we get to score a run: a batter "who becomes a runner and touches all bases legally" accomplishes that. But it's not all scoring because, of course, three outs are all an offensive team gets before having to go out onto the field to play defense while the opposition gets its three outs. [5.06 and 5.07]

Live Balls

The baseball concepts of "life" and "death" are among the first a Little Leaguer is taught. If hyperactive nine-year-olds, to whom concentration doesn't come naturally, can handle such diverse and difficult concepts, you would think that by the time a player reaches the majors, the notions of the ball's being alive or dead should be second nature.

Yet in stressful situations players, like other human beings, may get a little confused. Tempers may flare, and things may go wrong, and, well, a guy just forgets sometimes.

Early in the 1986 season, just such a combination of circumstances occurred. The game was played indoors at Seattle's Kingdome, and the Mariners were facing the Oakland A's. Jose Canseco, then only a rookie, led off the third for the A's by swinging at a third strike, only to see the ball get past the catcher. He reached first safely on the wild pitch.

Mariners pitcher Mike Moore was none too pleased at this turn of events. Perhaps he let his irritation affect him, because he proceeded to give up a double to the next hitter, Alfredo Griffin, and then to walk Bruce Bochte. In a few short minutes, Moore was faced with the pitcher's nightmare: the bases were loaded with none out.

At moments like that one, total concentration is called for. The pitcher simply must throw strikes, since a walk will force in a run, yet he can't give the batter too good of a pitch, since a grand slam is the biggest pitching mistake there is.

Moore walked the next batter. To compound his pitching troubles, he then made a mental mistake. He was so angry with himself that when his catcher threw the ball back to him, he bounced it off the turf in frustration. Since the ball was still in play, the runner moving to third on the walk alertly ran toward home plate.

Moore, already a little shaken by the previous events, picked up the ball and hurriedly threw to his catcher. The throw was no more catchable than the third strike he'd thrown to Canseco had been. Griffin scored. The other two runners moved to second and third. The next batter singled them in, and the Mariners lost 4–1.

If Moore had trouble keeping track of one ball in play, imagine how confused he would have been if there'd been two. That's happened a few times over the years, including once during the 1959 season at Wrigley Field.

Stan "The Man" Musial was the batter. The count was three balls and one strike when Cubs pitcher Bob Anderson threw wildly. As the ball rolled to the backstop, umpire Vic Delmore called ball four, and Musial headed up the first-base line. Cubs catcher Sammy Taylor took issue with the call, claiming the ball had hit Musial's bat. The Cubs manager came out to join the argument.

Since the call was ball four and no one had called time, the ball was still in play. But umpire Delmore, distracted by the argument, proceeded to pull another ball from his pocket and handed it to the catcher, though Cubs third baseman Alvin Dark had recovered the first ball at the backstop. There were two, count 'em, *two* balls in play.

Cardinals first-base coach Harry "The Hat" Walker immediately saw an opportunity and ordered Musial to dig for second. Anderson saw him take off, grabbed the new ball from his catcher, and threw to his second baseman. Alvin Dark also saw Musial begin his sprint, and he threw the original ball to Ernie "Let's Play Two" Banks at shortstop.

Anderson must have had a case of rag arm that day, because his throw went into center field. Musial watched it soar by and ran for third. To his surprise, he met up with Banks, who was waiting for him in the base line—with the ball. Banks tagged him out.

But was he out? After further discussion, the ruling was indeed that Musial was out, and the Cardinals played the game under protest— that is, until they made the issue moot by winning the game.

Dead Balls

In The Book there is a whole laundry list of situations in which the ball is automatically declared dead (starting with the umpire calling time, which Vic Delmore should have done when the argument began).

Hit Batsman. The ball is dead the moment a batsman is hit. For example, in none of the record-breaking thirty-five times Red Sox designated hitter Don Baylor was hit in the course of the 1986 regular season were the runners allowed to advance (unless, that is, they were forced to move up a base by Baylor's arrival at first). [5.09a]

Interference. The ball is dead and runners must hold when a catcher's throw is interfered with by the plate umpire (unless the runner is thrown out despite the interference, in which case the interference call shall be disregarded). [5.09b]

Balk. The ball is also declared dead when a balk is committed, though the runners advance (see Chapter 8 for more balk talk). [5.09c]

Illegal Hit. On the other hand, the runners must return when a ball is batted illegally—with an illegal bat, for example, about which there is more in Chapter 6. [5.09d]

Foul Ball. When a foul ball is not caught, the ball is dead. It wasn't always this way. Until 1881 runners had to make it back to their bases before the ball or risk being put out. [5.09e]

Today, the ball often carries out of play anyway, so there's no room for argument. But in one case in 1939, a Red Sox rookie named Ted Williams put a foul ball out of play—with his throwing arm.

It was a preseason game on, appropriately enough, April Fool's Day. The game was in Atlanta, against the Reds. A foul ball dribbled his way, and the Splendid Splinter moved over to field it. Almost as soon as he picked it up, the ball slipped out of his grasp. It must not have been Ted's day, because then he accidentally kicked it with his foot. When he finally did get a good grasp of the ball, he was so angry that he flung it over the fence. It struck a Sears store across the street. Red Sox manager Joe Cronin replaced his rookie right fielder for the remainder of the game.

Batted Ball. A fair ball that strikes a runner or umpire before a defensive player touches it is dead; on the other hand, if a fielder touches the ball and then it hits a runner, it is still a live ball. [5.09f]

Interference by a Uniform. This next variation isn't one that comes up every day: if a pitched ball gets stuck in the umpire's or the catcher's mask, the ball is dead and the runners may advance.

It comes up so rarely, in fact, that when it did happen in a Brewers-Athletics game, no one could find the rule that addresses it. [5.09g]

The game was in 1976, and the incident took place in the eighth inning. A pitch thrown by Oakland fireman Paul Lindblad bounced in the dirt in front of the plate, struck catcher Tim Hosley in the throat, and proceeded to get caught between his uniform and his chest protector. Home-plate umpire Dave Phillips, confident in his knowledge of the rule book, called a time out and waved in the runner from third. The score was 3–2, Milwaukee.

Oakland manager Chuck Tanner came running. He asked Phillips to explain the call, which he did; then he asked Phillips to show him where in The Book it appeared, which he could not. "I know you can't win a protest over an umpire's judgment," Tanner said later, "but you can win a protest if their decision is not in the rule book." Tanner lost both the game (4–2) and his protest (not least because, as we'll see in Chapter 9, anything not in The Book is up to the umpire's discretion).

Is the ball dead if it disappears inside a fielder's uniform? Although it probably couldn't happen with today's formfitting double knits, in older, baggier days it did, to Philadelphia Athletics shortstop Eddie Joost in 1948. He scooped up a ground ball at Fenway Park but then

The Book says, "The ball becomes dead when [the] umpire calls time . . . when an accident incapacitates a player"—as in this 1957 photo.

couldn't find it (it had rolled up his sleeve and inside his shirt). Ted Williams, the runner at third, froze, assuming that Joost was trying to fake him into making a run for the plate only to throw him out as soon as he left the bag. By the time he realized that Joost really had lost the ball—when the shortstop started flapping his arms and patting himself all over—Williams couldn't run anyway because he, like everybody else in the ballpark, was completely convulsed with laughter.

Runner Struck by Pitched Ball. The ball is also dead (though the runners may advance) when a pitched ball touches a runner trying to score. We haven't been able to find any instances of this happening, but it theoretically is possible if a runner on third got an extraordinarily good break on the pitch and beat it home. The rule also serves to discourage a pitcher in such a situation from throwing the ball at the runner. [5.09h]

The Time-out

According to The Book, only the umpires have the authority to call time, though sometimes Mother Nature (or mechanical failure) intercedes and does it for them. The umpire is empowered to call time when darkness or other conditions make play impossible; when light failure makes "it difficult or impossible for the umpires to follow the play"; when an accident incapacitates a player or an umpire; when time is requested for a substitution; and pretty much whenever an umpire feels it is appropriate. However, the umpire explicitly is not to call "time" while a play is in progress. [5.10]

Washington Senators first baseman Joe Cunningham pursues a foul pop and finds himself tumbling headlong into the dugout.

The Night the Park Went Dark

The Senators were playing a night game with the Tigers at old Griffith Stadium in Washington. With Tiger George Kell at the plate and the pitcher in his windup, the lights suddenly went out.

They remained off only briefly, but when they blinked back on, the crowd witnessed a strange sight. Everyone on the field except the pitcher was lying on the ground, and some of the prostrate players were even protecting their heads with their arms. It wasn't that they chose to catch a little shut-eye or even that they were afraid of the dark. The umpires, players, and coaches had hit the dirt because only the pitcher knew for sure whether the ball had been thrown. It hadn't, but no one was taking the chance of getting hit by a pitched or a hit ball.

The exceptional moments that aren't covered specifically by the rules are the truest tests of an umpire's resourcefulness. One such instance took place in the 1934 World Series between the Cardinals and the Tigers (the Series in which, by the way, a pair of brothers—Dizzy and Paul "Daffy" Dean—each won two games for the Cardinals, the only time in World Series history it has happened).

The seventh game was in Tiger Stadium, and by the sixth inning St. Louis had a 9–0 lead. As if the fans didn't have enough to be grumpy about, on a close play Joe "Muscles" Medwick slid into third with spikes high in an apparent attempt to spike the Tigers' third baseman. The fans booed and hissed. When Medwick tried to return to his left-field position for the bottom of the inning, the Detroit fans did more than boo. They bombarded Medwick with bottles, fruit, sandwiches, peanuts, popcorn, and assorted trash. The police intervened, but the food shower continued for nearly thirty minutes. Finally, baseball commissioner Judge Keneshaw Mountain Landis ordered Medwick out of the game. His absence had little impact on the result. The final score was 11–0.

Medwick himself summed up the bizarre situation cogently when he observed, "I know why they threw that stuff at me. What I can't figure out is why they brought it to the ballpark in the first place."

The last rule in this section of The Book spells out when the dead ball becomes live again: it is at the moment the pitcher assumes his place on the pitcher's plate, ball in hand, and the umpire calls, "Play." So we're back where we started, playing ball. [5.11]

Now batting for New York: Babe Ruth.

"The batter is one lone man playing the other nine men."

—Paul Gallico

Chapter 6

The Batter

The art of hitting cries out for comment. Ted Williams always said that hitting a baseball thrown by a professional pitcher is the single hardest thing to do in any sport, and we're not inclined to disagree with him. After all, even athletes who do it particularly well—Williams himself, to name one—get it right only about one time out of three.

Mickey Mantle often pointed out that his strikeouts and walks amounted to "five full seasons of never hitting the ball." First baseman Ted "Big Klu" Kluszewski waxed metaphorical in his description: "How hard is hitting? You ever walk into a pitch-black room full of furniture that you've never seen before and try to walk through it without bumping into anything? Well, it's harder than that."

In this chapter and in the two that follow—Chapter 7 concerns the runner, and Chapter 8 is about the pitcher—you'll come to understand and appreciate a little better how difficult hitting really is. You'll also see the rules of baseball at their most creative, most confusing, and most lively.

Batter Up

The Book says that the batter must take his position in the batter's box promptly. Of course, there's a fair amount of flexibility in the term *promptly*, as anyone who ever witnessed the antics of George Foster or Mike Hargrove (known as "the human rain delay") can attest. By the time batters have completed their prebatting ritual—tugging the shirt, arranging the helmet, adjusting the gloves, hiking up the pants, cleaning the shoes, saying a Novena—it's a wonder that there's still time enough to get in nine innings before curfew. (Check out Bernie Williams and Rickey Henderson. They're a mass of tics at the plate.)

It's up to the plate umpire to see that there is no unreasonable delay, but he's got enough to worry about without being a stickler about this rule. A violation is rarely called. However, The Book makes the ump's power clear: if the batter refuses to take his position promptly, the umpire may tell the pitcher to proceed and start calling balls and strikes. [6.02]

The Time-out

Once the batter has made himself comfortable, he may not leave unless the umpire gives him permission and calls time. Once the pitcher comes to the Set Position or starts his windup (see Chapter 8 for the details), the umpire will deny permission, no matter what reason the batter gives for wanting to step out of the box. If the batter leaves the box without permission, the pitcher may go ahead and pitch, and the ump calls balls and strikes as usual.

If a pitcher who has come to a Set Position or started his windup doesn't complete a pitch because a batter steps out of the box, no rule is broken; it's more of a standoff. Because both players have violated the rules, the play starts from scratch.

Naturally, when time is called, the ball is dead, but that doesn't necessarily stop pitchers from throwing and batters from swinging. In April of 1976 Milwaukee's third baseman Don Money did some serious swinging against the Yankees, but he might as well have stayed in bed. He hit a bases-loaded home run, but it didn't count—the umpire had called time. When Money went to bat again, he was unable to repeat himself and returned to the dugout hitless.

And in 1960 White Sox first baseman Ted Kluszewski was robbed of a three-run homer against Baltimore. In the top of the eighth it was 8–1 Orioles with two on and two out, and Kluszewski hit a ball out of the park. That was the good news. The bad news was that a moment before the pitch the umpire had decided that a couple of players throwing warm-up tosses on the field were too close to the action, so he called time. Kluszewski's homer didn't count. When he batted over, he killed the rally with a fly ball.

One last tearjerker: in the spring of 1913 the Philadelphia Athletics and the Giants were locked in a scoreless tie in the bottom of the tenth at the Polo Grounds. However, it looked as though everybody would be able to go home and have some dinner when the Giants managed to get a runner, Fred Merkle, to third with nobody out. Pinch hitter Moose McCormick was called to drive Merkle in.

According to the usual ritual, umpire Bill Klem turned away from his duties at the plate to announce the change in the line-up to the official scorer in the press box, but he took a little longer than usual. That's why he didn't see Grover Cleveland Alexander's fastball or Moose McCormick's answer to it—a solid single to left field.

Fred Merkle scored easily, and for a few sweet moments the Giants fans were able to celebrate. Both teams headed for the club-house, but because he had called time, Klem had no choice but to chase them back onto the field to take the play over. This time McCormick grounded out, and a long afternoon got longer still. After eleven innings the game was called on account of darkness.

Batter Out

Rule 6.04 says that a batter has completed his time at bat when one of two things happens: either the batter is *put out* [6.05 and 6.06] or he *becomes a runner* [6.08 and 6.09]. Let's cover the bad news first.

All's Well That Ends Well

Not all time-outs end in tragedy. The St. Louis Cardinals and the Brooklyn Dodgers were fighting for the pennant one afternoon in September. The Dodgers were winning by two in the bottom of the ninth when Cardinals outfielder (and future Hall of Famer) Stan Musial came to the plate with the bases loaded and two out. A ball rolled onto the field, and the third-base umpire called time. But the pitch came in anyway, and Stan the Man hit it over the right-field screen. The fans went crazy with happiness, and Musial circled the bases.

By the time Musial touched home, the word was out: the run didn't count. Musial took the news like a gent, but others reacted differently. In fact, before the argument was over, a coach and five or six Cardinals players had been ejected, and the police had to be called onto the field. But there was really nothing to argue about; the third-base ump had quite clearly raised his hands before the pitcher had start-ed his delivery. Eventually Musial returned to the plate—and smashed a game-winning triple.

Carl Yastrzemski once said: "You don't always *make* an out. Sometimes the pitcher *gets* you out." In fact, there are so many ways a batter may be put out, it's a wonder anyone ever reaches home. Rule 6.05 takes fourteen separate subsections to spell them out.

In the 1920 Brooklyn Dodgers–Cleveland Indians World Series, pitcher Charley Mitchell learned about several of the ways firsthand on his way to one of the least edifying World Series performances in history. Although the Dodgers reliever came to bat only twice, he made five outs for his team.

The first time he was up, there was a man on base, and Mitchell hit into a double play. The second time up the bases were loaded. Mitchell connected with a pitch, but he hit the ball straight into the waiting glove of Cleveland second baseman Bill Wambsganss, who stepped on second and tagged the runner making his way to

Going, going, gone! At 8:18 P.M. (Central Time) on September 8, 1998, Mark McGwire broke baseball's biggest record by belting home run No. 62. Roger Maris's children were on hand to celebrate the historic event. But Big Mac wasn't done. The Cardinals slugger kept going deep until he belted No. 70 in his last at-bat on the last day of the season. (Elsa Hasch/Allsport)

Talk About an Easy Inning!

These are the players who have made unassisted triple plays in the major leagues in the twentieth century:

NEAL BALL—Cleveland Indians shortstop, July 19, 1909

BILL WAMBSGANSS—Cleveland Indians second baseman, Game 5 of the World Series, October 10, 1920

GEORGE BURNS—Boston Red Sox first baseman, September 14, 1923

ERNIE PADGETT—Boston Braves shortstop, October 6, 1923

GLENN WRIGHT—Pittsburgh Pirates shortstop, May 7, 1925

JIMMY COONEY—Chicago Cubs shortstop, May 30, 1927

JOHNNY NEUN—Detroit Tigers first baseman, May 31, 1927

RON HANSEN—Washington Senators shortstop, July 30, 1968

MICKEY MORANDINI—Philadelphia Phillies second baseman, September 23, 1992

JOHN VALENTIN—Boston Red Sox shortstop, July 15, 1994

second, thus completing the first and only unassisted triple play in World Series history. It's a good thing for Mitchell that there are only three outs to an inning.

Here are some of the ways a batter may be put out:

The Fly Ball and the Strikeout. Even toddlers know these two: (1) if a ball (other than a foul tip) is caught on the fly, whether it's fair or foul, the batter is out; and (2) it's one, two, three strikes, you're out at the old ball game. [6.05a and 6.05b]

The only complication that may arise here is that in both cases the ball must be *legally* caught—that is, it must be caught in the glove or mitt before the ball touches the ground. The ball may not be "trapped," and a catch isn't legal if the ball lodges in somebody's clothes or if it first touches the umpire and is caught on the rebound. If a foul tip first hits the catcher's glove and then is caught by both hands against his body or protector before it hits the ground, it's a strike. And if a player deflects a batted ball and if he or another fielder catches it before it hits the ground, it too is an out.

The Force-Out. As in most things, the race goes to the swift. If a batter hits a fair ball and he or first base is tagged before he gets there, he's out. It is also considered a force if a catcher drops a third strike when first base is empty and the batter attempts to beat the throw to first. [6.05j]

The Dropped Third Strike. If a third strike is not caught by the catcher when first base is occupied before two are out, the batter is out. If first base is not occupied, it's a whole different story, as catcher Mickey Owen well knows. There is more about that (and especially about Mickey Owen's nightmares) later in this chapter. [6.05c]

The Intentionally Dropped Ball. The batter is out if an infielder intentionally drops a fair fly ball or line drive when first, first and second, first and third, or first, second, and third base are occupied before two men are out. When this does happen, the ball is dead, and the runners go back to their original bases. [6.05l]

If this sounds like a close relative of the infield fly rule, it is. An extension of that rule, it's designed to protect the poor defenseless runner from the actions of unscrupulous fielders. In one game, on May 20, 1960, it protected the runners on base when Stan Musial of the Cardinals went up against Joe Nuxhall, the pitcher for the Cincinnati Reds. Musial hit a bases-loaded line drive to Nuxhall, who dropped the ball. Although the infield fly rule was not in effect, in the opinion of umpire Ed Vargo, Nuxhall did it on purpose. Musial was out, and everybody stayed put.

This rule goes on to say that if the fielder lets the ball drop *untouched* to the ground, the batter is not out except when the infield fly rule applies. This aspect of the rule becomes a little easier to understand with the following actual play in mind.

On September 17, 1974, the Baltimore Orioles visited Yankee Stadium. In the bottom of the sixth the game was scoreless. Yankee second baseman Sandy Alomar was at the plate, and shortstop Jim Mason was the runner on first. With nobody out Alomar tried a sacrifice bunt, but he popped it to first. Orioles first baseman Boog Powell, noticing that Alomar was not exactly sprinting to first base and that Mason was staying around to tag up, stopped short and let the ball hit the ground. He then forced Alomar at first and tagged Mason out when Mason was unable to go into reverse quickly enough.

The Foul Bunt. If the batter bunts foul on a third strike, he's out. [6.05d]

Close Encounters. When there's a bat, a ball, a runner, and six defensive players protecting the infield at the same time, anything can happen, and it often does. Balls hit batters and/or fielders, bats hit batters, balls, and/or fielders, batters trip over bats, balls, and/or fielders. Several clauses in Rule 6.05 cover these eventualities.

If the batter is trying to hit a third strike and the ball touches him, he's out. (This is not to be confused with the Hit Batsman Rule, which is described later in this chapter [6.05f].) He's also automatically out if he hits the ball fair and it touches him before it touches a fielder. [6.05g]

If the batter hits a fair ball and then his bat hits the ball a second time in fair territory, he's out as well. (If this does happen, the ball is dead, and no runners advance.) However, if the batter drops his bat in fair territory and the ball rolls against it and the umpire thinks that the interference was an accident, the ball is alive and well (and in play). [6.05h]

Even if the ball goes foul, the batter may find himself in trouble. If a batter hits or bunts a ball foul and then tries to alter the course of the ball in any way, he's out, the ball is dead, and any runners stay put. [6.05i]

Batters don't usually have anything to do with the ball once they've hit it, of course. Much more often it's the defensive fielder who tries to alter the course of a ball. For example, Seattle Mariners third baseman Lenny Randle once tried to "talk" a ball foul.

The incident took place in a game against Kansas City in May of 1981. It was 8–5 Kansas City when Royals outfielder Amos Otis tapped the ball down the third-base line. Randle went down on all

Maybe We Should Call It a "Sacrifice Tim!"

One story has it that the bunt was "invented" by Tim Murnane, an infielder who played for the Athletics for a while before joining the Boston Braves. Murnane had great speed, but he wasn't much of a hitter. One day he swung at a pitch, and what was undoubtedly a triple in Murnane's mind turned out to be a dribbler in front of the plate. Thanks to a combination of his wheels and the fact that the opposition was caught unawares, Murnane made it to first. Recognizing a good thing when he saw one, Murnane never looked back. He went on to become one of the greatest bunters in the game.

fours, and the next thing you know, the ball dribbled foul. Kansas City manager Whitey Herzog had a few words to say about the play—notably that Randle had been blowing on the damned thing—and the umpire eventually decided that Randle had indeed been too close for comfort to the ball. Amos Otis got a hit. (*Postscript:* Randle said that he hadn't been blowing on the ball— he had been *pleading* with it.)

If a bat breaks and part of it ends up in fair territory and is hit by a batted ball or hits a runner or fielder, the ball is in play. If the same thing happens in foul territory, it's a foul ball (and the ball is dead). If a whole bat is thrown into fair territory and interferes with a defensive player who's trying to make a play, it's interference, whether the batter meant to let the bat fly or not.

It's a big playing field but obviously not big enough. Cubs batter Al Heist tried to lay down a bunt, but the ball—and Phillies catcher Al Kenders—had other ideas. Despite the collision, Kenders made the catch. Batter out.

Economy Measures

The foul strike rule was passed by the National League in 1901, supposedly as a response to Phillies outfielder Roy Thomas and Oriole-turned-Cardinal-turned-Giant John McGraw. Apparently both players could foul off balls at will, and they ended up wasting a lot of time, not to mention balls. In one game in 1900, Roy Thomas fouled off twenty-two balls before he eventually walked.

Sometimes there's just no telling what can happen to a bat, as Dave Winfield, Tony Oliva, Paul O'Neill, and other notorious bat-flingers can attest. Ted Williams knows all about it, too. The Splendid Splinter didn't much like striking out, and one day when he did, he let his temper get the best of him. Flinging his bat away in disgust, he stormed back toward the dugout. But something went wrong. Instead of slamming into the dirt, the bat flew into the air and landed more than seventy feet away in the box seats, on Gladys Heffernan, Red Sox manager Joe Cronin's housekeeper. Fortunately for everyone concerned, Mrs. Heffernan wasn't badly hurt, and she was a big, non-litigious Ted Williams fan.

The rule is the same for batting helmets: if a helmet is accidentally hit by a batted or thrown ball in fair territory, the ball is in play; in foul territory, the ball is foul—and dead. If a base runner interferes with a play by throwing a helmet, the runner is out, the ball is dead, and any runners must return to the last base legally touched. [6.05h]

While we're on the subject of being struck by flying objects, let us mention what happened on June 20, 1999. It was the bottom of the seventh, and the Yankees were losing to the Angels. Hoping to turn things around for New York, first baseman Tino Martinez stepped up to the plate while Paul O'Neill waited in the on-deck circle. Martinez popped up, his bat snapped, and a piece of the bat made a beeline for O'Neill's left leg. The barrel hit him just above the knee. The good news: O'Neill wasn't badly hurt. In fact, after being checked out by manager Joe Torre and the Yankees trainer, he singled to right field. The bad news: the Yanks still lost the game, 4–2.

Leaving the Base Path. The base lines are there for several reasons, not the least of which is to show the batter the way to first base. According to The Book, if a batter leaves the base paths on his way there, he's automatically out. (In practice umpires let batters run outside on a clean hit, but if there's any question that the runner was attempting to dodge a tag, he's out.) The diagram on page 6 has all the details of the playing field, but for these purposes the base paths refer to the second half of the distance between home and first. The batter may not run outside the three-foot line or inside the foul line in that area, with one exception: as much as he may not want to, a batter may (in fact, must) leave the base paths to get out of the way of a fielder who is trying to field a batted ball. [6.05k]

Interference by a Runner. Sometimes a batter is out because of what one of his teammates does. The Book says that if a runner intentionally gets in the way of a fielder who is either trying to catch a thrown ball or throwing a ball to complete a play, the batter shall be out. [6.05m]

The most common violation of this rule comes when a runner tries to break up a double play at second base. A certain amount of aggression on the base paths is permitted—and encouraged in some quarters—but if an umpire thinks such behavior is excessive and/or unsportsmanlike, he may call the batter out. In actual play, however, interference by a runner is almost never called.

Interference by a runner was the specialty of Detroit Tigers outfielder Ty Cobb. The sight of Cobb sliding into second with his spikes high was a familiar one indeed in the first thirty years of the twentieth century, and there was many a bloodied and scarred second baseman who wished that the umpires would be a little stricter in their rulings.

Every once in a while Cobb outdid even himself. During one game he must have been feeling more aggressive than usual on the base paths. He was on first, and there was a man on second. When a long fly ball was hit to the outfield, both runners tagged up and then took off. Cobb, tearing into second, was apparently not content to spike the shortstop. This time he slid into the bag on his back with his legs spread wide, and when he made contact with the fielder, Cobb clamped his legs around him. Surprised (at least) and powerless to move, the shortstop looked on as the front runner scored.

One of the most controversial plays in the history of the game brought together this rule and one of the most famous umpires of all time, Bill Klem. It involved a critical decision against the New York Giants, and manager John "Little Napoleon" McGraw always maintained that the call cost his team the pennant.

The date was September 27, 1928, and the National League pennant race that year was still undecided. The Giants, only a half-game behind the league-leading St. Louis Cardinals, were playing the first game of a doubleheader against the Chicago Cubs at the Polo Grounds.

The score was 3–2 Cubs in the bottom of the sixth, with one out; the Giants had runners on second and third. Giants catcher Shanty Hogan came up to the plate and hit the ball back at the pitcher, Arthur Nehf, who swiveled around and fired the ball to third.

By the time the ball got there, the runner, Andy Reese, was on his way home. Moving into position, Cubs catcher Gabby Hartnett lowered his shoulder and rammed Reese before he started his slide. Then, for good measure, Hartnett threw his arms around Reese and held him until the Cubs third baseman could tag him—or so it seemed to some reasonably objective witnesses to the play. Umpire Bill Klem clearly didn't see it that way, since he called the runner out.

All hell broke loose. McGraw screamed interference, and Klem screamed back. The fighting went on and on, but Bill Klem stood his ground. The Giants played the game under protest, but the Cubs won the game—and the next one as well.

Instant replays were still a few decades away, but a picture was already worth a thousand words, or so John McGraw thought. In the next day's paper he saw a picture of the incident—a close-up of Reese trapped by Hartnett—and he went ballistic.

He had the photo enlarged and took it with him to the league office the next day. Visual aids notwithstanding, the league officials

So There!

"American League catchers were out to stop my base running. The St. Louis receiver Paul Krichell had a vicious habit of hooking my leg when I slid into the plate and flipping me over so that I scraped up dirt with my face. The second or third time it happened, I advised him, 'Don't ever do that again.'

"Krichell gave me the hook once more, and this time I scissored my legs, caught him under an arm and almost detached it from his body. The arm was forced back and badly torn at the shoulder. Krichell's career ended right there, after only two major league seasons.

" 'I'm sorry about it,' I told the St. Louis players, 'but I warned him.' "

—From *My Life in Baseball,* by Ty Cobb

upheld Klem, and the Giants' loss stood. New York finished the season behind the Cardinals—by two games.

Hit While Stealing Home. Under certain circumstances, if a runner on third is hit by a thrown ball while trying to steal home, the batter is out. The circumstances are: there must be two out, a runner on third, and two strikes on the batter; a runner must attempt to steal home on a legal pitch; and the ball must hit the runner in the batter's strike zone. If all of the above apply, then it's strike three, the batter's out, and the run doesn't count. If all of the above apply except that two are not out, it's strike three and the batter's out, but the run counts. [6.05n]

The Infield Fly Rule. In 1895 the rule said that the batter is automatically out on an infield fly when there is one out and first and second or first, second, and third bases are occupied. In 1901 the rule was expanded to cover a situation when there are no outs. (For more on the infield fly rule, see Chapter 2.) [6.05e]

Illegal Action

Some of the countless ways in which a batter may be put out have little to do with action on the field and a lot to do with technicalities, what The Book calls "illegal action." In a general sense, they're rather like the batter's equivalent of the pitcher's balk. [6.06]

According to The Book, a batter is out for illegal action when:

He's Out of Position. The batter must take his position in the batter's box promptly, and he's not allowed to leave the box once the pitcher gets into position. (He may also not switch batter's boxes once the pitcher is ready.) If a batter hits the ball with one or both feet entirely out of the batter's box, he's automatically out. So much for the fantasy of stepping out of the box when you're being intentionally walked and hitting a game-winning run out of the park—and the ending of the movie *The Bingo Long Traveling All-Stars and Motor Kings.*

If you've never seen the first couple of innings of a baseball game, you might well wonder what we're talking about when we say "batter's box." The truth is that after an inning or two, thanks to the ministrations of the batters, there's not much left of the white lines that delineate the official batter's box. For obvious reasons, it's up to the plate umpire to remember where it used to be.

The out-of-position call is rare, and for good reason. After all, imaginary or not, the batter's box is plenty big—six feet by four feet—and if even part of a batter's foot is on the line, it's considered in. Even so, this rule was once broken by one of the greatest batters ever, Hammerin' Hank Aaron. If he'd been standing where he was supposed to be, it would have been home run number forty-four for the season. Fortunately he didn't need it to pass Babe Ruth.

Of course, the umpire has to see the batter step out of the box in order to call him out. And that brings us to "the illegal hit that won the 1933 World Series," as this story has been somewhat excessively described.

It happened in Game 2 of the Series between the New York Giants and the Washington Senators. In the sixth inning, with one out and men on base, Francis J. "Lefty" O'Doul, who had been the National League batting champ the previous year, came in to pinch hit—O'Doul's first and only appearance in the Series. Lefty hit a foul ball and then took a called strike. Then came a ball, another foul ball, and, finally, a single. Two runs scored, and the Giants won the game. (They also won the Series, in five.)

Lefty O'Doul was unquestionably the hero of the game, but according to the *San Francisco Chronicle*, Lefty had a (belated) confession to make. Here's what he told the press at the time: "I wasn't going to let Crowder throw a ball past me, you can bet on that. So with each pitch I crowded the plate a little closer, a little closer. Finally I was darn near standing on the thing, and when Crowder threw the pitch I wanted, I went out after it as though it was the pot of gold at the end of the rainbow. It was on the outside corner, and I know now that in my anxiety to hit it, I stepped across the plate." Fortunately for Lefty, baseball rules don't allow for *ex post facto* confessions. His triumph over Alvin "General" Crowder remains on the books.

He Interferes with the Catcher. The batter has the right to stand anywhere he likes in the batter's box—officially it's the catcher's job to get out of the batter's way—so a batter really has to go out of his way to be called out for interference. If a batter interferes with the catcher's fielding or throwing by stepping out of the box or making any movement that hinders the catcher's play at home (there doesn't absolutely have to be contact between catcher and batter, but there usually is), the batter is out, and the ball is dead. No runners advance on the play. The defensive team can't have its cake and eat it too, though. If the catcher puts out the runner despite the batter getting in his way, the batter isn't out.

Every once in a while a batter makes contact with the catcher on his backswing or follow-through. If the umpire thinks that the catcher was clobbered unintentionally—that the batter didn't mean to interfere with the catcher's motion—he may call a strike instead of interference (in this case the ball is dead, and the runners must return to their bases). If the ump decides that the catcher was hit on purpose, the call is interference, and the batter is out. [6.06c]

In May of 1986, the Yankees, playing against the Rangers, had some experience with this rule. Yankees outfielder Henry Cotto was up, and there was a runner on first, designated hitter Gary Roenicke. Cotto swung at and missed a 1–1 pitch. Roenicke was running on the play, and catcher Don Slaught tried to fire the ball to pick off Roenicke. But Cotto's bat hit him on the head, and he ended up throwing to center field. Fortunately for Slaught, he came away with something more than a splitting headache. Cotto was called out for interference, and Roenicke was sent back to first.

He Uses an Illegal Bat. Practically everything you want or need to know about bats—length and weight and composition and the particulars of The Pine Tar Incident, for instance—can be found in Chapter 1. However, this rule—about illegal bats—covers a very special case, and a serious offense.

An illegal bat is one that has been altered or tampered with in such a way that something unusual happens when the bat makes contact with the ball. The tampering usually involves filling, sanding, nailing, hollowing (and then filling with cork), grooving, flat-surfacing, shaving, and waxing. Any player caught using or trying to use an illegal bat may be thrown out of the game. [6.06d]

And that's just what happened on September 7, 1974, to Yankees third baseman Graig Nettles. In the fifth inning of a game against the Tigers in Yankee Stadium, Nettles hit a single to left field and the end of his bat fell off. When Tigers catcher Bill Freehan took a look at the bat, he saw that it had been tampered with—two pieces had been sawed off the end of the bat, a hole had been drilled, and the

Hide and Seek

A rookie pitcher once asked Cleveland shortstop Lou Boudreau if it was okay to pitch Ted Williams low. Hall of Famer Boudreau responded, "Yeah, you can pitch him low, but as soon as you throw the ball, run and hide behind second base."

hole had been filled with cork. Rumor has it that cork filling may add about fifty feet to a long drive.

As you can imagine, Freehan didn't waste much time pointing out his discovery to plate umpire Lou DiMuro. DiMuro declared the bat illegal and sent Nettles packing. It's just too bad for the Tigers that Nettles's bat didn't break a little sooner. In the second inning he'd used it to hit a home run, the one that won the game.

Batting out of Turn

It doesn't seem like much to ask: the manager makes out a lineup card, in which he informs the umpire (and the opposition) of the batting order for the game, and then batters come to the plate in that order. The first batter of each inning after the first is the player whose name follows that of the last player who legally completed his time at bat in the preceding inning (remember, a time at bat is completed when a batter is out or when he becomes a runner). [6.07]

In fact, that's the way it usually does happen. Each year there are only a couple of violations of the batting-out-of-turn rule, and what few there are usually result from clerical errors: the official lineup cards given to the umpire don't agree with those posted in the dugout.

But it does happen, and it did happen on April 29, 1977, in a game between the New York Mets and the San Diego Padres. But before we describe the events of that night, it would be helpful to spend a few moments on the finer points of the batting-out-of-turn rule:

A batter is out when he fails to bat in his proper turn. Note that the player who takes the proper batter's place isn't out; the one who was *supposed* to bat is out.

The umpire may not call attention to a mistake in the batting order. It is up to the opposition to call the rule violation to the attention of the ump. Batting out of order is one of only a few "appeal plays" in baseball—ones that must be called to the attention of the umpire by the opposing team. Other appeal plays are failure to touch a base and leaving a base too soon after a fly ball is caught. (For more about both see Chapter 7.)

If the mistake in the order is discovered before the wrong batter is put out or becomes a runner, the right batter may come to the plate. If he does, he assumes the ball-strike count of the wrong batter.

Viva Sammy! Ordinarily, shattering Roger Maris's thirty-seven-year-old home run record by five dingers would make a guy King of Baseball. But no, that seat was taken by Mark McGwire. In 1998 Slammin' Sammy Sosa had to settle for leading his Cubs to the playoffs and being named the National League's MVP. (Tom DiPace)

⚾ If the wrong batter becomes a runner or is put out and the defensive team appeals to the umpire before the first pitch to the next batter of either team or before any other play, the right batter will be out, and the umpire nullifies any effect that the appearance of the wrong batter had in the game. (Exception: if a runner advanced on a stolen base, a balk, a wild pitch, or a passed ball, it counts.)

⚾ If there's no appeal on the play, the wrong batter officially becomes the right batter, and the results of his time at bat are legal. The next batter will be the one whose name follows his in the official lineup.

All of these considerations may seem unnecessarily exacting and technical, but even with all the details spelled out, the umpires didn't get it quite right when the situation arose. The foul-up in the 1977 Mets-Padres game was a genuine comedy of errors.

On that April night, outfielder Dave Kingman hit two three-run homers, and Jon Matlack struck out ten Padres, but the next day all anyone could talk about was the screw-up in the batting order. The mistake didn't exactly decide the outcome of the game—in the seventh inning it was 8–1 Mets, and the final score was 9–2—but it sure made it interesting.

It all started with a clerical error. The lineup card posted in the dugouts had Mets John Stearns batting sixth, Roy Staiger seventh, and Bud Harrelson eighth. On the official lineup card, however, Staiger's and Stearns's names were reversed. The game began, and the players followed the dugout card. The first time through the lineup, no one said anything about players batting out of turn. When Stearns led off the fourth inning with a home run (making the score 5–1), still no one said anything.

(Later, Padres manager Joe McNamara said that he noticed the discrepancy in the fourth inning, but by the time he did, they had already started pitching to Staiger. Since Staiger made an out, McNamara saw no point in appealing the play.)

The next time the men came to bat, both were out, but in the seventh inning Stearns walked and Staiger singled. McNamara decided that it was time to have a chat with the umpire. What happened then was: the umpire nullified Staiger's single, called Staiger out, and told Harrelson that he would be the first batter up in the next inning. What *should* have happened then was: the umpire *should* have called Harrelson out, since Staiger took Harrelson's place improperly. And he *should* have kept mum about who was supposed to lead off the next inning. An umpire is not supposed to discuss the batting order with either team. Furthermore, he was wrong about Harrelson anyway.

When Harrelson led off the eighth and walked, technically McNamara could have protested the play. Since Harrelson should have been called out, the hitter should have been Matlack, who followed Harrelson in the lineup. But the game proceeded as if nothing was amiss.

Becoming a Runner the Easy Way

There's no such thing as a free lunch, but every once in a while a batter gets a free pass—that is, he is entitled to first base without what The Book calls "liability to be put out." There are many ways in which a batter may become a runner; these are the ones that don't involve making contact with the ball. [6.08]

The Base on Balls. "Oh, those bases on balls," is what Boston Braves manager George Stallings said when asked what his epitaph should be. Needless to say, he wasn't the first or the last manager to feel that way.

By the 1920s, when Stallings was a manager, walks were relatively common, but once upon a time a guy could get to be an old man before getting a walk. In 1879 it took nine balls to do it, but over the next seven years it got a little easier—from eight to seven to six to five, in 1886. By 1889 it was down to four balls, and there it stayed. [6.08a]

The Hit Batsman. The batter gets a free pass when he's hit by a pitched ball, on two conditions: the ball has to be out of the strike zone when it hits him (if it's not, a strike is called); and he has to try to get out of the way (a ball is called if he doesn't). If he is hit by a ball but not given a base, the ball is dead, and no runners advance. [6.08b]

You may think it's easy to make a hit batsman call, but it's not always so. In Game 5 of the 1969 World Series—between the Miracle Mets and the heavily favored Orioles in Shea Stadium—there were two arguments about whether a batter had been hit by a pitch.

The first one came in the top of the sixth, when the Orioles were leading 3–0. Orioles outfielder Frank Robinson was apparently hit by a Jerry Koosman pitch, but the umpire ruled that the ball hit the bat before it hit Frank. The Orioles disagreed, but the ruling stood.

In the bottom of the same inning, when Mets outfielder Cleon Jones faced Dave McNally, Jones claimed he had been hit by a pitch, too—on the foot. The umpire was inclined not to agree with

Yogi Berra Wins a Bet

According to Joe Garagiola, Yogi Berra used to have a lot of trouble fielding bunts, so much so that one day, when Joe and Yogi were with the minors in Norfolk, Virginia, the Norfolk manager bet Yogi a steak dinner that he couldn't throw a batter out at first during the game. Yogi took the bet. As the game progressed, Yogi wasn't fielding any better than usual, but he was determined to prove his manager wrong. Yogi came up to the plate and hit a little bunt out in front of the plate. Before the opposing catcher and pitcher could field the ball, Yogi himself grabbed it and fired it to first. Then, having been forced out at first, Yogi went to the dugout to collect his steak.

Jones, but like the baseball version of Perry Mason, Mets manager Gil Hodges came storming out of the dugout to point out some impressive physical evidence: the ball had shoe polish on it. Convinced, the ump sent Cleon Jones to first on a free pass.

Of course, most batters hit by pitches would take issue with people who call the trip to first a "free" pass; they would maintain that they earn their base and then some. As Ron Hunt, who held the major league record for being hit by a pitched ball (243 times) until Don Baylor took it away in 1988, said, "Some people give their bodies to science. I gave mine to baseball."

Interference by the Opposition. As we said earlier, the batter's box belongs to the batter, and if the catcher or any other fielder interferes with him after the pitcher delivers the ball, he may take his base. However, if the batter reaches first (on a hit, an error, a base on balls, a hit batsman, etc.) and all runners advance at least one base despite the interference, the interference call doesn't count.

If the catcher interferes with the batter before the pitcher delivers the ball, it's not considered interference. The umpire calls time, and the play starts over from scratch. [6.08c]

Ron Hunt in a familiar pose. Infielder Hunt, who took his bases for the Mets, the Dodgers, the Giants, and the Expos during his twelve-year career, held the major league record (243) for times hit by a pitched ball until Don Baylor assumed the crown in 1988 just before retiring.

When the Ball Touches a Runner. If a fair ball touches an umpire or a base runner in fair territory before it touches a fielder, the batter may take first (although the runner is out). However, if it touches one of them after it passes a fielder other than the pitcher or after it has touched any fielder, including the pitcher, the ball is in play. [6.08d]

Becoming a Runner the Hard Way

Sometimes the batter becomes a runner the old-fashioned way: he earns it. Rule 6.09 counts the ways:

A Hit. The batter becomes a runner when he hits a fair ball. Of course, he has to remember to run to first base when he does so. Larry Gardner, a third baseman for the Red Sox from 1908 to 1917, once lined a hit off the left field wall, but he was thrown out at first because he didn't run. His explanation? "I thought it was foul." [6.09a]

A Dropped Third Strike. There are a lot of ifs involved with this rule, but it does happen. *If* it's a third strike and *if* it's not caught by the catcher and *if* first base is empty or *if* first base is occupied and there are two out, a batter may make a run for first. If the batter-runner beats the throw, he gets the base.

The most famous missed strike of all time. In the fourth game of the 1941 World Series, Dodgers catcher Mickey Owen couldn't hold on to Hugh Casey's curve. Proving that it pays to know the rules, Yankee Tommy Henrich made it safely to first.

The most famous missed third strike of all time occurred in Ebbets Field in the fourth game of the Brooklyn Dodgers–New York Yankees World Series game of 1941. It was October 5, and the Yankees had won two games to the Dodgers' one. The Dodgers hadn't been in the Series since 1920, so the Brooklyn fans were hungry for a win.

In the ninth inning Brooklyn was ahead 4–3, with two out and the bases empty. Dodgers relief pitcher Hugh Casey was doing a great job, and it looked good for The Bums. Yankees right fielder Tommy Henrich was up, and the count was 3–2. The next pitch decided the game, or so it seemed for a minute; Casey delivered a fast-breaking curveball (some say that it was a well-loaded spitter), Henrich swung—and missed.

But then there was another miss. Dodgers catcher Mickey Owen couldn't hold onto the ball, and while he chased it, Tommy Henrich—no doubt familiar with The Book—bolted to first, where he was safe. From there all it took to break the collective heart of the Brooklyn fans yet again was a big inning for the Yankees. When the Dodgers came up in the ninth, the score was 7–4, and the Dodgers were through. The Yankees led three games to one, and the next day they made it official. The name of Mickey Owen, who had played 128 games in that season with only two passed balls and three errors, went down in history. [6.09b]

A Home Run. When a batter hits a fair ball that passes over a fence or into the stands at a distance from home base of 250 feet or more, he's entitled to take four bases as slowly and as showily as he dares. (Outfielder Jimmy Piersall ran part of the way backward once.) The only thing he has to worry about is touching all the bases legally, but as you'll discover in Chapter 7, even that is sometimes too much to ask.

A Ground-Rule Double. In the 1961 World Series, when Leo Cardenas of the Cincinnati Reds pinch hit against the Yankees, he hit a long ball that could have won the game, but instead it hit the scoreboard. Ruling: it was a ground-rule double. The Reds lost the game and the Series.

Then there was the time in Baltimore that a fair ball was hit out of the park for an out. The fence was being repaired, and the workmen hadn't quite finished—at one spot in the outfield the fence sloped outward at a forty-five-degree angle, rather like a launching pad. Naturally, a ball came soaring into the outfield, and naturally the outfielder gave chase. When he reached the ramp/fence, the enterprising fielder kept on running, and he caught the ball just as his momentum carried him out of the park. Ruling: Great catch, batter out.

And then there's the one about the Boston Braves, who used to play in a park that backed up to a railroad track. The fence was in pretty bad shape, so some empty tin cans had rolled under it onto the field. In a turn-of-the-century game between Boston and Cleveland, Indians outfielder Jimmy McAleer hit a long drive over the opposing outfielder's head and straight into a tomato can. The Braves' Hugh Duffy fielded the can, but he couldn't pry the ball loose. In the end he gave up and threw the whole shebang toward the infield. The third baseman couldn't get the ball loose either, so he fired it, can and all, toward home, where McAleer was preparing to score. The catcher tagged the runner with the can. Ruling: McAleer was safe. Tagging the runner with a can doesn't count, even if it's got a ball in it.

These stories lead us into a discussion of one of the least satisfying rules in The Book, 6.09 (c through h, the regulations that govern the ground-rule double.) We say "least satisfying" because practically everyone who witnesses a ground-rule double thinks either that the batter was robbed or that he was given an undeserved gift. Of course, ground rules serve a useful purpose, probably more so in the old ballparks, with their shrubbery and statuary and other ornamental but intrusive paraphernalia. Stadiums today are more uniform and conventional, and so are the ground rules.

Specific ground rules for each park are set by the home team (and approved by the league), and sometimes it takes a while to get the bugs out. For instance, in the first twenty-five games played in Candlestick Park (in 1974) there were a whopping eighteen ground-rule doubles—fair balls that bounced over the low fence. Naturally, the Giants made the walls higher, but not until the next year. Ground rules may not be changed once the season starts.

As we saw in Chapter 3, there is some leeway in ground-rule regulations, depending on the vagaries of the individual ballparks, but The Book spells out several standard rules for all parks. A play is considered a ground-rule double:

When a fair fly ball leaves the playing field at a point less than 250 feet from home base. If it's farther than 250 feet, it's a home run. In 1888 the number was 210 feet, and in 1892 it grew to 235 feet. It became 250 in 1926.

◯ When a fair ball touches the ground and then bounces into the stands, goes over or under a fence, over or under a scoreboard, or through or under the shrubbery.

◯ When any fair ball, whether it touches the ground or not, passes through or under a fence, through or under a scoreboard, through any opening of the fence or scoreboard, or through or under vines or shrubbery, or if it sticks in the scoreboard or fence.

◯ When any bounding fair ball hits a fielder and goes into the stands or over or under a fence in fair or foul territory.

◯ When any fair fly ball that's hit more than 250 feet from home plate is deflected by a fielder into the stands or over the fence into foul territory. If it's deflected into fair territory, the batter gets a home run. If it's hit less than 250 feet, it's still a ground-rule double.

BALTIMORE GROUND RULES

Foul poles with screens attached are outside of playing field.

Thrown or fairly batted ball that goes behind or under the canvas, also canvas holder, and remains: 2 Bases. Ball rebounding in playing field: In Play.

Ball striking yellow concrete surfaces, pillars or facings surrounding the dugout: In Dugout.

Fly ball striking yellow line or beyond in left and right field: Home Run.

Fly ball hitting fence or padding on fence, between foul pole and yellow line in left center or right center, then caroming over wire fence beyond yellow line (on fly): Home Run.

A fly ball that strikes iron pipe on top of wall in both right and left field and rebounds on to playing field: In Play. Leaves playing field or sticks under pipe: Home Run.

Thrown or fairly batted ball hitting photographers' bench or photographers seated on same, and rebounding on to playing field: In Play. Ball remaining on or under bench: 2 Bases.

The flip side of a lineup card lists the ground rules for the team's playing field. This relic describes a ballpark that's no longer with us: the Baltimore Orioles' Memorial Stadium.

The Designated Hitter

Legendary *New York Times* sportswriter Red Smith called the designated hitter (DH) a "corruption." Bill "Spaceman" Lee, who pitched for Boston and Montreal, once said that it serves only one useful purpose—to relieve the manager of all responsibility except for posting the lineup card and making sure everybody gets to the airport on time.

But others say that having a hitter instead of a pitcher come to the plate keeps fans from falling asleep. The pro-DH faction pointed to studies showing that the number of hits in a game was decreasing steadily—in 1930 a fan saw an average of 11.1 runs per game; in 1940 he saw 9.6; in 1950, 9.7; in 1967, he saw only 7.5. Clearly, they concluded, something had to be done to get more runners on base.

The DH was only one of the many recurring ideas for solving the "problem" of too few hits. There have been numerous other suggestions along the way—make the plate narrower, allow a walk on three balls (a favorite of Oakland owner Charlie Finley in the late sixties), use an eight-man batting order, allow a man to pinch hit more than once, move the mound farther away from the plate (this would probably increase runs, but heaven knows what it would do to pitchers' arms), lower the rubber, make the strike zone smaller, and make a pitcher finish any inning he starts.

But as of 1973 the DH became the designated solution, at least in the American League. It became official: a hitter may be designated to bat for the starting pitcher and all subsequent pitchers in a game without otherwise affecting the status of the pitcher or pitchers in the game.

In 1976 Commissioner of Baseball Bowie Kuhn caused an uproar when he required both leagues to use the DH in the World Series. (He got no complaints from Yankee Lou Piniella, who had the dubious distinction of being the first DH in World Series history. Playing against the Reds in the first game of the Series, Piniella came up in the second and hit a double.) Nowadays in a World Series game the home team may choose whether or not the DH rule will apply—a rule change made by Peter Ueberroth in response to a plea from Hal McRae of the Kansas City Royals. In All-Star Games the DH is used only if both leagues agree to it.

No doubt providing for the unlikely event that the National League reconsiders its current anti-DH stance, the rule book states that either league may use the DH rule. It then goes on to give the specifics. [6.10]

◎ A DH must be selected prior to the game and must be included in the lineup cards presented to the umpire.

◎ The DH named in the lineup must in fact come to bat at least once unless the opposing team changes pitchers. This could be called "The Earl Weaver Rule," after the Orioles manager—and troublemaker. When the DH was first established, Weaver, as usual, found a way to make it work for him. He got into the habit of naming a pitcher whom he had no intention of using that day as his DH, then sending up somebody else when the time came.

His strategy made a mockery of the DH. One day he penciled in pitcher Steve Stone as the DH against the Tigers in Detroit and turned in the lineup card. The problem was that Steve Stone had already gone ahead to Toronto to get ready to pitch the next day. Another time he said that Tippy Martinez would be the DH against the Blue Jays in Toronto. Unfortunately, when it was his turn to bat, Tippy was in Colorado at a funeral. Weaver used this strategy twenty-one times in 1979, twelve of them with pitcher Steve Stone.

◎ A pinch hitter may be put in for the DH, and so may a pinch runner. (The DH may not pinch run, however.) A substitute for the DH does not have to be announced until it's his turn to bat.

◎ The DH doesn't have to take the field, but he may be used defensively if the manager so chooses. The pitcher must bat in place of the substituted defensive player unless more than one substitution is made.

◎ Unlike other players in the lineup, the DH is locked into the batting order. No multiple rotations may be made that will alter the DH's position in the lineup.

◎ There are a few situations in which the DH role is terminated, all of them quite rare: if the game pitcher is switched from the mound to a defensive position; if a pinch hitter bats for any player in the batting order and then enters the game to pitch; if the game pitcher bats for the DH; and if the DH assumes a defensive position.

The DH rules are clear, but the arguments persist. Perhaps the DH is, as one cynic has said, just another reason for the two major leagues to disagree.

Fear Strikes Back

In 1953, when Jimmy Piersall played outfield for the Red Sox, he made a play that sportscaster Warner Wolf has called one of the smartest in baseball. It was the bottom of the ninth, and Boston was tied with the Washington Senators 2–2. Piersall was playing center field that day, and the Senators had a runner on first. The Senators' batter hit a line drive that Piersall knew he couldn't catch on the fly. Since a triple would win the game, Piersall tipped the bouncing ball over the fence for a ground-rule double. The strategy worked. The runner made it to third, but the Sox held the Senators there and went on to win the game.

Batting Rule Changes: The Highlights

1845 An official diagram of the field is finally drawn.

1858 The "called strike" rule is first written into the record books.

1870 The batter is given the right to call for a high or a low ball. (For more about the strike zone, see Chapter 2.)

1879 All pitched balls must be called strikes, balls, or fouls. The number of strikes in an out is officially three. There are nine balls in a walk.

1880 A base on balls decreases to eight. The catcher must catch a ball before it hits the ground to retire the batter on a strikeout.

1881 The batter may take a base on seven balls.

1883 A foul ball caught on the first bounce is no longer an out. It must be caught before it touches the ground.

1884 For a base on balls the magic number is six.

1886 The countdown continues. A base on balls is five.

1887 The batter is no longer allowed to request a high or low pitch. If he is hit by a pitched ball, he is entitled to first base and not charged with a time at bat. For inexplicable reasons, a strikeout is called on four strikes, but this rule lasts only one season.

1888 The strikeout is back to three strikes again. It is a ground-rule double instead of a home run if the ball is batted over the fence in fair territory where the fence is less than 210 feet from home plate.

1889 The sacrifice bunt is statistically recognized, but the batter is charged with a time at bat. A base on balls is four, and there it remains.

1892 The distance cited for a ground-rule double increases: now it's a ground-rule double instead of a home run if the ball is hit over the fence in fair territory if the fence is less than 235 feet from home plate.

1894 The batter is charged with a strike for hitting a foul bunt.

1895 The infield fly rule is adopted: the umpire may call an infield fly when there is one out and first and second or first, second, and third bases are occupied. A strike is charged to a batter for a foul tip.

1900 The shape of home plate is changed, from a twelve-inch square to a five-sided figure seventeen inches wide.

1901 The infield fly rule is in effect when there are no outs as well as when there is one out. The American League joins the majors (the National League was founded in 1876), and the rule discrepancies begin. For instance, the National League declares that any foul ball not caught on the fly is a strike unless the batter has two strikes on him. The AL does not agree—at least not right away.

1903 The American League agrees—any foul ball not caught on the fly is a strike unless the batter has two strikes on him.

1909 A foul bunt on a third strike is a strikeout, and the catcher is credited with the putout.

1926 The ground-rule double distance changes again. It is a ground-rule double instead of a home run if the ball is hit over the fence in fair territory if the fence is less than 250 feet from home plate. And at 250 feet it has remained.

1931 A fair ball that bounces through or over a fence or into the stands is considered a ground-rule double instead of a home run.

1971 All major league players have to wear protective helmets at bat.

1973 The year of the DH. The American League votes to accept the designated hitter rule on a three-year experimental basis. The National League does not.

1976 The American League accepts the DH as a permanent part of the rules. The National League reaffirms its opposition.

Ty Cobb, aggressive base runner.

"Never trust a base runner who's limping. Comes a base hit and you'll think he just got back from Lourdes."

—Joe Garagiola

Chapter 7

The Runner

Having dissected the actions of the batter in the previous chapter, The Book now quite logically takes up the terms and conditions of what the successful batter becomes: the runner.

According to The Book, it sounds pretty simple: "A runner acquires the right to an unoccupied base when he touches it before he is out." Yet as easy as that opening line makes it seem, the lot of the runner is, like almost everything else in the game of baseball, a veritable minefield of requirements and limitations.

Whose Bag Is It, Anyway?

"Possession is nine-tenths of the law" is a cliche that's been around as long as private property. It's just as true in the game of baseball as it is in life.

A good baseball example is found in the leadoff rule in this section of The Book: the base runner must head out for greener pastures when someone else becomes legally entitled to the base on which he is standing. Possession, therefore, becomes crucial in the everyday circumstance in which a batter hits a single and the man on first must go to the next base. [7.01]

A corollary to this is another rule, one that prohibits two runners from occupying the same base. Should it happen, it is the second runner who is out when tagged. Consistent with common laws of possession, the owner is the one who got there first and took "possession" of the bag. [7.03]

One example of two runners taking possession of the same base occurred in the 1917 World Series. At the start of the play, second base was occupied by White Sox pitcher Urban Faber. When the opposition pitcher took his sweet time delivering the ball to the plate, Faber thought fast—maybe too fast—and took off for third.

Unfortunately, a teammate was already occupying the base, so Faber was tagged out. That kind of empty-headed base running may well have been one of the earliest arguments for the DH rule—perhaps it is only proper that pitchers be banned from not only the batter's box but the base paths, too.

Another famous instance of one-too-many runners at a base occurred during the 1963 World Series. Tommy Davis was on first when Willie Davis came to the plate and promptly hit one down the right-field line. Willie, who was said by some to have had more raw speed than anyone in the game at that time (including his fellow Dodger Maury Wills), took off around the bases. Tommy Davis had better than average speed, but he was no match for Willie.

Unfortunately for the Dodgers, Willie had his head down, so when he pulled up at third, he didn't notice that the bag was already occupied by Tommy Davis. Yankees shortstop Tony Kubek, having taken the throw from the outfield, came over to make the tag. First he tagged Willie Davis. Then he tagged Tommy Davis. For good measure, he tagged the umpire and said, "One of you guys is out." (It was Willie.)

Those certainly weren't the only times a team ended up with two runners on one base, since careless base running, like jaywalking, is a fact of life. But three men on one base? The Brooklyn Dodgers managed that one in a game in August 1926.

The game was at Ebbets Field against the Boston Braves. The bases were loaded when Babe Herman, then a rookie, came to the plate and hit one deep to right. The man on third scored easily, but the runner on second held up until he was sure the drive wasn't going to be caught before he proceeded to third.

When he reached the bag, he made a big turn, but on taking a second look at the ball being relayed to the infield, he second-guessed himself, stopped, and started back to third. The man who had begun the play standing on first base was running with less caution, so he arrived at third at about the same time.

The two of them had only a moment or two to share a stunned silence before Babe Herman arrived. So did the ball, and the Braves' third baseman tagged everyone in sight. Herman tried to get back to second, but a quick throw later he was tagged out, too.

Perhaps that embarrassing scene was on Lou Gehrig's mind a few years later when he narrowly escaped the same situation. The Yankees were down 6–4 in the bottom of the ninth to the Washington Senators, but all was not lost. Gehrig was on second, Dixie Walker on first. Tony Lazzeri was at the plate and hit one deep into right-center. Gehrig wanted to be sure it wasn't catchable, so he paused before breaking for third. Walker, with a better angle on the flight of the ball, took one look and ran for glory. The two of them arrived at third like a man and his shadow.

As one, they slowed for a moment as the ball was thrown in from the outfield, but they quickly realized they had no choice but to proceed to the plate. Lazzeri was halfway between second and third and closing fast.

The play did not have a happy ending. When Walker and Gehrig reached home, they were met by Senators catcher Luke Sewell. He held the baseball in his hand. Both runners were tagged out, and the game was over.

Advancing the Runner

The runner may advance from one base to the next in many ways, but doing so "without liability to be put out" is one subset of possibilities. In each case the ball is declared dead. Rule 7.04 contains the following:

A balk is the first option cited in this rule. After a balk, all base runners advance one base. [7.04a]

A runner (or runners) also is given a free base when another base runner is hit by a batted ball. The runner who is struck is out, but other runners move up one base. A base on balls, too, forces the runners to advance when no base is available for the batter who has just walked. [7.04b]

When a fielder falls out of play after making a legal catch, the runners may take a base. However, in such circumstances the dugout is not out of play, so runners may advance only at their own peril when a defensive player steps off the field into either bench area, since the fielder can come out of the dugout firing. On the other hand, if a fielder falls down in the dugout

One of Baseball's Little Mysteries

"I don't know why, but I can run faster in tight pants."

—Phil Linz

after making the catch, the runners may advance without liability. [7.04c]

The runner gets a base when he is stealing and the batter is interfered with by the catcher or another fielder. [7.04d]

Not only base runners but "batter-runners" (as The Book calls them) as well advance on a home run. A home run is a hit that leaves the park in fair territory, or one that would have if it weren't "deflected by the act of a fielder in throwing his glove, cap, or any article of his apparel." [7.05a]

Runners and batter-runners get three bases when a fielder uses his cap, mask, glove, or uniform "detached from its proper place" to field the ball. Obviously, runners on base are guaranteed to score in this situation, but the hitter has a chance, too, since the ball is still regarded as playable. If the batter-runner elects to, he may try to score "at his peril." [7.05b and 7.05c]

These rules have produced a few oddities over the years. One occurred in 1947 in a Red Sox–St. Louis Browns game. BoSox first baseman Jake Jones hit a slow roller down the third-base line. The ball was foul, but the opposing pitcher, Fred Sanford, came off the mound to field it. When he didn't field the ball cleanly, he apparently lost his temper and bunged his glove at it. The umpire ruled it a triple. No doubt the play was one reason why the rules now state that in order for a rule-book triple to be declared, the ball must be fair.

What if the fielder uses his cap to catch not a batted ball but one thrown to him by a teammate? In such instances, each runner gets two free bases. The same penalty is assessed if a fielder throws his glove at and interferes with the flight of a thrown ball. There's no penalty if the glove doesn't touch the ball, or if the glove leaves the fielder's hand accidentally as he attempts to make a legitimate catch. [7.05d and 7.05e]

It's also illegal for a catcher to touch a thrown ball with his mask. That proved a painful lesson for rookie catcher Angelo Encarnacion and his Pittsburgh Pirates teammates. It was the bottom of the eleventh in Los Angeles on a Saturday night in August 1995. With runners on second and third, the Dodgers' batter swung and missed a pitch in the dirt. Encarnacion barely kept the ball from getting past him by scooping it up with his mask.

Manager Tommy Lasorda came charging out of the dugout. He complained to the crew chief, umpire Harry Wendelstedt, that the catcher is forbidden to touch a thrown ball with his mask when it is "detached from its proper place." Wendelstedt saw it Tommy's way, and his ruling sent the runner on third home to score. That ended the game, breaking the 10–10 tie.

If a fair ground ball bounces or is deflected into the seats in foul territory, it is automatically a ground-rule double, worth two bases to the batter and base runners alike. The same is true of a ball that rolls under a fence or the scoreboard. The Book also awards two bases for a ball that gets stuck in or under shrubbery or vines, but that's a recent change to the rule. [7.05f and 7.05g]

Throwing Errors

In the simplest possible terms, if a fielder throws a ball out of play, the ball is dead, and the runners get two bases. [7.05h]

It sounds simpler than it is. Consider the frustrations of Cubs manager Leo Durocher, who, within one ten-day period in 1969, appealed two decisions regarding overthrows of first base. He took one side on the first, the other on the second, and National League president Warren Giles denied both.

The first instance was at Wrigley, with the Giants beating the Cubs 3–2 in the eighth. The Cubs' Don Kessinger was on first, and on a hit-and-run play he headed for second as the ball was pitched. The batter, Glenn Beckert, grounded the ball to short. Hal Lanier (who went on to manage the Houston Astros to a division title in 1986) was the Giants' shortstop. He had moved to his left when he saw Kessinger break for second, but he recovered in time to field the ball to his right. He had no play at second, however, and his hurried throw to first went into the dugout.

The official scorer gave Beckert a hit, since the throw was too late to get him even if it had been accurate, and Lanier was given an error. But the argument got underway when umpire Al Barlick ruled that Kessinger could go to third and Beckert to second. He cited the portion of the rule that reads, "When such wild throw is the first play by an infielder, the umpire, in awarding such bases, shall be governed by the position of the runners at the time the ball was pitched." [7.05g]

Leo didn't get to be called "The Lip" because he pouted quietly. He put up the best verbal fight he could. Among other things, he told the umpire that he was invoking the wrong part of the rule. He explained that the ump should be looking at the part that reads, "If all runners, including the batter-runner, have advanced at least one base when an infielder makes a wild throw on the first play after the pitch, the award shall be governed by the position of the runners when the wild throw was made."

Durocher felt that "two bases" meant that Kessinger, who was already safe (or nearly so) at second when the wild throw was made, should have been allowed to score. The umpire disagreed. The game went on, but it was played under protest.

A little more than a week later, the Cubs were playing the Dodgers. This time Durocher's club was on the field, with Dodger Willie Crawford on first and Willie Davis at bat. Davis bounced a ball to second baseman Beckert, who threw the ball into the dugout.

The circumstances were much the same. First-base umpire Paul Pryor ruled that Crawford had passed the bag before the throw. But this time the ruling sent Crawford in to score and Davis to second.

"Now I've got Giles cornered," said Durocher, filing another protest. "He can't have it two ways."

Giles proved The Lip wrong when he refused to uphold either protest, saying that while the ruling in the Dodgers game was "not consistent" with the first one, "the ruling did not affect the outcome of the game." Durocher did get some satisfaction out of the whole situation, however. The next time he saw umpire Paul Pryor, he argued the issue further and, having gained no ground, returned to his dugout and publicly tore up his copy of The Book.

The Book also provides for a runner to get a free base if a pitcher's wild pitch or a pick-off throw goes out of play. The same one-base bonus is offered on ball four or on a third strike if there is a wild pitch or if the ball lodges in the umpire's mask or paraphernalia. [7.05h and 7.05i]

Another rudimentary base-running rule is that the base runner must touch each base in succession as he proceeds around the bases both backward and forward. That is, if a runner is required to retrace his steps, he must do so in reverse order as long as the ball remains in play. So a base runner who misjudges a fly ball and runs when he thinks it will fall in for a hit only to find that a fielder has caught it must retouch the bases he passed as he returns to the one that was justly his at the start of the play. [7.02]

Obstruction

The major concerns of The Book are the misdemeanors of the game, misdeeds of mostly minor kinds, as well as a multitude of

The Thinking Man's Game

This one was told by Adrian "Pop" Anson, legendary Cubs first baseman and manager before the turn of the century. He had a pitcher on his staff who was a little less quick-thinking than he was hard-throwing. "His greatest fault was he never watched base runners," recounted Anson. Apparently, he had the arm to be a major leaguer, but he was so short on concentration that the opposition could steal virtually at will.

One day Anson came up with a solution. He and the slow-witted pitcher and Cubs catcher "Pop" Schriver conferred before a game. Anson told his pitcher, "You pay more attention to base runners today. Don't let them get such long leads."

"I can't watch the plate and base runners, too," was the reply.

Anson gave him these instructions. "Since you say you can't watch the bases and the plate, too, just don't look at first base. Just look at the plate. Watch Schriver. When you see him take off his mask and spit some of that tobacco juice, you let fly with that ball to me at first base. Understand that?"

They decided to give it a try. But as the first batsman for the opposition came to the plate, Schriver noticed the plate was partially obscured with dirt. He took off his mask, squirted a little excess tobacco juice, and brushed off the plate.

As Anson concluded the story, "That dumb pitcher saw Schriver take off his mask, spit—and he remembered something. But he forgot that the game hadn't started. He fired to first. I wasn't expecting anything . . . It hit me in the Adam's apple and knocked me cold . . . I couldn't swallow food for a week. But long before the week was over, I decided not to take any more chances with that kind of ballplayer, and released him."

matters of interpretation. Yet a significant number of the rules concern higher crimes, the felonies of the baseball world.

One variety is obstruction. Obstruction can take numerous forms, but at its simplest, obstruction is defined as any situation in which a fielder without the ball interferes with the progress of a runner. An old story of the ever-clever John McGraw illustrates it well.

In the rough-and-tumble, turn-of-the-century days in which McGraw played, the game was more physical than it is today. With but one umpire on the field to oversee the action, it was possible to get away with illicit acts that would surely be witnessed by a man in blue today, and nowhere was this more evident than on the base paths.

McGraw's Orioles were known as among the toughest teams, bumping and pushing and even tripping base runners as they made for home. McGraw himself had a special trick: as a third baseman, he would slip his fingers through a base runner's belt and hold the runner just long enough for a teammate to get the ball back to the infield in time to prevent the runner from scoring.

On this particular afternoon, Louisville's Pete Browning was on third. Having fallen prey to McGraw's hold-the-runner trick before, Browning went McGraw one better: he undid his belt buckle. When the batter made contact with the next pitch, Browning headed for home—and left McGraw holding his belt.

McGraw didn't get called for it that day, but when an obstruction occurs, the umpire raises both arms in the air, calls time, and declares the ball dead. The obstructed runner gets a base, and any runner forced to advance will do so. If no play is made on the obstructed runner, then the umpire is not obliged to call time and

Some Guys Have All the Luck

Back in April of 1998, Chicago White Sox hitter Ray Durham did exactly what leadoff men are supposed to do: he got on base. On this particular evening he tied the major league record by reaching base on errors three times. His biggest ally seems to have been Cleveland first baseman Jim Thome, who made errors in the first and fifth that enabled Durham to get on. Pitcher Charles Nagy was responsible for the other miscue. Durham also did the other thing leadoff guys are supposed to do: he managed to score runs all three times.

may assess such penalties "as in his judgment will nullify the act of obstruction." Any runner may be obstructed, not only one trying to score; and any defensive player may be guilty of obstruction. [7.06]

Catcher's Balk

No doubt because he has the most to protect, the catcher is often the felon involved in interference calls. In fact, the catcher even gets a rule all his own to address what is commonly called the "catcher's balk," which occurs when a runner is trying to score from third on a steal or squeeze play and the catcher steps on or in front of home without possession of the ball.

According to the catcher's balk rule, the catcher is forbidden to leave his place behind the plate and to touch the bat or batter. If this rule is violated, the penalty is a balk call. Thus, the runner from third will score, any other base runners advance a base, and the batter goes to first. [7.07]

Catcher's balks occur so rarely that umpires seem to be lax in calling them even when they do. In fact, the perpetrator in the instance we came across in our research admitted he was guilty but got away scot-free. The guilty party was White Sox catcher Jim Essian, a ballplayer whom Thomas Boswell of *The Washington Post* once described as "a catcher with a penchant for rule-testing plays."

On the night in question, the score was tied in the bottom of the ninth in a game between Chicago and Baltimore. There were two down, and Oriole Pat Kelly was at third. Dave Hamilton was on the mound, and, never suspecting that Kelly would try to steal home, Hamilton took his time going to the plate.

Kelly got an enormous jump. The batter was as surprised as Hamilton and stepped out of the way of the oncoming Kelly. By abandoning the batter's box, he also gave Essian an opening, which the catcher took, leaping onto the plate. He awaited the pitch with one foot on home and his glove held well out in front of the base.

"If Smith [the batter] had swung, my head would have been a line drive to center field," said Essian after the game. "But the play was so close I couldn't have gotten Kelly any other way." Get him he did.

The call was "out," but it shouldn't have been. It should have been a catcher's balk, with the runner safe at the plate and the batter given first. As it was, the game went into extra innings, and the White Sox won in the eleventh on two unearned runs.

(Not only did Essian manage to get away with illegally blocking Kelly at the plate, but the previous week he had found another way to stretch the rules. On a double steal, he threw a white sponge he keeps in his mitt toward second, deceiving the runner at third. Then he threw the ball to third, easily picking off the confused lead runner.)

Interference

Catchers and other fielders aren't the only players who can be guilty of interfering with the opposition. It can go the other way, with batters or base runners interfering with fielders.

There's a blanket statement in The Book that addresses this area in a general way: "The . . . offensive team shall vacate any space . . . needed by a fielder who is attempting to field a batted or thrown ball." [7.11] And there are numerous specific situations covered, too. But even with all the carefully written rules and descriptions of situations, interference calls are still among the trickiest in the game.

Here's an example. In a game in 1976 in Oakland, Sal Bando hit a high pop into foul territory. The A's were playing Baltimore, and the Orioles' catcher and third baseman both hurried over to catch the ball, which was dropping from the sky near the Athletics' on-deck circle.

Larry Haney, the next scheduled hitter for Oakland, tried to make himself scarce as the two Orioles fielders positioned themselves under the ball. It all happened very quickly, of course, but somehow Haney was unable to get out of the way, the ball fell to the ground, and the Orioles immediately commenced to argue that an interference call should be made on Haney.

The interpretation of the rule would seem to be pretty straightforward. The on-deck hitter didn't "vacate" the space, so he's out, right? Wrong, said the umpires, and Bando, given a second life, tripled and eventually scored the winning run.

After the game, the umpires said they didn't call interference because in their judgment Haney had tried to get out of the way. But do the rules allow for that? Not the way we read it. The Book says, very simply, that Haney or whoever the potential interferer is "shall vacate"—not try to vacate. Our call would be that Haney was guilty of interference, and Bando was out.

If interference calls are among the most difficult to make in the game of baseball, they definitely are among the most likely to be made wrongly, as this next and more famous World Series situation points out.

Few baseball fans have forgotten the image of Boston Red Sox catcher Carlton Fisk sidestepping down the first-base line, his arms windmilling the air in the sixth game of the 1975 Series between Boston and Cincinnati. You know the scene: it was as if the ball Pudge had just smashed down the left-field line needed an extra whisper of wind to stay in fair territory, and he was going to make damn sure it got it. It worked.

However, here we are concerned with a tableau in that Series that was much more controversial. Fisk was again on stage, this time weighed down by his mask and leg and chest protectors. Cincinnati's speedy Cesar Geronimo was on first, and a journeyman outfielder named Ed Armbrister was at the plate, pinch hitting for the pitcher. The score was 5–5, with nobody out in the tenth inning of Game 3.

Armbrister was instructed to bunt, which he did, knocking the ball hard off the artificial turf in Riverfront Stadium. The ball bounced high, and Fisk lunged for it, only to get tangled up with Armbrister, who, in the words of *New York Times* columnist Red Smith, "dallied near the plate." Fisk hurriedly separated himself from the runner and rifled a throw to second, only to see it soar high over the bag and into center field.

The runners made their way to second and third, and Fisk turned to home-plate umpire Larry Barnett, waiting for an interference call. None was forthcoming. Needless to say, an argument ensued. The Red Sox lost their argument and, three plays later, the game.

The argument raged long after the last out, however. In the locker room, on TV, and in print the discussion centered not only on the interpretation of the rule—but also on which rule applied.

Umpire Barnett did not refer specifically to any rule, either during or after the game. But he did talk about "intent": if the runner had intentionally obstructed the fielder, said Barnett, then it would have been interference. As he explained it to the press later, his conclusion was that since Armbrister's collision with Fisk was unintentional, there was no call to be made.

Students of The Book disagreed, and two different but applicable rules were cited. The first, Rule 7.08b, states that a runner is to be called out when he "hinders a fielder attempting to make a play on a batted ball." (The replays offered incontrovertible evidence that

Armbrister "hindered" Fisk in his attempt to field the ball.) The second rule, 7.09l, asserts that it is interference if a batter or runner "fails to avoid a fielder who is attempting to field a batted ball." Here again, Armbrister seemed guilty of the crime (as did Haney in our first example).

On the basis of this evidence, more than a few partisans were heard to call for Barnett's head: there was nary a mention of "intent" in these two relevant rules, so where did Barnett get off? A bad judgment call is one thing, a bad call based on an incorrect reading of rules is quite another.

There were voices to be heard in support of Barnett as well. A National League official, Fred Fleig, said that in the supplemental instructions umpires are given there is a clarification to rule 7.06 that reads, "When a catcher and batter-runner going to first base have contact when the catcher is fielding the ball, there is generally no violation and nothing should be called." Rule 7.06 pertains to catchers interfering with runners rather than the reverse, but Fleig saw it as supporting Barnett.

Another member of the pro-Barnett faction was John Johnson, chairman of the Official Playing Rules Committee. He cited still another rule, 7.09h, which says that the batter or runner is guilty of interference, "If, in the judgment of the umpire, a batter-runner willfully and deliberately interferes with a batted ball or a fielder in the act of fielding a batted ball, with the obvious intent of breaking up a double play." As Red Smith pointed out the day after the game, the problem with that interpretation is that the particular "subsection was written in to cope with Jackie Robinson, a base runner who used to let an obvious double-play grounder hit him. That rendered the ball dead and eliminated the double play, although Robinson was out automatically."

Was Barnett's call the correct one? You can make up your own mind on the basis of the rules cited above. But you should also know that after the 1975 Series, 7.08b was adorned with a new addendum that reads, "A runner who is adjudged to have hindered a fielder who is attempting to make a play on a batted ball is out whether it was intentional or not." If the same situation occurred today, Barnett would be obliged to call Armbrister out for interference.

In Boston they still remember this one, not least of all because if it had gone the other way, that home run of Fisk's in Game 6 could have been a Series winner instead of a gamer.

Willful Interference

While the mention of the "Jackie Robinson" rule is fresh in your mind, let's review. In short, the rule prohibits "willful" interference by the base runner or batter-runner with a batted ball or fielder. The penalty is that the interfering runner shall be called out along with the runner who has advanced closest to scoring, whether he started the play on the bases or as the batter. In no case, states The Book, may a run or runs be scored as a result of the interference. [7.09g and 7.09h]

A couple of different sets of circumstances are often cited as contributing to the introduction of these rules. One occurred on opening day in 1955 when Robinson was on the base paths and he let the batted ball hit him while running the bases. Another case often mentioned as the precedent is the time Don Hoak, a third baseman in the National League in the mid-fifties and early sixties, actually fielded a ball while he was a base runner to ensure that the defense wouldn't be able to turn a double play. (Some recall that he stopped the ball with his foot, but either way, the result was the same.) These acts led to the criminalization of "willfully and deliberately interfering" with a double-play ball. [7.09h]

As you have probably come to realize, this section of The Book is complicated. Rule 7.09 alone is divided into thirteen subsections, and each addresses a type of interference by the batter or runner. Some are obscure, others Little-League obvious, but let's review them.

The batter-runner is not allowed to "hinder" the catcher in his attempt to field the ball after a third strike. [7.09a] The batter is allowed to hit the ball only once (he may not touch either a foul or fair ball a second time). [7.09b] And he is out if he intentionally "deflects the course" of a ball hit foul. [7.90c] Those seem pretty straightforward.

Let's get a little more complicated: with a runner on third, if the batter or runner interferes with a fielder making a play at home before two are out, the runner is automatically out. [7.05g] Another situation covered in The Book that you probably haven't seen come into play (though it does occasionally) concerns "confusion." This rule says that members of the offensive team may not "stand or gather around a base . . . to confuse . . . the fielders." [7.09e] The penalty is that the runner shall be called out.

Next comes a rule that provides umpires with considerable leeway in interpretation. In summary, it prohibits a batter or runner who has just been declared out from impeding any following play on another runner. Here are two situations to which this rule applies. In one, the call was made correctly; in the other, not. See if you can decide which is which. [7.09f]

One circumstance involves Carl Yastrzemski. The bases were loaded (with Yaz on second) in a crucial game against the Orioles late in the Red Sox's pennant-winning 1975 season. The batter was Jim Rice, who grounded to third. Brooks Robinson fielded the hard-hit ball, stepped on the bag, and threw to first. His throw was off the mark.

While Orioles first baseman Lee May pursued the errant throw, Yastrzemski, who had been called out on the force play at third, kept running. He ran past third and was hustling down the home stretch when May, who apparently hadn't seen Robinson touch third, gunned the ball toward home to catch Yastrzemski. His throw, too, was wild, and the runner who started on first, Fred Lynn, came in to score. Was Yaz guilty of interference?

A variation of Yaz's decoy play occurred once in a minor league game between teams representing Elmira (New York) and Williamsport (Pennsylvania). With one out, Elmira had three men on. Once again, the batter grounded the ball toward third, and again, the third baseman stepped on the base before throwing wildly to first.

This time, however, when the first baseman caught up with the ball and threw to the plate, his throw was on the money. With a flourish, the catcher tagged the runner, and the umpire signaled him out, completing the double play.

Elmira immediately protested: both outs were called on the same man, and a runner can only be called out once in an inning, right? Wrong, said the umpire, calling the next runner out for the interference of his predecessor.

The answer is hidden in the fine print of the rule: "If the batter or a runner continues to advance after he has been put out, he shall not by that act alone be considered as confusing, hindering, impeding the fielders." As seems appropriate, the major league umps called it right. Yaz was indeed "safe," and the winning run Lynn scored on the play was legitimate. The ump in the Elmira-Williamsport game blew the call.

Interference with a Thrown Ball. Another variation of offensive interference occurred in the World Series in 1978. Reggie Jackson was on first, Thurman Munson on second. The batter, Lou Piniella, lined a shot to Dodgers shortstop Bill Russell, who dropped the ball. Russell quickly picked it up and stepped on second, forcing Jackson, and then threw to first.

Jackson, who had stopped when it looked as if Russell would catch the liner for the out, was well toward first. He saw the throw coming his way and leaned into it. The ball hit him and bounded away, and Munson scored.

Tommy Lasorda raced out of the Dodgers' dugout and argued for an interference call on Jackson. The first-base umpire, Frank Pulli, said, "From the angle I had, I couldn't tell whether Reggie moved into the ball. I saw it as not intentional interference on Reggie's part . . . [and] there has to be intent in the judgment of the umpire."

Despite the fact that the TV replays revealed that Jackson had angled his hip and thigh into the throw, there was no interference call. The disputed run made the difference in the game; the Yankees won, 4–3, in ten innings. (The Yanks won the Series, four games to two).

Base Coach Interference. This portion of The Book also forbids coaches at third and first to interfere with the action on the field when the ball is in play. They can neither physically assist the runner in any way nor act "in any way to draw a throw by a fielder." [7.09i and 7.09j]

A case of base-coach interference took place in the minor leagues in 1972. In a game between Shreveport and Arkansas, base runner Mike Vail slipped rounding third. Vail, who went on to a major league career, was helped to his feet by Arkansas Travelers manager/third-base coach Fred Koenig while the ball was still in play. Shreveport manager Norm Sherry immediately protested, and the umpires upheld his objections. Vail became the third out of the inning (instead of a run scored), and the Travelers lost 2–1.

Moving Violations

Many of the rules that follow restate what we learned in our first lessons about the game. They concern not the assault and battery by base runners or fielders but rather matters that might better be characterized as "moving violations."

Leaving the Base Line. The runner must stay outside but within three feet of the base line while running the last half of the distance to first; if he fails to do so and interferes with a fielder, he can be called out for interference. [7.09k] This rule was not invoked (though some said it should have been) in the 1986 National League playoffs.

The playoff was all even at one game apiece, but the Houston Astros were leading the New York Mets 5–4 in the ninth inning of Game 3 at Shea Stadium in New York. Mets second baseman Wally Backman led off the bottom half of the inning with a drag bunt up the first-base line.

Houston first baseman Glenn Davis raced in, grabbed the ball, and lunged at Backman as he ran past. Backman slid, his body in foul territory, and reached back to tag the first-base bag with his hand.

The umpire ruled Backman safe, and Houston manager Hal Lanier shot out of the Houston dugout to argue. Despite his argument, the umpires didn't change their decision, and after the game even Lanier agreed that they'd made the right decision. ("The

Tigers base runner Harvey Kuhn arrives at home in a cloud of dust, scoring before Yankees catcher Yogi Berra can tag him out. If only Yogi had jumped into that dust bowl, too, the umpire would really have had a tough call to make. (UPI)

umpires made the right call, but I've got to go out and question it," he said.)

It was Mets manager Davey Johnson who summed it up best: "It was a borderline case. We've had plays where the guy almost came into the dugout to get away from the tag." Since Backman was only two to three feet into foul ground, he was safe.

The play had an important impact on the game, too. One batter later, Mets center fielder Len Dykstra homered; Backman's run tied the game, and Dykstra's hit won it, 6–5. (And the Mets won the playoffs in six games.)

Another classic instance of leaving the base line is the situation in which a runner at first blatantly abandons the base line when sliding into second in an attempt to break up a double play. It's happened many hundreds of times over the years without being called, but the rule was invoked in the Yankees' home opener in 1978.

Chris Chambliss was on first, and a ground ball was hit to second. Rangers shortstop Bert Campaneris took the toss from his second baseman to force Chambliss at second, then prepared to throw the ball to first. The ball had been hit hard enough that Campaneris had plenty of time not only to make the throw but also to take two full strides toward right field to avoid the oncoming Chambliss.

Despite his evasive action, Campaneris found himself on a collision course with the much heftier Chambliss, who, seeing he was out anyway, bodychecked Campaneris. Campaneris could not make his throw to first.

The umpires gave the Rangers their double play anyway. The key to the decision was that the umpire—and, on instant replay, the fans at home—could see that Chambliss turned sharply from the base path and veered into Campaneris.

Appeal Plays. We'll see more of these kinds of "moving violations" shortly, but before we do, it is important to understand the mechanism of the "appeal," since it is by appeal plays that most of these rules are enforced. (See Chapter 6 for discussion of appeals regarding the batter-runner.)

Appeal plays occur, for example, when a runner advances on a fly before the ball is caught, or when a runner fails to touch a base, or overslides first and does not return immediately. In each case, the defensive team must tag either the runner who is allegedly guilty or the base he left. The tag must be made while the ball is live, except

Why Keep It a Secret?

The scoreboard in left said 4–1, Yankees. As the Yankees took the field for the top of the eighth on July 1, 1989, nobody in the Stadium—including the Yankees—seemed to realize they had just scored a run to make it 5–1.

Larry Barnett knew, though. It was his job as home-plate umpire to recognize that a run had just scored on an inning-ending double play.

What happened was this. With one out, Mike Pagliarulo was on third, Bob Geren was on first, and the squeeze was on. Pags got a good jump off third and the batter, Wayne Tolleson, turned to bunt.

Tolleson's bunt wasn't very good, and the Brewers' pitcher caught it in the air and fired to first to double up Geren. The inning was over, but before the runner at first was called out, the runner at third had crossed the plate.

Barnett said nothing. "I can't signal the run has scored while the Brewers are still on the field," the veteran umpire said afterward. "That would be coaching, since they do have the right to appeal at third on Pagliarulo before they leave the field."

Because it wasn't a continuous-action double play, in which the third out is collected as a force or at first base, the Brewers could have appealed at third, saying that Pags left too early. As Barnett explained later, "That's covered in Rule 7.10d . . . It's the apparent fourth-out rule, where the defense has to appeal the play and take the out that is to their advantage. The Brewers left the field without an appeal, so the run counted." Final score, 5–1 Yanks, although no one but the umpiring crew knew it until the game was over.

Word got out eventually, of course, and in the papers the next day Yankees skipper (but not for long) Dallas Green was quoted as saying, "I've been in this [game] for 33 years, and I've never, ever seen that play . . . You keep saying you've seen everything in baseball, but it's obvious you haven't seen anything."

in the case of a play at home plate, in which case the appeal must be made before the next pitch. [7.10]

In a game during the New York Mets' first season, Mets first baseman "Marvelous Marv" Throneberry made an error in the first inning, booting a ground ball that led to an unearned run. When he came to bat in the bottom of the inning, Throneberry attempted to undo the harm he had done and hit the ball a country mile. It didn't go out of the park, but it did roll to the wall in the deepest part of the Polo Grounds.

Throneberry, not known for his foot speed, churned around the bases and, with a slide worthy of a more graceful man, was safe at third with a triple. However, one of the opposition infielders had observed that the Marvelous One had failed to touch second on his way by. He called for the ball, got it, and tagged second. The umpire called Throneberry out.

The Mets manager in those early years was, of course, the inimitable Casey Stengel. He emerged from the Mets' dugout to argue the call with the umpire, but he never got the chance. On his way to second, his own first-base coach stopped him. "Don't bother, Casey," the coach warned. "[Throneberry] didn't touch *first* either."

One of the most famous incidents in baseball history falls within the jurisdiction of this rule. The protagonist is a New York Giants infielder named Fred Merkle. Despite an otherwise respectable sixteen-year major league career, he is known to history as "Bonehead" Merkle.

The pennant race in the National League came down to the wire in 1908, with the Giants, Cubs, and Pirates in a close race. It ended with the Cubs on top by a single game, thanks in large part to a base-running error by Merkle that cost his Giants a game. The game they lost was to the Cubs.

Merkle probably wouldn't have played that day except that the Giants' regular first baseman, Fred Tenney, complained of lumbago and asked manager John McGraw for the day off. Merkle was inserted into the lineup.

On that September afternoon, he played creditably until the bottom of the ninth. Even then, he got off to a good start by singling. He stood on first, and the game was tied with the winning run at third. Al Bridwell, the Giants' shortstop, stepped to the plate.

Bridwell got a base hit to center. The runner on third sprinted home, and Merkle, who was approaching second, saw his teammate cross the plate. With the winning run having scored, Merkle headed for the dugout, too, in order to avoid the crowd of hometown fans that was swarming onto the playing field to celebrate the winning of the pennant.

Cubs second baseman Johnny Evers saw Merkle take off for the bench and alertly called to his teammates to throw him the ball. The center fielder, Solly Hofman, threw it to him, but his throw was off target.

Apparently Giant Joe McGinnity was the next player to control the ball, but as to what happened thereafter, accounts vary greatly. McGinnity may or may not have thrown the game ball into the left-field bleachers; the ball may or may not have made it to second base to force Merkle. Merkle may or may not have gotten to second before the ball did (if the game ball—or any ball—made it there at all).

What everyone does seem to agree on is that the field was crowded with players, police, and fans, and that the umpires did not see the play. Nonetheless, the decision was that Merkle was out, the run did not count, and the score remained tied.

Because the furor was such that resuming play was impossible, the umpires further ruled that the game ended in a tie. The president of the National League was then appealed to, and seven days later his decision came down: the game was to be played over.

Why is this man smiling? After all, it's Fred "Bonehead" Merkle, the man who is remembered best for one ill-considered moment on the base paths. In the bottom of the ninth of a game crucial to the 1908 National League pennant race, he headed for the showers after the winning run had scored—but before he touched second. On appeal, he was called out, and his team lost both the game and the pennant.

When the season ended with the Giants and Cubs tied, the two teams met to replay the Merkle game—and this time the Giants lost, 4–2. The Cubs won the pennant.

In the decades since Merkle's mistake, there has been no small amount of ink invested in defending him. In fact, within weeks of the event, *The New York World* reported that "many veteran players have come to the front and spoken in behalf of Fred Merkle . . . They call attention to the fact that ever since the rule was adopted under which a game ends when the team last at bat scores the winning run, players have run for the clubhouse as soon as the runner crossed the plate, without advancing to next base." But despite such defenses, Merkle is still remembered as "Bonehead."

Here are some other key base-running rules:

The runner must stay on the bag; if he is tagged while off the base and the ball is in play, the runner is out. Overrunning first base is an exception. [7.08c]

Overrunning or oversliding first is an exception to the rule that a runner must remain on base or risk being tagged out, but it is not without limitations. The runner who overruns first must "return at once" to first. Umpire Nick Bremigan once said of outfielder Mickey Rivers, then of the Yankees, that he "can run from home to first as fast as anyone in baseball, but once he has beaten out an infield hit, it seems like it takes him a year to amble back to first base. But he is never called out for it." [7.08j]

Another familiar regulation is that a runner must return to "tag up" at his base after the catch of a foul or fair ball. If he does not return or if he leaves the base before the ball is caught, the runner is subject to being put out. [7.08d]

A runner who starts toward the dugout or his position can be called out on appeal. The same is true of a runner who misses home plate; he must come back and touch it or, on appeal, the umpire may call him out. [7.08k]

The force play is another early lesson: a runner who is forced to advance when a batter hits the ball must reach the next base before the ball does or he's out. However, if a preceding runner is put out, the force is removed on the lead runner—just the way we learned in elementary school. [7.08e]

◇ A runner hit by a batted ball also is out, but if a batted ball hits two runners, only the first is out; after a runner is struck, the ball is dead. [7.08f]

◇ If a fair ball hits a runner immediately behind an infielder, the runner will not be called out unless in the umpire's judgment the runner intentionally interfered with the ball. [7.09m]

◇ The batter may not interfere with a play at the plate; if he does, the runner is out if there are less than two down in the inning. If there are two outs, then the batter is out, and the run does not count. [7.08g]

◇ Passing another base runner is punishable by declaring the passer out. [7.08h]

This last situation seems most often to happen on home runs: the happy slugger, contemplating what a wonderful thing he's accomplished, makes his way around the base paths, running past another runner along the way. Detroit Tigers infielder Dalton Jones did it in 1970 on a grand slam, turning his clout into a three-run single.

That simple mistake can sometimes take on the complexities of high drama. In 1931, Lou Gehrig passed a fellow Yankee after a home run—and it cost him sole possession of the home run title (he and Ruth tied with forty-six).

Advanced Tagging Techniques 101: Here Twins third baseman Rich Rollins, having tagged out Yankees base runner Phil Linz, finds himself at one with Linz's posterior.

The Iron Horse passed Lyn Lary on the base paths of Griffith Stadium—but only in a technical sense, as Lary had run directly across third base and into the dugout because he thought he had seen outfielder Harry Rice catch the ball. Sure enough, Rice had caught it, but only after the ball had rebounded out of the stands. Gehrig was credited with a double. [7.08h]

A similar base-running error—committed by the great Hank Aaron—occurred in an unusual game played on May 26, 1959. The Pirates' Harvey Haddix had pitched twelve perfect innings but, leading off the thirteenth, Milwaukee Brave Felix Mantilla reached first on a throwing error. He was sacrificed to second, then Aaron was given an intentional pass. Up came intimidating Joe Adcock, who proceeded to drive the ball over the fence in right-center. Three-run homer, Braves win 3–0, right?

Incorrect. Mantilla did score the winning run, but Aaron took a short cut across the diamond. Adcock was then called out for passing Aaron on the base paths. The final score went into the record books as 1–0, and Adcock's clout was reduced to a double. Sadder still, after a remarkable one-hitter, Haddix got the loss.

Another variation of the thou-shalt-not-pass-another-base-runner rule was acted out one day by Indians Lou Boudreau and Oris Hockett in a game against the Philadelphia Athletics during World War II. Hockett was trying to score from third, but finding himself caught dead to rights at home, he reversed himself and headed back to what he thought were the safe confines of the hot corner. There he discovered teammate Lou Boudreau. With a shrug, Hockett, for reasons known only to himself, walked toward left field. The opposition catcher alertly tagged both Hockett and Boudreau, who was standing on third base.

The defense argued that the call should be a double play, but the umpires disagreed. They ruled that Hockett was out but declared Boudreau safe, since he had been standing safely on the base when he was tagged. Not so fast, said the opposition's manager, one Cornelius McGillicuddy, *a.k.a.* Connie Mack, as he emerged from the Athletics' dugout. Mack inquired of the umpire, "Don't you think the play went this way? When Hockett ran back past third, that put Boudreau ahead of him. So Boudreau is out for passing a preceding runner. Hockett, of course, was tagged in left field, so he's out. Double play." The umpire's response to Mr. Mack? "Keerect, and thank you, sir."

The Merkle Moral

"The game of baseball takes nothing for granted. Because the play happened to be a final one does not make it excusable to slur the rule. It is just as much a crime against the baseball code to fail to complete a play at the end of a game as in the middle. Merkle was asleep and worked his little dab of gray matter very poorly. He paid the penalty of thoughtlessness, just as he must have paid the penalty had he been caught asleep off base."

—From *The St. Louis Post-Dispatch*, September 24, 1908

Reverse Base Running. Baseball is a game that is to be taken seriously, and The Book is poised to admonish those players foolish enough to make fun of our national pastime.

However, one rule in The Book makes it difficult to keep a straight face. The rule in question says that the runner must not run the bases in reverse order, for if he does so for "the purpose of confusing the defense" or "making a travesty of the game," the umpire shall call time—and the runner will be out. [7.08i]

In the early years of this century (before the introduction of the rule), reverse base running had an occasional strategic use. In a 1902 game between the Orioles and the Athletics, the A's had men on first and third. In an attempted double steal, the runner on first, Harry Davis, broke for second. While he managed to steal the base, the run did not score.

Apparently Davis wasn't a man who took no for an answer. On the second pitch he sprinted back to first, and on the third, he ran to second again. The second time he stole second he drew a throw from the Orioles catcher, and the man on third scored the winning run.

Perhaps the strangest wrong-way move of all took place in Peoria in 1883. Dan O'Leary, playing for the home team, was at bat in the bottom of the ninth with two down and the score tied, 7–7. He was badly fooled by two pitches, swinging wildly and cleaving the air. But on the third pitch he connected. Though he fell to his knees, the ball jumped off the bat.

O'Leary got up and ran—the wrong way. He'd lost his sense of direction and headed up the third-base line. When he reached third, he turned toward second. He heard his teammates yelling at him, but he thought they were encouraging him to run faster as the ball was being relayed in from the outfield. He continued around the horn, only to be called out when he reached home plate—not because the ball beat him but because he ran the wrong way. Though the "travesty of the game" rule wasn't inserted into the rule book until 1920, common practice apparently dictated the call on O'Leary.

Running Rule Changes: The Highlights

1848 First basemen are required to hold the ball in order to put out a runner. Before this the base runner was out if the ball hit him. (Part of this rule change was that the batter-runner could be put out merely by tagging the bag before he reached it.)

1864 Base runners are required to touch all bases in circling the bases.

1870 The batter-runner is allowed to overrun first base.

1880 The runner is called out if hit by a batted ball. (This rule reportedly cured base runners of the habit of running into the ball to prevent infielders from making a play.)

1920 Running the bases in reverse order "for the purpose either of confusing the fielders or making a travesty of the game" is prohibited.

1956 Thanks to Jackie Robinson and Don Hoak, the 1880 rule regarding a base runner's interference with a batted ball is broadened to include double plays. Both the batter and the interfering runner are to be ruled out.

Satchel Paige, 1942.

"Just take the ball and throw it where you want to. Throw strikes. Home plate don't move."

—Satchel Paige

Chapter 8
The Pitcher

In the beginning the man with the ball was simply called the thrower—the term *pitcher* didn't come into common use until about 1858—and for a short while he was not considered any more important to a baseball team than any other player. Eventually, though, it became clear to everyone involved with the game of baseball that the pitcher's role was pivotal and that he had a clear advantage over the batter. In order to balance things out a little, the powers that be began tinkering with the rules.

Naturally, there was a fair amount of experimentation along the way and not a few changes of mind and heart. For one thing, the distance from the pitcher's box to the plate kept increasing—from 35 feet to 45 feet to 50 feet to 60 feet, 6 inches, where it remains. For another, they kept altering the height of the pitcher's mound. The strike zone went through various periods of adjustment, and the number of strikes in an out and balls in a walk fluttered up and down more than a Phil Niekro knuckleball.

One of the most significant ways in which a pitcher's unfair advantage over the batter was limited was by regulating the manner in which he was permitted to throw the ball. There were many strange experiments. At one point he was allowed a running start (shades of cricket); at another he had to pitch from a standing position. Today's standard Windup and Set positions evolved over many decades.

Delivery

In 1845 it was declared that the pitchers had to "pitch" a ball, not just throw it. In 1868 pitchers were forbidden to bend their

Neither Would We

When asked if he ever gets tired of talking about pitching a perfect game for the New York Yankees in the 1956 World Series, Don Larsen said, "No, why should I?"

elbows—they had to use the straight-arm delivery—but in 1872 things loosened up somewhat: a pitcher could throw any way but overhand. In 1879 he had to bring his arm below his hip on delivery, but four years later he had to pass it only below his shoulder.

It was around this time that pitchers gave batters—and rule makers—something else to worry about: the curveball. There's some disagreement about when it was first thrown and by whom—in 1867 by William Cummings or 1877 by Arthur Cummins—but the one thing people do agree about is that when it was first thrown, no one knew what to make of it. In fact, despite the evidence of their own eyes, many experts maintained that a pitcher simply could not make a ball do that; it had to be the wind. Eventually, of course, they did believe it, and they declared it eminently legal.

The rules regarding pitching delivery do not make for the most fascinating reading, but an understanding of them is essential to an appreciation of the game. So here goes.

The pitcher basically has a choice of two positions—the Windup Position and the Set Position—and either may be used at any time. [8.01]

If he chooses the Windup Position, the pitcher holds the ball with both hands in front of his body and faces the batter with his pivot foot on or in front of and touching the pitcher's plate (same thing as the rubber). The other foot is "free." He may take a step backward and a step forward (but not to either side) with his free foot when he delivers the pitch, but otherwise both of his feet must remain on the ground.

From the Windup Position he may do one of three things: pitch the ball, step and throw to a base in an effort to pick off a runner, or drop his hands and leave the rubber, pivot foot first. He may not go into a Set or Stretch Position from there. [8.01a]

If a pitcher opts for the Set Position, he must begin the motion by placing one hand on his side. Then he faces the batter with his pivot foot on or in front of and touching the rubber. His other foot is in front of the rubber, and again he grips the ball with both hands in front of his body.

(The Set Position is often used in combination with the Stretch Position. According to The Book, the Stretch is permitted provided that after the Stretch the pitcher holds the ball with both hands in front of his body and comes to a complete stop before assuming the Set Position. However, if you watch tapes of Phil Niekro, you'll see that he never came to a complete stop with men on base—and he got away with it.)

From the Set Position a pitcher is again allowed to do one of three things: pitch the ball, throw to a base to pick off a runner, or step backward off the plate with his pivot foot. [8.01a]

Regardless of which position he chooses, the pitcher must always step *ahead* of the throw. If he snaps the throw and then steps toward the base, it's a balk. (There's much more about balks later in this chapter.) And clumsiness is held against him, too. If a pitcher drops the ball—either by accident or on purpose—with men on base, it's a balk. If there's no one on base, it's either a ball or no pitch, depending on whether the ball crosses the foul line (ball) or not (no pitch).

When a pitcher throws any illegal pitch with no one on base, a ball is called; if a base is occupied, it's a balk.

Once the pitcher leaves the rubber, he becomes a regular infielder and may throw anywhere, and in any way, he likes. [8.01e]

Naturally, no two pitchers have identical pitching motions, and no two umpires are exactly the same in the way that they interpret the pitching delivery rules. That fact was very apparent in the 1975 World Series, when one of the many things people found to argue about was Red Sox pitcher Luis Tiant's moves on the mound. Did

"I just felt like I was playing catch."

That's what Chicago Cubs rookie Kerry Wood said after striking out twenty Houston Astros in one game. The big day was May 6, 1998, and the game ended in a one-hit 2–0 victory for the twenty-year-old phenom, who set a record for the National League and tied (with Roger Clemens) the major league record for strikeouts. Twelve of the twenty Ks went down swinging, and eight were called out by plate umpire Jerry Meals.

he balk or didn't he? Several million viewers of that thrilling Series had an opportunity to make the call.

Remember the old Jerry Lee Lewis song "A Whole Lotta Shakin' Goin' On"? That was Luis Tiant on the mound. Start, jerk, stop. Start up again, look up, look down. Jerk, pause, pitch. And that was with nobody on base! As sportscaster Curt Gowdy once said, "Luis Tiant comes from everywhere except between his legs." There doesn't seem to be much question that Tiant didn't always step ahead of the throw, but perhaps because his motion was consistent, the American League umps didn't often come down hard on him.

It may seem that every eventuality about pitching delivery has been provided for, but that's not quite true. At the moment there's no rule governing which hand a pitcher may use and whether he may be allowed to switch once he has declared himself. There's already been one ambidextrous pitcher in major league baseball—Greg Harris of the Rangers/Red Sox, who pitched with his right but hinted that he could switch without notice—and there's no reason to think there won't be another one coming along one of these days. Some provision may eventually have to be made for listing on the lineup card not just the starting pitcher's name but also his throwing arm of preference.

There's no business like show business. Rip Sewell's "blooper pitch."

Ask a Silly Question . . .

When asked why his peculiar lob pitch was called the "Ephus Pitch," Rip Sewell responded crisply: "I don't name 'em. I just throw 'em."

The Book also has nothing to say about the trajectory of the ball once it leaves the pitcher's hands, which was just fine with Truett "Rip" Sewell. Because there was nothing in the rules to prohibit it, in 1943 Sewell stepped on the mound and made baseball history. He threw a lob.

Sewell was facing the Detroit Tigers, and Dick Wakefield was the batter. Sewell delivered the ball from his usual position, but from then on things got very strange indeed. After leaving Sewell's hands the ball soared high in the air—some viewers said it went up twenty-five feet—and then, after what seemed like an eternity, it floated down in front of the hapless Wakefield. He struck out.

Wakefield's strikeout was the first of many that Sewell eventually chalked up with the lob—or the "Ephus Pitch," as it was quickly christened for reasons no one seems to recall. No one had ever seen anything like it, but batter after batter was convinced that he could send it out of the park. Fairly drooling over the slow, dangling pitch, with visions of home runs dancing in their heads, most batters swung away with all their might. And most missed.

One day, out of the frustration that was typical of the batters who had to face the Ephus, Boston Braves shortstop Eddie Miller caught the ball as it came across the plate and threw it back in Sewell's face. Sewell caught the ball, and the umpire called a strike.

But not everyone was cowed by the ridiculous Ephus. In the 1946 All-Star Game Ted Williams, who was never intimidated by anything, took a good long look at Sewell's best pitch and sent it into the right-field bleachers. Sewell's reaction: "That was the first homer ever hit off that pitch, and I still don't believe it."

Spitters, Defaced Balls, and Other Trick Pitches

Every once in a while it is boldly suggested that if an athlete can cope with curves, sinkers, screwballs, sliders, knuckleballs, and ninety-five-mile-per-hour fastballs—all of which are perfectly legal pitches—he can probably handle spitters, shine balls, mud balls, grease balls, and emery pitches.

What's more, it is often argued, since rules don't seem to keep determined pitchers from loading the ball anyhow, we may as well do away with the rule and stop making cheaters of some of the finest players in the game. But so far, the rule remains, and pitchers continue to discover ingenious new ways to get around it.

There was a time, before the spitball was outlawed, when pitchers took a certain amount of pride in doctoring the ball. For instance, Pirates pitcher Marty O'Toole was one of the best spitball pitchers of his era—he played in the majors from 1908 to 1914—and he didn't believe in subtlety. Before he pitched, he had the disconcerting, and insanitary, habit of holding the ball up to his face and licking it with his tongue. Since it was a perfectly legal pitch, there wasn't anything anyone could do to stop him. Or was there?

One day in 1912 O'Toole was pitching to the Phillies, and at least one Philadelphia player, first baseman Fred Luderus, had finally had enough of seeing O'Toole use the game ball for a lollipop. When the Phillies took the field, Luderus took a tube of liniment to first base with him, and he gave the ball a little rubdown every chance he got. Within a few innings, O'Toole's tongue was so inflamed and raw that he had to leave the game.

When Pirates manager Fred Clarke protested, Phillies manager Charlie "Red" Dooin countered with a hygiene lesson and a plea of self-defense. He said that since O'Toole was putting millions of germs on the ball, it was only fair that the Phillies should be allowed to disinfect it.

Those sorts of hijinks disappeared in 1920, when what is now Rule 8.02 went into effect. Officially, a pitcher may rub the ball between his bare, untainted hands, but that's about it. He may not bring his pitching hand to his mouth (except in cold weather, when the pitchers are allowed to blow on their hands if both managers agree). He may not deface the ball or apply any foreign substance to it. And he may not rub the ball against his body or his uniform. The first time a pitcher does any of the above, the umpire may call a ball and issue a stern warning. If he does it again, the umpire may throw the pitcher out of the game. [5.02a]

A pitcher may also be disqualified if he's caught with any "foreign substance" on his person. One occasional exception is the rosin bag. It usually stays on the ground behind the pitcher's plate, but if it's raining or the field is wet, an umpire may tell the pitcher to carry the bag in his hip pocket. But no matter where the rosin bag is, the rosin may touch only the pitcher's hands, not the ball, his glove, or his uniform. [8.02b]

In the old days the "defaced ball" rules were such that an umpire actually had to catch the pitcher in the act of doctoring or defacing the ball, and it was a common sight to see umpires out on the mound frisking the pitcher, looking for Vaseline or sandpaper or thumbtacks or whatever. However, as of 1974 the umpire became more of a judge than a detective, since he no longer had to discover evidence that a pitcher was throwing an illegal pitch. Now if an umpire suspects that a pitcher is throwing an illegal ball (based solely on his observation of how the ball travels), he may warn him and, if it happens again, eject him from the game.

Of course, that doesn't mean that the pitcher has to be happy about the call. In August of 1978 Don Sutton certainly wasn't. He was accused of throwing a defaced ball—the umpire maintained that he had scratched it with his fingernail—and ejected from the game. The umpire didn't see Sutton scratch the ball, but he maintained, correctly according to The Book, that the scratches on the ball were evidence enough of Sutton's crime.

But Sutton's ejection was only act one of the drama. Act two involves a conflict in The Book. Rule 8.02 says that the punishment for the crime is the pitcher's disqualification, but Rule 3.02 calls for a ten-day suspension. In the end Sutton was spared suspension, perhaps because he announced that if he was suspended, he was planning to sue umpire Doug Harvey and the National League for preventing him from making a living. (On the other hand, the umpires working in the 1986 National League playoffs saw no reason to eject Astros pitcher Mike Scott, despite the postgame complaints of ball-tampering that came from the Mets' dugout.)

An earlier bit of drama about the spitball was enacted in 1968, and that time the result was a change in the rules. As the rule stood then, a pitcher was forbidden to spit on his hands before any pitch, including warm-ups.

The Phillies were up against the Mets at Shea Stadium. In the bottom of the seventh inning reliever John Boozer came in for Woody Fryman. Bud Harrelson waited as Boozer prepared to take his eight warm-up throws. Before Boozer threw his first warm-up, he spat on his hands. The umpire called ball one.

Not surprisingly, manager Gene Mauch came flying out of the dugout to protest, but umpire Ed Vargo stuck to his guns: as long as Boozer was in the pitching circle, he was not allowed to wet his hand. And as Mauch and everyone else could clearly see, Boozer was in the pitching circle.

Livid, Gene Mauch proceeded to cut off his nose to spite his face. He ordered Boozer to go to his mouth; Vargo called ball two. Still defiant, Mauch gave the order again; this time Vargo called ball three and threw Boozer out of the game. Mauch followed Boozer to the locker room a few minutes later. When the smoke cleared and Bud Harrelson finally faced a pitcher, reliever Dick Hall, he started with a 3–0 count.

Gene Mauch lost the battle, but he eventually won the war. His argument with Vargo focused attention on what was obviously a counterproductive and foolish aspect of the hand-to-mouth rule. Soon thereafter the rules committee voted to exempt warm-ups from the rule.

When is a spitter not quite a spitter? If there is a play on the ball. If a violation is called but the batter reaches first on a hit, an error, a base on balls, a hit batsman, or any other legal method, and no other runner is put out before advancing a base, then the play continues. However, the pitcher is still charged with a violation of the rule, and he still gets a warning from the umpire. [5.02a and 5.02c]

Scuffing the Ball

If you look up the word scuffball in the dictionary, don't be surprised if you find a tiny picture of Richard Alan Rhoden. Rick Rhoden, an impressive right-hander whose reputed ball-tampering created a major stir in both leagues—first with the Dodgers and Pirates in the National League and then with the AL's New York Yankees—is practically synonymous with ball-scuffing. There was never a dull moment when he was on the mound: opposing players and managers would fling accusations; umpires kept him under constant scrutiny; fans made threats or hollered encouragement from the stands.

In 1987, Rhoden's first season with the Yankees, AL president Bobby Brown threatened to suspend Rhoden for ten days if the umpires ejected him for scuffing the ball. But it didn't happen. Suspecting that somebody is scuffing the ball is one thing. Proving it is something else. And no one—least of all the umpires—wants to

Who Says This Is a Game?

"Pitching is the art of instilling fear by making a man flinch."

—Sandy Koufax

eject a pitcher without incontrovertible proof.

Like the brushback pitch and the spitter, the scuffball is part of the game—some say a big part of the game. Yankees pitching coach Mark Connor once estimated that twenty-five to thirty percent of all pitchers deface the ball to make it move. Others put the percentage even higher than that.

The Beanball

"To pitch at a batter's head is unsportsmanlike and highly dangerous. It should be—and is—condemned by everybody," says The Book. On the other hand, we have the immortal words of Ty Cobb: "Every great batter works on the theory that the pitcher is more afraid of him than he is of the pitcher."

It's been illegal since 1881, but for all that, the "purpose pitch"—*a.k.a.* the beanball, the brushback, the message pitch, or what Don Drysdale called his "brushback slider"—has always played an important role in the rhythm and strategy of the game. In fact, many members of an earlier baseball generation, among them Drysdale, Lou Boudreau, and Jimmy Piersall, say that if today's players can't stand the heat, they should stay out of the kitchen. After all, those batting helmets aren't there for decoration.

In the good old days, Dizzy Dean, who still holds the record for consecutive knockdowns, flattened eight New York Giants batters in a row, then skipped the ninth man (pitcher Carl Hubbell), and knocked down the lead-off man again.

No one was badly hurt that day, but there have been other, grimmer days. The grimmest of all was a day in mid-August of 1920, when Cleveland Indians shortstop Ray Chapman was beaned by a Carl Mays pitch. He died in a hospital several hours later.

Ray Chapman is the major league's only fatality, but there have been plenty of close calls. Detroit Tiger Mickey Cochrane took a pitch in the ear from New York Yankee Bump Hadley; Philadelphia Athletics pitcher Marion Fricano almost put Cass Michaels of the White Sox out of commission; and in an accident eerily reminiscent of the Ray Chapman tragedy, Tony Conigliaro was hit in the eye by a Steve Hamilton pitch in Fenway Park in 1967. Dickie Thon of Houston was hit in the face by the Mets' Mike Torrez in 1984. Milwaukee's Kevin Seitzer was beaned by New York's Melido Perez in 1994. In 1995 Kirby Puckett suffered a broken upper jaw when he was hit by a pitch from Cleveland's Dennis Martinez. It comes with the territory.

There has always been and always will be a fine line between a pitcher who is simply demonstrating his territoriality and a pitcher who's breaking the rules. No one would argue that a pitcher is entitled to control the plate—not to let a batter lean into the strike zone, for instance. (One of Don Drysdale's Dodgers teammates once said of him: "Don didn't like to see a hitter crowding the plate. Of course, he took the position that you were crowding the plate the

How's the weather up there? Mariners pitcher Randy Johnson—nicknamed the "Big Unit" because, at six-foot-ten, he's the tallest pitcher in major league history— earned a prominent place in the record books when he pitched a no-hitter—Seattle's first—against the Detroit Tigers. On the way to the 2–0 victory the intimidating Johnson, who signed with the Diamondbacks for the 1999 season, struck out eight and walked six. (Tom DiPace)

Did He or Didn't He?

Scuff the baseball, that is. Not surprisingly, Rick Rhoden never would say for sure. "Why should I?" he told reporters. "If they want to believe I do it, let them." When Rhoden left baseball in 1989 he took his secret with him.

moment you left the hitters' circle!")

No one would argue, either, that even the very best pitchers can't always throw the ball where they want it to go. (When someone accused Grover Cleveland Alexander of throwing a beanball, he said: "All I did was throw a curve, but it kept following him.")

Determining whether a pitcher has crossed that fine line is what Rule 8.02d is all about. If an umpire suspects that a pitcher is intentionally pitching at the batter, he has the authority to eject both the pitcher and his manager. Under normal circumstances, he first issues a warning to the pitcher and managers of *both* teams; the second time it happens, he may eject the offending pitcher. ("*Unfair!*" is the general response to this rule. If the umpire warns both teams when only one has committed an offense, the offender is, in effect, getting a free ride.)

In modern times the response to the beanball is often a rush to the mound and ensuing fisticuffs, but in days past the players tended to let their bats do their fighting for them. One of the most memorable examples of this came on a day in Ebbets Field when Willie Mays went up against Brooklyn Dodgers pitcher Sal Maglie.

The first Maglie pitch to Mays was a brushback, and the second was so close that Mays went down in the dirt. The umpire warned Maglie, but Sal said that he couldn't help it—it was so hot that his hands were slippery. Maglie asked the ump to tell Willie he was sorry.

The umpire gave Willie the message, and Willie sent back one in return: a four-hundred-foot home run. As Willie rounded second, he decided to add insult to injury. "*Hey, Maglie! I'm sorry!*" he hollered.

"I'm a very moody person," pitcher Randy Johnson once told a group of reporters. No doubt Cleveland Indians outfielder Kenny Lofton would second that emotion. In April 15, 1998, Lofton got on the Big Unit's nerves when he took his time returning to the batter's box after Johnson threw a slider that was more than a little inside. When Lofton finally did step up to the plate, his reward was yet

Cleveland hurler (some say "headhunter") Jaret Wright clobbered eleven batters in the 1998 season and beaned ten more in 1999. (Tom DiPace)

another buzzball, this time a shot that cut even closer.

Not surprisingly, there was chaos on the field. When the dust settled, Johnson, Lofton, and Cleveland's Sandy Alomar were ejected, and Mariners manager Lou Piniella (who went after Lofton) was fined. In the short run Johnson's tactics benefited the Mariners, who won the game 5–3. In the long run the news wasn't so good for Seattle. After due deliberation AL President Gene Budig gave Johnson a three-game suspension.

Johnson didn't appeal Budig's ruling, but neither did he agree with the conclusion that he had thrown at Lofton on purpose. "It wasn't deliberate," he said. "It didn't hit him. I'm a good enough pitcher that if I'd wanted to hit him, I could have."

Clearly, "Keep an eye on pitchers who throw inside" is a key component of Gene Budig's job description. In June of 1999 he found it necessary to have a much publicized discussion with Cleveland hurler—some prefer the term "headhunter"—Jaret Wright about his deportment on the mound.

The seemingly reckless right-hander had clobbered a whopping eleven batters in the 1998 season, and with five hit batsman behind him already he seemed well on his way to beating his own record. Twice already in the 1999 season he had hit batters in the helmet with fastballs—and instigated bench-clearing brawls both times. He was suspended for five games for hitting Boston outfielder Darren Lewis in the head. After Wright hit Detroit's Tony Clark, Budig decided it was time for a heart-to-heart talk. What happened behind those closed doors was not made public. What's more, many observers felt that Budig should never have let it be known that he was even meeting Wright.

In defending his pitcher Cleveland manager Mike Hargrove, who attended the hush-hush meeting, said, "I agree he's hit a lot of people, but he's a twenty-three-year-old power pitcher trying to find his command and location." That may be true, but consider this: in his first three major league seasons, Wright has hit a batter every seventeen innings he pitched. Over the same period, the major league average was one HBP for every twenty-eight IP. Want a little more perspective? For their careers, Don Drysdale tagged a hitter every twenty-two innings, Bob Gibson every thirty-eight, and Clyde Wright (Jaret's father) every seventy-five.

There have been many proposals for eliminating the beanball. Perhaps the most frequently heard comment is that the abolition of the designated hitter would go a long way toward making the beanball obsolete. If a pitcher had to come to the plate himself, some cynics say, it would be a different story. (However, since batters routinely get beaned in the National League, this argument doesn't hold much water.)

Then there was Casey Stengel's modest proposal. To wit: "Any time a pitcher hits a batter with a pitched ball, let the batter go not to first but to third base. Giving the batter the equivalent of a triple, putting him in scoring position, would be a penalty extreme enough to make the hurlers very careful."

Warm-up Pitches

The Book says that when the pitcher takes the mound before each inning, or when he comes in to substitute for another pitcher, he is entitled to take eight warm-up throws within a minute's time. If a substitute is brought in on what The Book calls a "sudden emergency"—usually when the pitcher of record is injured—and consequently has not had enough time to warm up, the umpire may let him take as many pitches as the ump deems necessary. [8.03]

One would think that this perfectly straightforward rule is tamper-proof, but one would be wrong. In 1911 the rulemakers in the American League decided that all those warm-up pitches were slowing down the game. The president of the league declared that pitchers could no longer take warm-up pitches at the beginning of each inning. He should have left well enough alone.

Despite the rule, most pitchers would manage to squeeze in a few throws as the fielders got into position, and the umpires let it pass. One day when Boston met the Philadelphia Athletics, pitcher Ed Karger took his place on the mound and tossed a couple to his catcher as his fellow Red Sox took the field. Stuffy McInnis, the Philadelphia first baseman, came to the plate and watched as the Sox took the field and Karger continued to warm up.

Suddenly, McInnis stepped up and sent what was supposed to be a warm-up pitch far into the outfield. The fielders, not yet in position, had no chance to do anything but admire the hit, and McInnis circled the bases. The ruling? Since warm-ups were officially not allowed, the home run counted. The rule, never a popular one anyway, was off the books by the end of the year.

Delaying the Game

There is no end to the things a pitcher must remember. For example, not only must he pitch properly; he has to do it within a time limit. The Book says that a pitcher may not delay the game; specifically, when a batter is in position, the pitcher may not throw the ball to any player other than the catcher unless he's trying to pick off a runner. And when there's no one on base, the pitcher has twenty seconds from the time he receives the ball to send it back to the catcher. If the pitcher does delay the game, the umpire calls a ball. [8.04]

The fact is, the twenty-second rule is often violated, but it's almost never called. For one thing, the umpires have enough to worry about without spending time watching the second hand of the clock between pitches.

In general the National League is much more lenient about the twenty-second rule than the American League. In 1969 American League president Joe Cronin decided that it was time to get tough, and he declared that all AL parks would install timers—called "pitchometers"—in their scoreboards. However, there were loud protests from many teams in the league, and in the end only two teams, the White Sox and the Indians, went along with the plan. The rest of the American League made do with their usual timing method—a third-base coach with a stopwatch—but to this day the

National League has neither stopwatch nor pitchometer.

Another time-saving rule change had to do with the introduction of a new ball into the game. In the old days the pitcher or the batter could put in an order for a new ball any time he felt like it, but now a new one may be brought into the game only if it hits a wall or gets muddy, and then only at the umpire's discretion. Pitchers may ask the umpire to look at an old ball in the hopes that he'll get rid of it, but they can't officially demand a new one.

Every once in a while someone suggests that the biggest waste of time in baseball is the throwing of four wide pitches for an intentional walk. Why can't the manager just tell the umpire to let the batter take a base? But then that someone is reminded that a free pass takes less than a minute, and besides, the fans would miss out on a perfect opportunity to boo the opposing pitcher.

Other students of baseball think that all this fuss about pitchers delaying the game is itself a waste of time. After all, most pitchers are just as eager as anyone else to keep the game moving. At least the best ones are. (Just ask Greg Maddux.) Maybe it's coincidence, but if you rattle off the names of the dozen best pitchers of the last decade, you'll note that there's not a dawdler in the bunch.

As Grover Cleveland Alexander once said, when asked why he liked to pitch so fast: "What do you want me to do? Let them sons of bitches stand up there and think on my time?"

The Balk

A friend of ours recalls the first time he went to a ballgame with the woman who later became his wife. It was only their third date, and he was still getting to know her. They were sitting behind the third-base dugout in Wrigley Field, and the Cubs had men on first and second in the top of the third. Suddenly our friend's companion leaped to her feet and hollered, "Balk!" Sure enough, the umpire agreed, the runners advanced, and our friend knew for sure that he had met the woman of his dreams.

The point here is not to define true love but rather to demonstrate that a balk is hard to spot and even harder to explain. The Book has a go at it (in 8.05), and so, therefore, must we.

When a base is occupied, it is a balk if the pitcher pitches when he is not touching the rubber. When he *is* touching the rubber, it's a balk if the pitcher makes any motion naturally associated with pitching without delivering the goods. The Book gives some examples, such as if the pitcher:

- Fakes a throw to first.
- Fails to step ahead of the throw to a base.
- Drops the ball, accidentally or intentionally.
- Fakes a throw to an unoccupied base.
- Does not face the batter when he delivers the ball.
- Unnecessarily delays the game.
- Pitches or seems to pitch when he isn't touching the rubber.
- Stands on the rubber without the ball.
- Pitches to a batter who's not ready.
- Pitches to a catcher who's not in the catcher's box.

Did he or didn't he? Balk, that is. One of the many things that fans found to argue about during the exciting 1975 Red Sox– Cincinnati World Series was Luis Tiant's move to first. (AP/Wide World Photos)

Pitches from the Set Position without coming to a stop.

Takes his hand from the ball for anything other than to pitch or pick a runner off after he's in position.

The above list is long, but it all sounds pretty simple, right? Wrong. The balk is probably the most misunderstood of all rules, and perhaps the most erratically called. In 1978 during a Cardinals-Giants series in San Francisco, four balks were called in one game, eight over the three games. Yet some teams go for weeks without a balk.

The technicalities of the balk rule can sometimes befuddle the spectator, but the spirit of the rule is clear. The purpose of the balk call is *to prevent the pitcher from deceiving the base runner.* Foremost in the umpire's mind should be not the precise placement of the pitcher's pivot foot (although that does matter) but his "intent" when he makes his move.

While we're on the subject of deception, let's discuss a perennial favorite: the hidden-ball trick. An infielder hides the ball in his glove while the pitcher pretends to take it to the mound and prepares to pitch. As soon as the runner takes his lead off the base, the infielder tags him out. It sounds like the perfect crime.

But on August 12, 1961, the San Francisco Giants discovered that crime doesn't pay. José Pagan, the shortstop for the Giants, hid the ball in his glove, and pitcher Jack Sanford pretended to take it to the mound. Pagan prepared to tag the runner—Cincinnati catcher Johnny Edwards—as soon as he stepped off second. But the umpire had done his homework. As soon as Sanford stepped on the rubber without the ball, the umpire was entitled to declare a balk, which is exactly what he did. Edwards was awarded a free pass to third. [8.05l]

The Book instructs that when a balk is called, the ball is dead, and each runner takes a base. However, in 1954 the already somewhat intricate rule was amended. Before that a one-base advance had been mandatory when a balk was called, but the rule was expanded to give the batter an option to ignore the balk call if he reached first on a hit, an error, a base on balls, or a hit batsman, provided that all the runners advanced at least one base. In a burst of logic, Jim Gallagher, chairman of the rules committee, said, "If a pitcher commits a balk, he violates the rules. There is no reason why the offensive team should be penalized."

Three years later the logic of this rule change became crystal clear. Detroit was playing Baltimore. The score was tied 1–1, and the Tigers had runners on second and third. Baltimore pitcher Connie Johnson began his pitch to Tiger Charlie Maxwell. The umpire signaled for the balk, but Maxwell hit the pitch for a single. All the runners advanced a base, so the balk was ignored. Under the old rule, Maxwell would not have been credited with a hit or an RBI, though the runners would have advanced.

Twenty years later, a similar situation arose in Yankee Stadium, but this time it wasn't solved quite so simply. The Yanks were hosting the Toronto Blue Jays in April of 1977. In the bottom of the fourth inning with two out, Lou Piniella was at the plate and Jim Wynn was on third. A balk was called on Blue Jays pitcher Jerry Garvin, but on the pitch Sweet Lou hit a line drive that bounced out of the center fielder's glove. Piniella made it to second, but Wynn, who had tagged up at third, was held there.

According to the balk rule, because Jim Wynn did not advance a base, the balk call had to be honored. Wynn was awarded home, but Piniella—robbed of his double—had to bat again. (He struck out, and the Yanks eventually lost, protested, and lost again.)

Every once in a while when the baseball rulemakers gather, someone brings up the subject of balk lines, lines that would be drawn on the pitcher's mound to help umpires determine if a pitcher is using a trick move to first or third base.

In fact, during spring training of 1974 they decided to give the balk lines a try. The lines were three inches wide, drawn with chalk or lime. They started fifteen inches from the pitching rubber and extended to the edge of the pitching circle. The idea was that the pitcher had to step across the guideline if he wanted to throw to first or third. Naturally the pitchers hated balk lines—especially lefties, who claimed that they were being discriminated against ("How many pitchers throw to third?" asked Mets southpaw Jon Matlack), and no one else thought much of them either. The lines were rejected for regular season play.

Umpires seem to do fine without visual aids. As Tom Seaver has said, "Maybe in high school games the umpires need a line to tell a balk, but the big league umpire should know a balk when he sees one, without lines."

Visits to the Mound

This is a rule for which most pitchers are probably grateful. Some of them, notably Bob Gibson, think that any visitor to the mound is

Spare the Rod and Spoil the Pitcher

The time came when Cardinals superstar Bob Gibson stopped pitching and started coaching. One day during a stint with the Braves, he went out to the mound to calm down a pitcher who was getting well and truly shelled. Whatever he said definitely worked; the pitcher got through the inning with his ERA intact. When asked after the game what he had said to encourage the beleaguered pitcher, Gibson answered, "I just told him that if there weren't fifteen thousand people watching, I'd hit him in the head."

one too many. Tim McCarver is one of Bob Gibson's biggest fans, but McCarver is the first to say that Gibby could be a little prickly sometimes, particularly when he had visitors on the mound. "I remember one time going out to the mound to talk with him," recalls McCarver. "He told me to get back behind the batter, that the only thing *I* knew about pitching is that it's hard to hit."

The Book says that a coach or manager may make one trip per inning to the mound—the area falling within the eighteen-foot circle around the pitcher's rubber—without removing the pitcher. If a coach or manager makes a second visit, the pitcher must be replaced. What's more, the coach or manager is allowed only one trip to the mound per batter. If he does make a second trip while the pitcher is facing the same batter, the manager is ejected from the game, the pitcher finishes pitching to that batter, and then the pitcher too is out. [5.06]

If a coach or manager tries to get a message to the pitcher without visiting the mound, there's a rule to cover that as well. If a manager or coach talks to any player and that player talks to the pitcher before there has been an intervening play, the umpire considers it an official visit to the mound.

Anyone who watches a coach or manager or a pitcher's teammate go to the mound for a conference with his pitcher cannot help but speculate about what in the world they're *saying* out there. Umpire Jim Farley has a story about that: "Baseball fans are given to speculation about what goes on in mound conferences during tense moments in the national pastime. Many years ago I made it a point to find out after a huddle between Lefty Gomez, the great Yankee pitcher, and Tony Lazzeri, his second-base teammate.

"With the bases loaded and no one out, Lazzeri called for time and walked to the pitcher's box. He looked Gomez squarely in the eye and said, 'You got yourself into this; get yourself out.' "

Substitute Pitchers

Relief pitching as a major factor in baseball strategy is a comparatively new phenomenon. In the early days a pitcher was expected to go nine innings, and if a starter had to leave a game, another starter would usually take his place. It's instructive to note that of the 867 games that Cy Young started, he finished 751, and Walter Johnson finished 631 of his 822 starts. And Joe "Iron Man" McGinnity, who played from 1893 to 1925 and had his greatest success with the New York Giants, pitched both games of a doubleheader five times during his career.

They just don't make 'em like this anymore. Joe "Iron Man" McGinnity of the Giants, who pitched both games of a doubleheader five times during his career.

A Pitch Only a Mother Could Love

On Mother's Day 1939, Bob Feller's mother traveled from her home in Van Meter, Iowa, to see her son pitch against the White Sox. It was the first time she'd seen him play in the big leagues, and Mrs. Feller got the royal treatment—a private box along the first-base line in Comiskey Park with all the trimmings. What better gift could a mom ask for? However, soon after the game got started, Mrs. Feller might well have wished she'd gotten a candy-gram instead. A foul ball hit by Sox third baseman Marv Owen sailed into the stands and knocked her out cold. The story had a happy ending, though. Mrs. Feller came to not long afterward. She needed a few stitches, but otherwise she was as good as new.

There was a time when the guys in the bullpen were broken-down starters or pitchers without the talent to win starting jobs. In the old days, if you got into another team's bullpen, you had the game won. In today's bullpen you might just find a Trevor Hoffman, a John Wetteland, or a Rob Nen.

Only after World War II did a team have to have a bullpen to be a contender. A case in point was the big seven-game 1947 World Series. No starter finished a game, and the games ultimately became a battle between Dodgers reliever Hugh Casey, who played in six games, and Yankee Joe Page, who made an appearance in four. The Yankees beat Brooklyn four games to three.

There has on occasion been some resistance to the emphasis on relief pitching, in large part because of the time that some people say is wasted along the way. One of the rule changes that has been recommended to streamline the game says that any pitcher who starts an inning must finish it, at least in the first seven innings of the game. But restrictions or no, relievers are unquestionably an indispensable part of today's game, and among the most celebrated. As famous reliever Sparky Lyle has said, "Why pitch nine innings when you can get just as famous pitching two?"

Pitching Rule Changes: The Highlights

1858 The called strike is introduced. The pitcher is allowed to make a short run in his delivery.

1863 The pitcher is not permitted to take even a step in his delivery.

1867 Pitchers are allowed to take as many steps as they like before delivery.

1872 The pitcher is allowed to snap the ball during delivery, but he's restricted to a below-the-waist motion.

1879 The pitcher is required to face the batter.

1881 The pitcher is fined for deliberately hitting the batter with the ball.

1883 Pitching is allowed from anywhere up to shoulder height.

1884 Almost all restrictions on a pitcher's motion are lifted. He may throw the ball with virtually any motion he chooses provided that his delivery is no higher than his shoulders and he is facing the batter at the moment of windup. He is allowed only one step before delivery.

1887 A pitcher must keep one foot on the rear line of the box and may not take more than one step in delivering the ball. Before delivery he must hold the ball in front of him so that it is visible to the umpire.

1893 The pitcher's box is replaced by the rubber—a slab twelve inches long and four inches wide. The pitcher is required to place his rear foot against the slab. The pitching distance is lengthened to sixty feet, six inches, where it remains today. (According to some sources, it was meant to be sixty feet, but when the original planner wrote *60'0"*, the final *zero* was thought to be a *six*. Six it stayed.)

1898 The first official balk rule: a pitcher is compelled to throw to a base if he makes a motion in that direction.

1899 The balk rule is refined: a pickoff throw may not be faked; a pitcher must complete his motion.

1903 The height of the pitcher's mound is established. It must not be higher than fifteen inches above the base lines.

1908 Pitchers are forbidden to scuff or soil a new ball.

1920 The abolition of the spitball. Exception: each team is allowed to appoint two spitball pitchers for the 1920 season.

1921 Eight National League and nine American League pitchers are officially designated as spitball pitchers and allowed to use the spitter for the rest of their careers. The lucky fellows in the AL: Doc Ayers and Hub Leonard (Detroit), Ray Caldwell and Stan Coveleski

(Cleveland), Urban Faber (Chicago), Jack Quinn (New York), Allan Russell (Boston), and Urban Shocker and Allen Sothoron (St. Louis). In the NL: Bill Doak and Marv Goodwin (St. Louis), Phil Douglas (New York), Dana Fillingim and Dick Rudolph (Boston), Ray Fisher (Cincinnati), and Burleigh Grimes and Clarence Mitchell (Brooklyn).

1925 Pitchers are allowed to use a rosin bag.

1939 The pitcher is allowed to have his free foot in front of or behind the rubber, with his pivot foot in front of or on the rubber (but always in contact with it).

1940 The pitcher is permitted to take two steps—one forward, one backward—as long as his pivot foot remains in contact with the rubber at all times. It is a balk if a pitcher throws or fakes a throw to an unoccupied base.

1955 When a base is occupied, a pitcher must deliver the pitch within twenty seconds of receiving it from the catcher. If he fails to do so, the umpire may call a ball.

1968 If a pitcher "goes to his mouth" with men on base, a balk is declared. If the bases are empty, a ball is called.

1969 The pitcher's mound gets lower—to ten inches above the base lines and home plate, where it remains.

1974 Umpires are permitted to declare illegal pitches without physical evidence. If they think that the motion of a ball indicates that the pitcher is throwing a spitter or a defaced ball, they can issue a warning and eventually eject him from the game.

Umpire Art Gore takes on Leo Durocher in 1953. Gore won. (AP/Wide World Photos)

"It ain't nothin' *till I call it."*

—Bill Klem

Chapter 9

The Umpire

In the top of the seventh inning of a baseball game in October of 1981 in Yankee Stadium, an unthinkable event took place. In front of the 54,000 fans gathered to watch a contest between the Yankees and the Milwaukee Brewers, an angry, drunken fan jumped over the third-base rail and attacked the plate umpire, Mike Reilly. Within seconds help was on the way. Yankees third baseman Graig Nettles stepped in and pulled the fan off the umpire's back.

There was much to talk about afterward. Naturally, people discussed the play that brought on the disturbing assault—Reilly had called Dave Winfield out at third on a controversial tag, and the crowd did not exactly approve—but the more significant discussions had to do with the role of the umpire in today's game. In fact, when some players and reporters later kidded Nettles about coming to the aid of the "enemy," Nettles pointed out that while he may have had his differences with umps over the years, the bottom line is that the guys on the field have to stick together. And that includes umpires.

Many years later—on September 27, 1996, to be precise—the baseball world was once again shocked by a player's treatment of an umpire. This time the villain was Baltimore Orioles second baseman Roberto Alomar, and the wronged official was John Hirschbeck. The Orioles were in Toronto trying to clinch a wild-card playoff berth.

It started out like a run-of-the-mill disagreement. Hirschbeck called Alomar out on strikes. Alomar argued the call—and kept arguing from the dugout even after the next batter came up.

Eventually Hirschbeck ejected Alomar, and Alomar came out of the dugout to argue some more. Then it happened: Alomar spat into the umpire's face and left the field. Alomar claimed later that he'd been provoked, that Hirschbeck had called him a bad name. He also said that Hirschbeck had become "bitter" since the death of his eight-year-old son, in 1993. When he heard about Alomar's remarks, Hirschbeck stormed into the Baltimore clubhouse and threatened to kill Alomar.

League president Gene Budig suspended Alomar for five games but ruled that the suspension would begin at the start of the following season. Some experts opined that the punishment fit the crime, nobody was really hurt, and we should all go back to our lives. Others said it was a slap on the wrist for a heinous crime and cried out for Alomar's head. (Baltimore GM Pat Gillick courageously went on record as being against Alomar's actions. "From the Orioles point of view we don't condone spitting on people," he said.) The Alomar-Hirschbeck incident was the talk of sports for weeks, even after Alomar apologized (calling his own actions indefensible) and withdrew his appeal of the suspension.

The story had a happy ending. On April 22, 1997, just before the start of an Orioles–White Sox game, Roberto Alomar walked past second base and out to right field and offered his hand to John Hirschbeck. The crowd in Camden Yards went wild as player and umpire shook hands and made up. After the game Hirschbeck told reporters: "I hope that now that you've seen us shake hands, you'll let it go."

Umpire Harry Wendelstedt was probably right when he said, "Baseball regards umpires as a necessary evil. If they could play games without umpires, I'm sure the majority would vote to do so." But of course, we *can't* play baseball without umpires. There has to be someone on the playing field who is impartial, someone who knows the rules and is not trying to bend them to suit the purposes of one team. Perhaps most important, it is essential to have someone in the game whose job it is to honor not just the letter of the law but its spirit as well. As the saying goes, it's a dirty job, but *somebody's* got to do it.

Umpires have been doing it ever since 1845, when the rules of baseball were written for the first time. And ever since then umps have been criticized, reviled, second-guessed, even pelted with produce. While everyone knows that umps are only human, we can't help expecting them to perform superhuman feats. As

American League umpire Nestor Chylak used to say, "They expect an umpire to be perfect on opening day and to improve as the season goes on."

Job Description

According to a study done by an umpiring school some years ago, in an average nine-inning game the umpiring staff calls 288 balls and strikes, calls 64 players safe or out (56 of them at first), and gets hit with the ball once.

The Book doesn't provide these sorts of stats. It says simply that the umpire has two major responsibilities: he must make sure that a game is conducted in accordance with the rules, and he must keep order. Fortunately for the ump, along with this grave mission also comes a goodly amount of power—in short, the umpire is the boss of virtually everyone on the field.

The umpire may give orders to players, coaches, trainers, managers, and club officers, and if they don't do what they're told, he may enforce penalties for infractions of the rules. He may suspend or call a game, and if push comes to shove, he may declare a forfeit. (For more about called, suspended, and forfeited games see Chapter 4.)

And that's not all. An umpire may also eject any player, coach, manager, or substitute for complaining about decisions, demonstrating unsportsmanlike conduct, or using bad language—according to *his* judgment. If he has a mind to, he can even throw out members of the ground crew, ushers, photographers, reporters, broadcasters, and anyone else not authorized to be on the playing field. (For more about ejections, see Chapter 4.) What's more, in the unlikely event that something happens that's not covered in The Book, he may use his judgment and wing it. [9.01a through 9.01e]

(The only thing more powerful than an umpire is, apparently, television. In the 1972 World Series, Baseball Commissioner Bowie Kuhn forbade the umpires to eject Dick Williams and Blue Moon Odom from the game, lest the televised event be deprived of any of its star attractions—even ones who broke the rules.)

If you're thinking of becoming an umpire because you want a job without any paperwork, you'd better think again. There are the line-up cards to deal with and the results of a game to record. And then there are the reports. Within twelve hours of the end of every game the umpire must write a report to the league president listing all

Whistle While You Work

"Why do I like baseball? The pay is good, it keeps you out in the fresh air and sunshine, and you can't beat them hours."

—Tim Hurst, umpire

incidents worthy of comment, including the disqualification of any player, manager, coach, or trainer, and any rule violations. [9.05a] If someone was disqualified because of obscene or abusive language or because he attempted to inflict physical violence, that's considered a flagrant infraction of the rules, and the details must be reported even sooner—within four hours. [9.05b]

These interoffice memos don't just get filed somewhere, either. The league president supposedly rules on each report, determining whether any disciplinary action is called for and whether a fine should be levied on the offender and, if so, how much. Any such fine must be paid within five days. [9.05c]

Safety in Numbers

In the beginning two umpires and a referee ran the game—each team got to pick an umpire (presumably one who had a tendency to favor his employer), so the referee was needed to settle disputes between the umps—but ever since 1858, the arbiters have been independent.

In the 1870s there was usually only one umpire per game, and he called everything from behind the plate. In the 1880s there was still just one, but he was mobile—he usually moved behind the pitcher when there was a runner on base. In 1898 the work was divided between two umpires, and in 1933 three-man umpiring crews became the standard. It wasn't until 1952 that the four-man team became commonly used.

As the rule stands now, a game may be run by one or more umpires. If there happens to be just one, he has complete jurisdiction over the game, and he may stand wherever he wishes to carry out his duties. [9.01] If there are two or more umpires, one is appointed umpire-in-chief (the plate umpire), and the others are called field umpires. [9.03] Umpires in each crew usually take turns at the helm.

The Hierarchy

What would any job be without an organization chart? Even the men in blue have them. The umpire-in-chief is the master of all he surveys.

He takes full charge of the game, and he's responsible for seeing that it's carried out properly. More specifically his duties [9.04a] are:

He calls and counts balls and strikes. Actually, he doesn't need to call them—he may signal them and save his voice. There was a time when he had to wear out his vocal chords, but according to baseball legend, that all changed in 1888. That was the year that a ballplayer named William Ellsworth Hoy, a deaf-mute insensitively nicknamed "Dummy," came to the big leagues. Because Hoy, a left-handed outfielder who started with the Washington Senators, could not hear the plate umpire's call, he persuaded the authorities to introduce hand signals instead— the right arm for a strike. The new system was not only easier on Hoy and the umpire; it made it easier for the fans to follow the action as well.

He calls and declares fair balls and fouls except those normally called by the field umpires.

He makes all decisions regarding the batter.

He makes all decisions except those traditionally made by the field umpires.

He makes all decisions about time, forfeits, and rain delays.

It's all in the wrist. "Bill McGowan's School for Umpires," from a 1949 postcard.

179

◯ He receives a batting lineup from the manager of each team and passes on the information to the official scorer. He also informs the scorer about subsequent changes in the lineup.

◯ He announces special ground rules.

Granted, the umpire-in-chief runs the show, but field umpires are by no means second-class citizens. They make all decisions on the bases except the ones reserved for the umpire-in-chief; they work with the umpire-in-chief in making decisions about time, balks, illegal pitches, and so forth; and they help the umpire-in-chief enforce the rules. [9.04b] A field umpire's call is just as good as that of the umpire-in-chief.

The chief umpire is charged with settling any disagreements between umpires regarding a call. If umpires disagree, the chief must call them together in a huddle (no managers or players allowed) to discuss the matter. After the meeting is over, the umpire-in-chief announces his decision. [9.04c]

Viewers of the 1986 American League playoffs were able to see the umpiring staff—especially plate umpire Terry Cooney and third-base ump Richie Garcia—in action during Game 3 between the Boston Red Sox and the California Angels in Anaheim.

The score was 1–0 Boston in the bottom of the fourth. Oil Can Boyd was doing the pitching honors for the Red Sox, and the Angels had two out and two men on: outfielder Brian Downing on first and first baseman Wally Joyner on second. Third baseman Doug DeCinces came to the plate and hit what Jim Palmer called a "pool cue shot"—the ball meandered down the first-base line and bounced off the bag into fair territory. By the time Red Sox first baseman Bill Buckner caught up with the bouncing ball, his play was at the plate, where Wally Joyner was preparing to score. Buckner fired the ball to catcher Rich Gedman. It was a close call, but plate umpire Terry Cooney made it: *safe.*

Red Sox manager John McNamara argued the call, and Oil Can was predictably perturbed, but it's unlikely that even they could have predicted what happened next: Terry Cooney had second thoughts, conferred with third-base ump Richie Garcia, and changed his call. Joyner was *out.*

This time Angels manager Gene Mauch argued the call and then some, but he didn't get a new call for his trouble. He got thrown out of the game. (However, he did get some satisfaction later, when the Angels won the game, 5–3.)

Interviewed after the eventful game, umpires Cooney and Garcia explained what happened. Cooney said that because he'd gone to cover the play at first, he was able to see that Gedman had the ball in time, but he wasn't sure Gedman had actually tagged Joyner. He called the runner safe. When McNamara and virtually the entire Red Sox bench came at him, Cooney decided to check with Garcia.

Garcia said that Cooney didn't ask him to make a call or to decide whether Joyner had beaten the tag; Cooney simply wanted to know whether or not there had *been* a tag. Garcia answered in no uncertain terms—there had definitely been a tag. The umpiring teamwork resulted in a reversed call.

If Garcia had not been asked for his opinion, he would have had to keep mum. According to The Book, an umpire may ask for help from another umpire in making a call, but no umpire may volunteer an opinion. [9.02c] There's one near-exception, and a common one at that: if the plate umpire calls a ball on a checked swing, a manager or catcher may ask the plate umpire to request confirmation from the base umpire. In that situation, whatever the base umpire says goes. There's no appeal if the plate umpire calls a strike. [9.04]

Positions

The rules dictate that the umpire-in-chief stands behind the catcher, but exactly *where* he decides to position himself is up to him. Each umpire has his own style. Some like to get in really close to the pitch—too close, according to a few catchers. Umpire Shag

Complaint Department

In his book *Three and Two!* umpire Tom Gorman allowed himself a moment or two of justifiable outrage. One of the things that got his dander up was the fact that on the historic day in 1956 when Don Larsen pitched that perfect World Series game, no one even said thank you to the ump. After all, said Gorman, there wouldn't have been twenty-seven outs without him! For the record, the man who did the honors behind the plate was Babe Pinelli, who labored twenty-two years in the National League. Pinelli retired two days later.

Crawford, among others, used to squat down and put his hand on the catcher's back to keep his balance.

Field umpires may stand wherever they like in order to be in the best position to see a play. [9.04b] Of course, since every play is different, an umpire can never be absolutely sure about where that is. The truth of this was never more obvious than in the call made by ump Don Denkinger in the sixth game of the 1985 World Series—the St. Louis Cardinals against the Kansas City Royals. In the bottom of the ninth inning field umpire Don Denkinger ruled outfielder Jorge Orta safe at first base, a decision that led to a rally, which in turn led to a Kansas City win (at least that's what the Cardinals say). Manager Whitey Herzog and relief pitcher Joaquin Andujar complained so much about the call that both were thrown out of the game.

The scene was this. Denkinger was standing somewhere between six and nine feet behind first base. The first baseman, Jack Clark, fielded the ball and tossed it to pitcher Todd Worrell, who ran over

Ever vigilant, ump Bill Valentine keeps his eye on the ball, but the rest of his body is up for grabs. The fielder made the tag. (AP/Wide World Photos)

to cover first. The problem was that Worrell is six-foot-five. When Worrell reached for the Jack Clark throw—it was high—Denkinger couldn't possibly see the ball and the runner's foot at the same time. He called Orta safe, but the replays told the real story. Orta was definitely out.

Later on Denkinger explained what happened: "There isn't any way I can watch the ball being caught and watch the foot. It's completely out of my peripheral vision. Without question, had I been fifteen feet back or twenty feet back, I could have seen them both . . . I did the only thing. I watched him catch the ball, I looked down at the foot. The foot was on the bag, and I called him safe. Obviously, from watching the replay, the ball got there before he did, by a split second. I only did what I could do with what I had to work with."

Appeals and Other Feedback

Rule 9.02 says that an umpire's judgment is final, and no one may argue about whether a pitch is a ball or strike, a ball is fair or foul, or a runner is safe or out. No manager or coach is allowed to argue balls and strikes. In 1974 a rule was passed that the ump will brook no disagreements about balks, either. Any manager leaving the dugout to argue these calls will be ejected from the game.

A manager may not take issue with judgment calls, but he may differ with the umpire when it comes to interpreting the rules. If a manager believes that an umpire has made a decision that conflicts with the rules, he may appeal the decision—but only to the umpire who made it. (There's no going over or under the umpire's head.) If he is dissatisfied with the results of his appeal, he may take his case to a higher court. That is, he may register an official protest (for more about appeals and protests see Chapter 4).

Players are suspended for bad behavior all the time, but the suspension of an umpire for an on-field dispute is practically unheard of. It did happen at least once, though. In July 1999 umpire Tom Hallion was suspended for three games without pay for his actions during an argument with Colorado catcher Jeff Reed and pitching coach Milt May. It started with a complaint about a checked-swing call. It ended when Hallion appeared to get physical with May and Reed. NL president Len Coleman's call? Hallion was *outta* there!

Umpires were made an official part of baseball in 1845, and it didn't take long for guys on the field to start disagreeing with them. The first recorded player-ump argument took place in 1846. Needless to say, the umpire won the argument. (Umpires always win arguments.) Despite the fact that the umpire has the last word (except in those exceedingly rare instances in which they're overruled by league officials), baseball men have always tried valiantly to get a word or two in edgewise. There are hundreds of stories about what happens when a manager meets an umpire. Here are a few:

Durocher. Leo Durocher liked to give everyone a hard time, but umpires were his favorite target. When he was in New York with the Dodgers and then the Giants, he was especially mischievous. One day in Brooklyn he had mouthed off so much to umpire George Magerkurth—Durocher was third-base coach, and Magerkurth was officiating behind the plate—that the umpire finally put his foot down. He explained in no uncertain terms that if he heard one more word out of The Lip, Durocher would find himself in street clothes.

In the very next inning Durocher's self-control was tested when there was a close play at the plate on outfielder Pete Reiser. Magerkurth called Reiser out. Durocher felt pretty strongly that Reiser had been safe, but he didn't dare say anything. He knew that if he made a peep, he'd be ejected.

Durocher chose another strategy. He fell to the ground in a dead faint. The fans laughed uproariously, but Magerkurth didn't crack a

Who's on First?

One day in the Polo Grounds, the Giants were taking a beating from plate umpire Ted McGrew. Several close calls in a row went against them, and the Giants were getting steamed. The loudest complaints came from Bill Terry, who was doing double duty as manager and first baseman that day.

In the seventh inning Terry blew his stack, kicking up dirt, hollering at McGrew, and generally creating a ruckus. Right fielder Mel Ott came running in to calm Terry down, but the damage had already been done. McGrew had given Terry the thumb.

"You can't put me out," complained Terry. "I don't have anyone else to play first base!"

The ump was nothing if not a reasonable man. He turned to Mel Ott and said, "Okay, you're out of the game!"

smile. He simply looked down at The Lip's limp body and said, "Dead or alive, Durocher, you're out, too."

Frisch. Once when Frank Frisch, then managing the St. Louis Cardinals, got thrown out of a game, at least he exited laughing. After what Frisch thought was a bad call, he ran over to the plate umpire and started sputtering. "*Why, you blubber-head . . .*" he began. The umpire, red in the face, bellowed back, menacingly: "What did you call me?" For Frisch it was in for a penny, in for a pound. His last words in the game were: "Oh, so you're not only blind! You're *deaf*, too!"

Stengel. Baiting umpires was Casey Stengel's favorite sport. Perhaps his most theatrical moment took place when he was manager of the Braves. He trapped a bird, a small sparrow, under his cap and bided his time. When there was a close play at the plate that went against the Braves, Stengel made his move. He tipped his cap to the ump and gave the umpire the bird.

Stengel Again. It's up to the umpire-in-chief to decide if and when to call a game on account of darkness or when to have the lights turned on, but that hasn't prevented some players and managers from dropping broad hints when they were winning a game. Casey Stengel used to light matches in the dugout.

Once he took his tactics a step further. His team was winning, but his pitcher was getting tired, and it was getting late. Casey stalled for a while, but still the umpire showed no sign of calling it a day. Casey gave it one more try: he called time and visited the mound, using a flashlight to guide his way. He got a few laughs from the fans, but he got more from the umpire: an ejection and a fifty dollar fine.

Klem. No discussion of umpires would be complete without a story about National League umpire Bill Klem, the "patron saint of umpires," the man who is credited with the tradition of drawing a line in the dirt with his foot and "daring" a manager or player to cross it. (He supposedly also invented the thumb-up-for-out, palms-down-for-safe motions.) He was known to run a tight ship, but he managed to have a sense of humor as well.

Over the thirty-six years he umpired in the game, Klem threw a lot of people out of a lot of games, but there was general surprise one day when he ejected Pie Traynor, the mild-mannered third baseman for the Pittsburgh Pirates. Mystified by the ejection, reporters asked Klem after the game why Traynor had left the game.

"He wasn't feeling well," was Klem's answer. When one of the reporters pointed out that Traynor had looked fine before and during the game, Klem elaborated: "Well, that's what he told me. He said he was sick and tired of my darned mistakes."

Hurst. It's unusual but not unheard of for an umpire to change his mind. National League umpire Tim Hurst did it, as third baseman (and later umpire) George Moriarty learned to his dismay one sunny day. When Hurst called a strike, to make the count 3–2, Moriarty turned to him in disgust and complained that it was no better than the previous pitch, which Hurst had called a ball. Hurst's response: "Okay, then we'll call them *both* strikes. You're out."

The Show Must Go On

According to Rule 9.02d, an umpire may not leave during a game unless he's injured or becomes ill. It's certainly unusual for umpires to take their leave in mid-game—most of them take a great deal of pride in working even under adverse conditions—but once in a while it happens. Umpire Paul Pryor was an example, perhaps an extreme one, of devotion above and beyond the call of duty.

On a day Pryor was assigned as umpire-in-chief for a Dodgers game he discovered that he had food poisoning. Undaunted, he insisted on taking his place behind the catcher, but in the seventh inning even his iron will and stoic determination couldn't fight nature. He hollered a warning to Dodgers catcher Johnny Roseboro, and seconds later he threw up on home plate, in front of fifty thousand people. Pryor took the rest of the day off.

An umpire has never actually died on duty in the majors, but it's happened twice in the minors. The first incident took place in 1899, when two professional clubs were playing in Alabama. Samuel White was officiating, and he was not having a good day. All through the game both teams complained steadily about White's calls, and in a late inning one of the players actually threatened him with violence. At the end of his rope, White knocked the player down, but that just made things worse. The ballplayer hit White in the head with a baseball bat and killed him. A few years later the same thing happened to umpire Ora Jennings in Indiana.

So much for the golden age of baseball.

Instant Replays

Replays may be fine and dandy for the NFL and the NHL but not for major league baseball. This was made crystal clear in May 1999 after veteran umpire Frank Pulli, who was officiating a game between the St. Louis Cardinals and the Florida Marlins, left the playing field and went into the dugout to watch television. Florida's Cliff Floyd had hit either an RBI double or a two-run homer—Pulli wasn't certain which it was—so the umpire watched an ESPN replay before making his call: a double.

There's nothing about replays in The Book, so the Marlins, who lost the game, 5–2, filed a protest. After due deliberation National League president Len Coleman gave the instant replay a big thumbs down. His conclusion: "Use of the video replay is not an acceptable practice . . . Traditionally, baseball has relied on the eyes of the umpires, as opposed to any artificial devices, for its judgments. I support this policy." So did AL president Gene Budig.

A Bad Call

Television's slow-mo and opinionated broadcasters have unquestionably made life rougher for today's umpires, but long before technology allowed for such second-guessing, one umpire's call was proved wrong beyond a shadow of a doubt.

The fateful day was May 25, 1946, and the game was between Jersey City and Newark. In the top of the sixth inning Jersey City's Buster Maynard hit a line drive off the left-field fence, and the umpire, Scotty Robb, called it a double.

Maynard's Jersey City teammates started squawking, insisting that the ball had gone over the fence and into the crowd, then bounced back into the park. The way they saw it, it was a home run. Scotty Robb listened for a while, and then he talked it over with his colleague, umpire Art Gore, but in the end he stuck with his original decision. Maynard stayed on second base.

What happened the next day has to be every umpire's nightmare. A Newark newspaper carried the following story: "Late yesterday the faces of umpires Scotty Robb and Art Gore were a deep crimson. They learned that the Maynard drive hit a youngster on the head before rebounding to the field. The unidentified kid was sent to the hospital for observation for a possible fracture . . ."

On September 27, 1996, Baltimore Orioles second baseman Roberto Alomar—who disagreed with a call and was ejected from the game—spat in the face of umpire John Hirschbeck and left the field. (Manager Davey Johnson put in his two cents as well.) We can only hope that Roberto wasn't chewing tobacco at the time. (AP/Wide World Photos)

A Good Call

On the other hand, the umpire who called what was perhaps the most disputed play in World Series history—the catch that Sam Rice did or did not make on October 10, 1925—was vindicated some fifty years later. Or maybe he was.

The Series was between the Washington Senators and the Pittsburgh Pirates, and the long drive was hit to deep right-center by catcher Earl Smith. The fleet-footed Rice ran after the ball, caught it, and went crashing over the three-foot fence into the seats. According to all reports, at least ten seconds passed before Rice showed himself. When he finally did so, he had the ball firmly in his glove. The umpire, Cy Rigleer, called it a fair catch.

The Pirates begged to differ. They maintained loud and long that the fans had helped Rice with his play. In fact, some Pittsburgh supporters in the stands were prepared to sign affidavits to the effect that Rice dropped the ball and the helpful fans restored it to his glove. But despite all protestations to the contrary, the umpire stuck to his guns. Earl Smith was out. (The Senators won the battle, 4–3, but lost the war—the Series—also 4–3.)

As you can imagine, throughout the rest of his career—indeed, throughout the rest of his life—Sam Rice was asked countless times what really happened that day, but all he'd ever say in response was, "The umpire called him out, didn't he?" Eventually, though, he said one more thing—that he would write the truth, the whole truth, and nothing but the truth in a letter to be opened after his death. Sam Rice died on October 13, 1974, and sure enough, he left a letter in which he revealed the "truth." Dated July 26, 1965, the letter gave a detailed description of the play, the long-awaited punch line of which was "At no time did I lose possession of the ball."

The Twelve Commandments

The Boy Scouts may have their motto, but major league umpires have their "general instructions"—rules that govern their behavior on the field during a game. What follows is the "short form"—the twelve commandments of umpiring, which are written in small print under Rule 9.05.

1. Don't Talk to the Coaches or Players When the Ball Is in Play. Like several other umpires, ump Tom Gorman wrote a book about his life on the field—it's called *Three and Two!*—and in it he has a fair amount to say about chitchat on the baseball field, particularly at the plate. In his years of umpiring he discovered that many players liked to shoot the breeze during a game, but one of the biggest offenders in Gorman's view was Yogi Berra, who had a tendency to treat a trip to the plate like a cocktail party.

According to Gorman, every time Yogi came to bat, it was, "Hello, Tom. How's the wife and family?" until Gorman had finally had

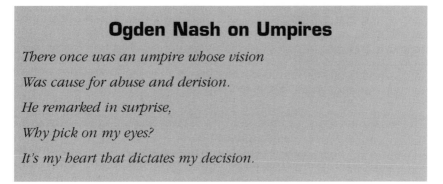

Ogden Nash on Umpires

There once was an umpire whose vision

Was cause for abuse and derision.

He remarked in surprise,

Why pick on my eyes?

It's my heart that dictates my decision.

enough. The next time Yogi inquired after his family, Gorman answered, "They died last night. Now get in there and hit."

On the other hand, sometimes it's the umpire who has loose lips—does the name Ron Luciano ring a bell? Most batters didn't mind his chattiness too much, but once in an important pennant race in 1974 it got to be too much for Carl Yastrzemski. When he stepped into the batter's box, he turned to Luciano and said testily: "I'm fine, my wife's fine, the kids are all fine. It's a nice day. Now let me hit in peace."

2. Be Polite to Club Officials, but Don't Fraternize with Them. After all, you never know when you're going to have to throw them out of the park or cause them to make good on fifty thousand rain checks.

3. Keep Your Uniform in Good Condition. Be Active and Alert on the Field. Most umpires wear specially made pants for working the plate—extra-wide so that they can squat down in comfort. When Harry Wendelstedt was a rookie umpire in the minors, he didn't know the drill, so he showed up on his first day of work wearing the uniform unaltered, just as the sporting goods catalog sent it. He took his place behind the plate in the Georgia-Florida League, hollered "*Play*," got into position for the first pitch, and

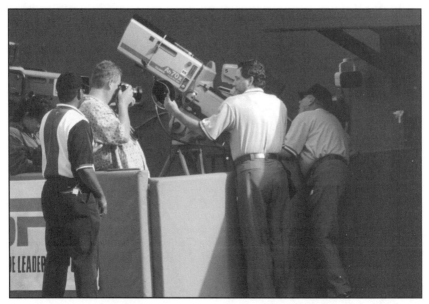

Was it or wasn't it? Evidently thinking he was refereeing an NFL game, umpire Frank Pulli resolved a disputed call by going to the videotape. (Tom DiPace)

Joe Garagiola was right: Baseball is a funny game. Pitcher Joe Engel, who played the game from 1912 to 1920, is a guest at a "Dinner for Umpires."

he—and everyone else around him—heard a loud rip. His uniform was *not* in good condition.

4. Take Your Time. Don't rush into any decisions; take as much time as you need. Carry a copy of The Book and don't be ashamed to refer to it when you have to.

5. Keep the Game Moving. After all, you're not being paid by the hour.

6. Don't Lose Your Temper. Most umps do pretty well at this one, all things considered, but veteran Tim Hurst, considered by many to be the toughest umpire of all time, was not a role model for his peers. He once told Eddie Collins, the Hall of Fame second baseman, that if he didn't get away from him he would spit in his eye. Collins didn't, so Hurst did—spit in Collins's eye, that is. (Hurst's temper proved to be his downfall. Ban Johnson, the American League president, eventually fired him for his excessive behavior.)

7. Two Wrongs Don't Make a Right. If you made a bad decision, don't try to "even things out" with the opposition. Each call must stand alone, on its own merits.

8. If You Have to Pick One, Keep Your Eye on the Ball, Not the Player. It's more important to know where the ball is than it is to know whether a runner missed a base. Of course, it's best to know *both.*

9. Remember That It Ain't Over 'til It's Over. Wait until a play has been completed before you make a "safe" or "out" motion. Even Golden Gloves sometimes have butterfingers.

10. When in Doubt, Check It Out. An umpire should call his own plays, but there's no disgrace in asking for a second opinion.

11. Be Where You're Supposed to Be. And that, of course, is the best position from which to see the play.

12. Be Courteous, Impartial, and Firm. Not necessarily in that order.

Umpiring Rule Changes: The Highlights

1845 The rules of baseball are written down for the first time, and the authors have the good sense to make provisions for an umpire. To wit: "When assembled for exercise, the President, or in his absence, the Vice President, shall appoint an Umpire, who shall keep the game in a book provided for that purpose, and note all violations of the By-Laws and Rules during the time of exercise." Their grammar wasn't great, but their hearts were in the right place.

1846 The first recorded argument between a player and an umpire, during a game between the Knickerbockers and the New York Club at Elysian Fields in Hoboken, New Jersey. The umpire wins. The player is fined six cents for swearing.

1858 The umpire may call strikes if the batter refuses to swing at good pitches. At a convention in March it is decided that one umpire, chosen by the home team, will be in charge of a game. (Before that each game had been run by two umpires and a referee.)

1860 The umpire of each game is selected by the captain of each team. The umpire is given the authority to suspend play, and he must make a call when a ball is foul.

1861 The umpire gets some paperwork to do. At the end of a game he must declare the winning club and record his decision in the scorebook of each team before he leaves the field.

1865 The umpire must record the score in the scorer's book before he leaves.

1876 To select an umpire the visiting team submits five names, and the home team is allowed to choose two names from among them. The umpire officially says, "*Play!*" for the first time. If either team fails to begin the game within five minutes of the umpire's call, the umpire may declare a forfeit. If an umpire is unable to see whether a catch has been fairly made, he may ask the spectators and players about it and then make his decision. (Believe it or not.)

1877 More changes in how an umpire is selected. Now the league "shall select three gentlemen of repute" in each city where there is a team. At least three hours before a game the visiting team chooses the umpire from among them.

1878 Umpires get paid, five dollars a game. The payroll is the home team's responsibility.

1879 Umpiring becomes bigger business. The National League (the only one at the time, remember) names twenty men living in or near cities where the league has teams as "fit" to be umpires, and each game is run by someone from the list. (This rule remained in force until 1883.) An umpire's fees and expenses are now paid by the visiting club. An umpire is given the power to impose fines—of not less than ten dollars and not more than twenty dollars—when he thinks it's necessary, and he may terminate a game after a rain delay of thirty minutes.

1880 The limits of the fines an umpire may impose change. Now it's not less than five dollars and not more than fifty dollars.

1881 A spectator who "hisses or hoots" at or insults the umpire may be ejected from the grounds.

1882 The umpire must make his own calls; he may not talk to spectators or players about a play. In fact, only the team captain may speak directly to the umpire. If an umpire imposes a fine or declares a game forfeited, he must write to the league secretary and tell him so within twenty-four hours. (If he doesn't do so, he may lose his job.) Corruption rears its ugly head for the first and only time in the world of umpires: a National League umpire, Richard Higham, is expelled from the league for collusion with gamblers.

1883 The league hires its first staff of salaried umpires, under the same system that is in use today. Officially, they report to the league secretary, and they earn one thousand dollars for the season. The four men hired came from cities not represented in the league: W. E. Furlong from Kansas City, Missouri; S. M. Decker from Bradford, Pennsylvania; Frank Law from Norwalk, Ohio; and A. F. Odlin from Lancaster, New Hampshire. It was decided that applications would be accepted each year until March 1, and that the umpires would be selected by the first of May.

1886 An umpire may introduce a new ball at any time. Before this year, when a ball was lost, the umpire gave the team five minutes to find it before he threw in a new one.

1887 The umpire has the authority to call a game if the spectators are disorderly. The league gets tougher about paperwork: if an umpire doesn't notify the league about fines within twenty-four hours, he himself is fined. The maximum fine for arguing with an ump or protesting a call is ten dollars.

1888 The mandatory fine for a coach who leaves the coach's box to protest a call is five dollars.

1889 A second offense results in a second fine or removal from the field.

1890 The umpire gets some respect; he's called "Mr. Umpire" for the first time.

1895 The limits on fines changes again—to not less than twenty-five dollars and not more than one hundred dollars. If the crowd becomes so rowdy that the game is stopped for more than fifteen minutes, the umpire may declare the visitors the winner. The score: 9–0.

1896 A twenty-five dollar fine is imposed on a coach or a player who uses vulgar language. It costs players five dollars to ten dollars for any other first offense, twenty-five dollars and possibly ejection for a second offense, and mandatory ejection for a third offense.

1897 The umpire has twelve hours to report a fine or an ejection to the league president, four hours for what he considers a "flagrant offense."

1901 The league president may add insult to injury; if the offense is "flagrant" enough, he may suspend a player or coach who has been fined and/or ejected by an umpire.

1903 If there is only one umpire in a game, he may stand anywhere on the field he likes.

1906 The umpire assumes authority over the groundskeeper; he may give him orders that have to do with getting the field ready for play.

1908 Four umpires are assigned to the World Series for the first time. Only two work in a game at a given time.

1909 Four umpires are assigned to the World Series. All four work in each game.

1910 The umpire organization chart is established. The plate umpire—the one who judges balls and strikes—is appointed the umpire-in-chief, and the others are field umpires. An umpire may not interfere with or criticize his colleagues' decisions; in fact, only if he is asked for his opinion may he give it. Only the umpire-in-chief may declare the game a forfeit. The captain of a team must notify the umpire-in-chief of any substitution, and the ump in turn informs the spectators. An umpire must warn players on the bench for excessive yelling before he can fine or otherwise punish them for it. Before a game begins, the umpire must announce any special ground rules.

1914 In the case of fire, panic, or storm, the umpire does not have to wait until the pitcher has the ball on the mound to call a time-out.

1920 A ball that hits the umpire is in play. The umpire may suspend play at any time for an accident involving a player or an umpire. After a thirty-minute rain delay an umpire may terminate a game—but only if he wants to.

1933 Three umpires to a daily game come into regular use.

1935 The first umpire school opens, and aspiring umps flock to Hot Springs, Arkansas.

1939 Six umpires are appointed to the World Series, two as alternates.

1940 The umpire gets still more power. As of this year, trainers fall under his jurisdiction.

1947 Six umpires are hired to work in the World Series, all of them on the field. The two who had been alternates are now posted in the outfield, on the left- and right-field foul lines.

1950 An umpire may no longer levy fines. That enviable job is reserved for the league president, who determines fines after receiving a postgame report from the umpire.

1952 Four umpires to a regular game becomes standard practice.

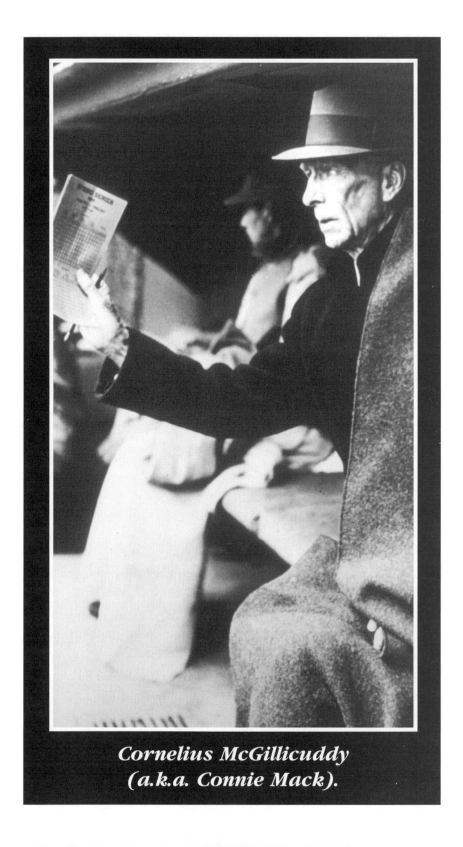

Cornelius McGillicuddy
(a.k.a. Connie Mack).

"Baseball fans love numbers. They love to swirl them around their mouths like Bordeaux wine."

—Pat Conroy

Chapter 10
The Official Scorer

Baseball wins its converts early and keeps them late. Few people of any age cannot lay claim to vivid recollections of their exploits on a baseball field: the game-saving catch, the ball hit over the center fielder's head with two men on in the last of the ninth . . . you know the stories we mean.

Yet one of the great appeals of the game has virtually nothing to do with the physical acts of pitching, hitting, or fielding a baseball. Baseball is not only a game of athletic accomplishment—it is also a matter of paperwork.

Lawyers talk about creating a "paper trail": if you need to demonstrate in a court of law that events unfolded as you claim, there is no better way to do it than with a series of documents that prove your story true. The game of baseball has its own unique paper trail, beginning with the lineup cards the managers present at home plate before the game, continuing during the game with the official scorecard maintained by the official scorer (and unofficially by innumerable fans in the stands), and ending with the box score in the newspaper the morning after. The cumulative information drawn from box scores, in turn, produces record books, encyclopedias, and other statistical summaries.

The box scores and the rest are more than formal records suitable for interment in dusty archives. They mean something to the millions of fans who refer to them. The very foundation of baseball's unique and satisfying paper trail is to be found in Chapter 10 of The Book. At the close of this chapter, we'll explain how to keep a scorecard and read a box score. But before we do, The

Book has much to tell about the elements of which both are assembled—and by whom.

The Official Scorer

At the ballpark, there is one person designated to be the "official scorer." Usually the role of scorer is rotated among members of the press corps. Though occasionally talk is heard about making the official scorer a full-time employee, it seems unlikely to happen, at least for now.

The official scorer is charged with making scoring judgments. The most common instances in which judgments are called for are in assigning errors, and the scorer is responsible for designating a particular play an error or a hit, and to pass the word on to the press box and public address announcer. The scorer must not interfere with any umpire's decisions, nor is he permitted to point out when a hitter is batting out of turn. [10.01]

The scorer is charged with recording a wide variety of events and actions, including the following:

⚾ For each batter-runner, records must be kept of runs, hits, runs batted in, doubles, triples, home runs, grand slams, total bases, double and triple plays, stolen bases, times caught stealing, sacrifice bunts, sacrifice flies, bases on balls, intentional walks, times hit by a pitched ball, bases awarded for interference or obstruction calls, and strikeouts. [10.02a]

⚾ For each fielder, putouts, assists, errors, double plays, and triple plays are to be recorded. [10.02b]

⚾ For a pitcher, the record must show innings pitched, batters faced, batters hit by pitched balls, strikeouts, wild pitches, balks, and the number of runs, earned runs, home runs, sacrifice hits and flies, walks, and intentional bases on balls allowed. In addition, the winning and losing pitchers, the starting and finishing pitchers, and any saves are to be recorded. [10.02c]

⚾ Other miscellaneous data required are passed balls, runners left on base, the number of outs when the winning run is scored if the game is won in the last half-inning, the inning-by-inning score, the umpires' names, and the length of the game. [10.02d through 10.02n]

Thanks a Lot, Dick

In a 1975 game at Candlestick Park in San Francisco, Giants pitcher Ed Halicki pitched a no-hitter. At least if you read the official box score, you'd think he did. However, if you were to take sportswriter Dick Young's word for it, you would think it was a one-hitter.

The key play was a grounder hit by New York Met Rusty Staub. The batted ball deflected off Halicki's leg and rolled toward Giants second baseman Derrel Thomas. He fielded it, dropped it, picked it up, dropped it, grabbed the ball once again, and threw to first—but not in time. Joe Sargis of the San Francisco office of United Press International, the official scorer, ruled the play "E-4." Halicki went on to complete his no-hitter.

Reportedly no one in the press box, including several New York writers, objected to Sargis's terming the play an error. However, Dick Young, three thousand miles away and watching the game on TV, certainly did. He went to his typewriter and accused Sargis of subscribing to the theory that, "the first hit off any starting pitcher should be 'a good one.'"

The upshot, of course, wasn't a change in the ruling—Halicki's name remains among the ranks of those who have officially pitched no-hit ballgames. But Sargis lost his job as occasional official scorer at Candlestick (and the fee of forty-five dollars the major leagues were then paying for the chore). UPI made him stop scoring, explained Sargis, ". . . not because the decision was wrong, but because UPI people are supposed to cover the news, not make it. As soon as I became controversial, because of the Young column, they decided I had become a newsmaker."

The official score is submitted to the league office within thirty-six hours of the end of a game. All of the data from all league games are collected and collated and assembled as part of baseball's permanent record. They are kept by the official statistician, who is appointed by the league president. [10.21]

Hitting Statistics

The Book gets pretty technical in defining what is or is not an RBI, base hit, stolen base, sacrifice, putout, assist, double or triple play, error, wild pitch or passed ball, walk, strikeout, and earned run.

These definitions provide the exactitude that makes scoring complex and challenging. Let's take each definition, one at a time.

Run Batted In. "RBI" may be the first acronym most of us learned in life—long before we came across the word "acronym"—so it's probably a safe bet you know not only what it means but that it's acceptable to pronounce it either "Are-bee-eye" or "Ribbee."

An RBI is the credit a batter gets when a run scores as a result of his hit, sacrifice, infield out, or the force produced by his being issued a bases-loaded walk, by his being hit by a pitch, or by a defensive player's interfering or obstructing his progress. No RBI is credited when a run scores on a ground-ball double play or what would have been one if an error hadn't been committed. (A historical note: For years, a stat called "game-winning RBI" was credited each time a batter gave his club "the lead it never relinquished." However, in 1989 the game-winning RBI was eliminated as an official statistic.)

Base Hits. Once again, we have an elementary concept: it is a hit when a runner reaches base on a batted ball that strikes the ground before being caught and when the batter reaches first base before the ball does. Seems simple enough, right?

This unofficial line score allowed Pirates fans to keep track of the 1960 World Series from the sidewalks of Pittsburgh. The Bucs beat the Yanks in this one, 6–4.

Needless to say, it's more complicated that that. One wrinkle is what the ever-watchful sportswriter Dick Young termed "the dumbest rule in baseball." Despite his feelings (and we're inclined to agree with him, by the way), The Book continues to credit a batter with a hit when a fair ball hits a runner or umpire (except in cases in which the infield fly rule has been called). [10.05]

Defining what isn't a hit is even more complicated. Here are some of the nonhits described in Rule 10.06:

⚾ It's not a hit when a preceding runner is out on the play (either by force-out or when he is simply attempting to advance).

⚾ It's not a hit when a fielder makes an error that, in the judgment of the official scorer, would have been an out if the ball could have been handled "with ordinary effort."

⚾ It's not a hit when a runner already on base is called out on appeal for failing to touch a base he should have reached in the course of his advance.

⚾ It's not a hit when the defensive team tries and fails to get a preceding runner but could have, in the judgment of the official scorer, gotten the batter.

⚾ And it is not a hit when another runner is out for interference with a batted ball unless, in the official scorer's judgment, the batter-runner would have been safe in any case. [10.06]

A single, a double, a triple, and a home run are one-, two-, three-, and four-base hits when the batter reaches those respective bases. Except, that is, for the following instances, as described in Rule 10.07:

⚾ When the batter-runner advances on an attempt by the defensive team to put out a preceding runner and, in the judgment of the official scorer, the extra base(s) gained by the batter-runner would not otherwise have been gained. The classic example of this is the batter who singles with a man on second and, when the defense throws to the plate in an attempt to prevent the runner from scoring, the batter takes second on the throw. The batter gets a credit for a single but not a double.

◇ A hit is not what it appears to be when the runner is called out on appeal for not touching a base. When a happy hitter misses a bag on his home-run trot and the defensive team appeals, the hitter is credited with the last base he reached safely; a successful appeal at second, therefore, reduces a homer to a single. In the same way, a runner who overslides second trying to stretch a single into a double and is tagged out is credited with a single: he is to be "credited with only as many bases as he attained safely."

◇ When a batter ends a game with a game-winning hit, he gets credit only for as many bases as the runner scoring the winning run advances on the play. A deep drive to the deepest part of the park that otherwise would have been a sure triple becomes a single in the event the winning run scores from third on the play; on the same play, the batter would be credited with a double if the winning run scored from second. The exception, of course, is the home run. The home-run hitter gets credit for all RBIs scored on his home run, no matter how few are needed to win the game. [10.07]

Batting Championships and Cumulative Performance Records

The Book establishes clear guidelines for winning championships and setting records. For batters, they are as follows:

Batting Championships. Each player's batting average is computed by dividing the total safe hits by total at-bats. [10.22b] The batting championship is won by the player with the highest average.

However, in order to qualify, the number of times a player must have appeared at the plate must be at least 3.1 times the number of games his team scheduled—that is, 502 in the case of a 162-game schedule. If a batter falls short of the required appearances, his batting average must be computed using the minimum number of plate appearances, even if he did not accumulate that many. (Plate appearances include at-bats, times hit by a pitch, sacrifices, walks, and awards of first due to obstruction or interference.) [10.23a]

Although this ruling has never been invoked in the major leagues, there was much discussion of it in 1980 when George Brett's batting average approached .400 near season's end. Because of an injury,

Brett had missed numerous weeks of the season, so as the season drew to a close, comments were heard from several quarters about the rule, most of them objecting to the "phantom" at-bats that would have to be added if Brett's total plate appearances fell short of the requisite number.

What would have been done, according to a clarifying statement from commissioner Bowie Kuhn, speaking on behalf of the Official Baseball Records Committee, would be that Brett's "real" average would appear in the records, but that if he failed to reach the necessary number of appearances, his average would also be recomputed by adding "phantom" at-bats to bring him to the required number. Fortunately, the case was moot, as Brett remained healthy and accumulated enough plate appearances (but fell short of his .400 goal, batting .390).

Slugging Championships. Slugging percentage is determined by dividing the total bases gained by all safe hits by the total times at bat. [10.22c]

On-Base Percentage. This statistic is determined by dividing the total of hits, walks, and times hit by a pitch by the total number of at-bats, walks, times hit by a pitch, and sacrifice flies. [10.22f]

Hitting Streaks. A batting streak in consecutive at-bats shall not be broken by a walk, being hit by a pitch, defensive interference, or a sacrifice bunt. However, a sacrifice fly does terminate a hitting streak. [10.24a]

In the same way, a consecutive-game hitting streak will not be terminated if in all of the player's plate appearances he walks, is hit by a pitch, is interfered with by a fielder, or sacrifice bunts. Further, consecutive-game hitting streaks are determined not by the games a team plays but the games in which the player takes part. [10.24b]

Consecutive-Game Playing Streaks. A streak shall be deemed extended if a player plays one-half of an inning on defense or completes a time at bat by reaching base or being put out. A pinch-hitting appearance alone is not sufficient to extend a consecutive-game playing streak, but being ejected by an umpire before meeting the above requirements will not terminate a streak. [10.24c]

Stolen Bases

The term "stolen base" wasn't even coined until 1871, and stolen bases didn't appear in the box scores or the official records until

1886. Even then they were so broadly defined that a stolen base was credited to a runner who, by his own volition, went from first to third on a single. (In large part this explains such performances as Harry Stovey's 1888 record of 156 stolen bases.)

The rules in The Book regarding stolen bases were changed slightly in 1888, but it was in 1898 that what we now know as a stolen base became recognizable: in essence, a stolen base was to be credited to the base runner whenever he reached a base he attempted to steal without the aid of battery errors, fielding errors, or a hit by the batter. This change was so sweeping that all career and single-season marks established under the earlier rule are no longer recognized in all-time records.

Further changes were made in 1909 and 1920: if either runner was thrown out on an attempted double steal, no runner was to be credited with a steal (1909); and no stolen base was awarded a runner if there was no attempt to get him out (1920).

The Book today instructs that a base runner is to be credited with a steal when he advances to the next base without the aid of a hit, out, error, passed ball, wild pitch, or balk. However, there are some other limitations in special circumstances.

A stolen base is credited when a base runner breaks for the next base before the pitcher throws to the plate and the pitch is a wild pitch or passed ball. If the runner is able to advance two bases on the play, both a stolen base and a wild pitch or passed ball are credited.

This situation came up in a game in Houston in 1971. The Astros were playing the Giants at home, and their catcher, John Edwards, was on third in a tight game. A suicide squeeze was called, and Edwards took off from third before the pitch.

The batter, Houston pitcher Don Wilson, missed the bunt, but the catcher also missed the ball. Edwards scored easily, and official scorer John Wilson alertly—and correctly—termed it a stolen base. A discussion ensued, however, because National League president Chub Feeney was in attendance, and he disagreed with the call: he thought the catcher had been guilty of a passed ball. Wilson pointed out rule 10.08a to Feeney, but that didn't satisfy him. Feeney asked Wilson to write him a letter describing the play, saying that he planned to take the matter up with the rules committee during the off-season. Either he thought better of it or the rules committee wasn't persuaded to change the rule. It remains the same today.

The fleet Jackie Robinson steals home in the first game of the 1955 World Series. (AP/Wide World Photos)

A stolen base is credited when, in the course of an attempted steal, the catcher unleashes a wild throw. The catcher gets no error on the play unless the runner gains two bases or a second runner also advances.

A stolen base is duly awarded to a runner who, on an attempted steal or a pickoff play, successfully avoids being put out in a rundown and no error is committed. If two runners advance on the play, two stolen bases are credited; if the runner in the rundown manages to return to his original base while another runner advances, the runner who gains a base is credited with a steal.

An instance of this occurred in a 1985 Yankees-Oakland game. Yankees outfielder Dave Winfield was on third, and he broke for the plate on a suicide-squeeze attempt. However, the batter missed the bunt, and Winfield found himself in no-man's-land, caught in a rundown between the plate and third. Winfield managed to evade the tag of A's pitcher Tommy John, and he slid home safely. He was credited with a steal on the play.

No stolen base is credited when on a multiple steal any runner is out; when a runner is tagged out after oversliding the base he is trying to steal; when a runner would have been out if the fielder catching the throw hadn't muffed it; or when a runner steals a base "solely because of the defensive team's indifference to his advance."

◇ "Caught stealing" is the official scoring entry for a runner who tries and fails to steal a base; who is picked off; or who overslides while stealing. [10.08]

Perhaps the most famous caught stealing of all was John Anderson's "steal" of second base. A well-liked player for the Washington Senators, Anderson found his reputation transformed overnight: for decades after, a stupid play was described as "a John Anderson."

Let Them Have Asterisks

When Roger Maris approached Babe Ruth's record for most home runs in a season in 1961, Commissioner Ford Frick was reported to make his familiar asterisk ruling: if Maris broke the record, it would not be recognized unless he did so within 154 games, the seasonal schedule in which Ruth had set his sixty-home-run mark. If Maris hit more homers in more games, said Frick, the line in the record book would have an asterisk.

Using the the same logic, in 1962 Frick ruled that Maury Wills's stolen-base record would also have to feature an asterisk if more than 154 games were required to break the old mark. But students of the game quickly pointed out to Frick one small inconsistency: Ty Cobb's record had been set in 156 games. So when Wills stole one more than Cobb, 97, in his 156th game, Frick had no choice but to erase Cobb from that particular line in the record book. (Wills went on to steal 104 for the full season.)

Yet this foolishness about asterisks just won't go away. In 1991 the commissioner's office determined that Roger Maris's single-season home-run record would no longer have an asterisk associated with it. That ruling seemed more than a little strange, given that a special records committee (which included a representative from the commissioner's office) had determined back in 1968 (!) that no asterisks should ever be placed next to any single-season record. Thanks to Mark McGwire, the issue regarding the home run record would seem to be moot . . . but don't be surprised if, one of these days, somebody brings it up again.

"Honest John" was on first in an important game. The Senators were down a run in the top of the ninth. Anderson wanted more than anything to help his team, but somehow he forgot one crucial fact: the bases were loaded. He broke for second and was promptly tagged out for the final out of the inning and the game.

Sacrifices

The sacrifice wasn't recognized in the statistics of the game until 1889. Even then, the batter was still charged with an at-bat. In 1893 a batter credited with a sacrifice was no longer given a time at bat for his selfless act.

There are two kinds of sacrifices: bunts and flies. Today neither kind of sacrifice counts as an at-bat, an important factor when it comes to figuring batting averages: he who advances or scores a runner on a bunt or fly is not penalized by being awarded a nonproductive at-bat. There are a number of variations on the theme of sacrifice bunts, so let's look at those first.

When, with less than two outs, the following situations occur, you should identify them on your scorecard as *sacrifices*:

The batter advances the runner(s) on base with a bunt even though he is put out in the process—or would have been, in the official scorer's judgment, except for an error. [10.09a]

The runner(s) is advanced on a bunt despite an errorless attempt by the defense to put out the advancing base runner. If the official scorer judges that the batter would have have been safe in any case, the batter is credited not with a sacrifice but with a hit. [10.09b]

It is *not* a sacrifice bunt under the following circumstances:

When any advancing base runner is put out trying to advance one base. [10.09c]

When the batter is, in the judgment of the official scorer, bunting for a hit, not just to advance the runners. [10.09d]

The concept of the sacrifice fly as we know it today didn't exist until after the turn of the century; it wasn't until 1908 that the batter was no longer charged with an at-bat for hitting a fly that scored a run. And the rule has gone through several changes since then. The sacrifice fly rule was removed entirely from the game from 1931 until 1953 except for one year, 1939, when it was reinstated. But since 1954, the rule has been as it is today.

Compared to the sacrifice bunt, the requirements for a sacrifice fly are simple: when a runner scores after having tagged up on a line drive or fly ball that is caught in the outfield, a sacrifice is credited to the batter. The only wrinkle is in cases in which a runner scores after a catch is muffed and, in the official scorer's judgment, the runner could have scored even if the ball had been fielded cleanly. [10.09e]

Defensive Statistics

There is little glory to be found in playing everyday defense. Great catches or throws make great replays on television, but a good defense is not measured by the number of exciting moves made by its fielders. It's the day-in, day-out methodical making of the routine

One record that requires no asterisk is the one for consecutive games. Cal Ripken Jr. broke Lou Gehrig's record—all he had to do was play in 2,131 games in a row. (AP Photo/John Dunn)

Assist, putout, or error? Wally Moon and Duke Snider of the Dodgers collide in pursuit of a fly ball. The ball popped out of Snider's glove, and he was charged with a two-base error. (AP/Wide World Photos)

plays and the accumulation of errorless putouts and assists—together with the odd spectacular play, of course—that distinguishes quality defense. So here's the nitty-gritty of the defense: the putouts, assists, and errors.

Putouts. Fielders are credited with putouts when they catch a batted ball in the air, whether it's fair or foul. Putouts also are earned by fielders who catch thrown balls and then tag or force out runners or batters, and when a fielder tags a base runner off his base. [10.10]

Catchers get special advantages in the putout category. They are credited with putouts on illegally batted balls, foul bunts on third strikes, and batters hit by their own batted balls. They also get putouts on calls of batter interference with the catcher and for outs called as a result of batting out of order. [10.10a]

When we come to leftover miscellaneous plays, there is a certain logic to the way putouts are assigned. For example, in rarely traveled, arcane areas of the game—such as when an infield fly is not caught—the putout is credited to the nearest fielder. The nearest fielder also gets the putout when a runner is hit by a batted ball. By the same rules of common sense, the fielder who gets the putout is [10.10b]:

The fielder the base runner avoids when the runner is called out for leaving the base line;

The fielder who is nearest the "point of passing" when a runner is called out for passing another base runner;

The fielder who covers the base abandoned by a base runner running the bases in reverse order;

The fielder who is interfered with on an interference call, except when it is on a throw, in which case the fielder who was to receive the throw is credited with the putout and the thrower gets an assist;

The first baseman gets the putout when the batter-runner is called out because of a previous base runner's interference.

Assists. Most often, fielders are credited with assists when their throws result in a putout. But it's not quite that simple.

Other situations in which fielders are given assists are as follows:

When a fielder deflects a batted or thrown ball so that a putout results or would have resulted if no subsequent error had been made. The classic example of this is a play in which the pitcher deflects a ball hit back to the box, and a fielder subsequently fields it and throws out the runner. The pitcher is credited with an assist. In the event a fielder deflects a ball in flight and it is caught by another fielder for an out, an assist is, again, credited to the deflector;

When a throw or deflection is involved in a play in which a runner is called out for interference or leaving the base line. [10.11a]

No assists are given to:

Pitchers on strikeouts unless the third strike is dropped and the pitcher makes the throw to first for the out. [10.11b]

⚾ Pitchers when, following a legal pitch, the catcher picks off a base runner or tags a runner trying to score. [10.11c]

⚾ A fielder who throws wildly, allowing the base runner to advance, even if the runner is subsequently put out on the same play. [10.11d]

Double Plays and Triple Plays. Players involved in a play in which two or three outs are made are credited with assists or putouts unless an error or misplay occurs between the beginning of the play (defined as the pitch) and its end (when the ball is declared dead or it returns to the pitcher as he assumes the position). [10.12]

Double plays are commonplace, often occurring several times in a game. But triple plays are much rarer—the 1990s have seen an average of about *five* per season while the double plays number more like *five thousand* in any given year. Most often a hard line drive caught by an infielder enables the defense to catch the runners off base, but triple plays can take all manner of forms. All that is required are two men on base and nobody out.

An unusual triple play took place in Philadelphia some fifty years ago. Eddie Waitkus was batting for the Cardinals, with Granny Hamner and Richie Ashburn on first and second, respectively. After missing two bunt attempts, Waitkus took a called strike three (out number one). Ashburn had been moving on the pitch, so catcher Joe Garagiola (today better remembered as a television commentator than a player), fired to the third baseman, who flipped to the shortstop, who tagged Ashburn (that's number two). Meanwhile Mamner was in no-man's-land between first and second and looking confused. A hard peg to first was grabbed by Stan Musial, who put the tag on Hamner (triple play!). The remarkable thing about this play was *no one hit the ball*. Yet in a matter of seconds, three men were out.

Errors. A misplay is defined as a "fumble, muff, or wild throw." An error is, in turn, defined as a misplay that prolongs a batter's time at the plate or a runner's presence on the bases or permits the runner to advance.

Errors are the area in which the official scorer's judgment comes most prominently into play. A call in the 1986 World Series makes the point clearly. Bill Buckner was playing first for the Red Sox, and Mets catcher Gary Carter hit a pop-up behind first base.

The ball rolls free, and only base runner Lee Walls of the Dodgers seems to know where it is. Walls scored, and catcher Chuck Hiller was charged with an error. (AP/Wide World Photos)

Buckner, hobbled for most of his career with leg and ankle troubles and reduced in the Series to wearing high-top baseball shoes, turned and "ran" back to get under the pop. Misjudging the ball, he overran it, and when he tried to come back for it, he slipped and fell. The ball landed foul.

Buckner should have caught it (a muffed catch), and his failure prolonged Carter's at-bat. Therefore, it's a error, right?

The official scorer at Fenway Park thought not. No error was charged, and few people who watched Buckner's pained moves would complain.

An error is (ordinarily) charged in the following situations:

🟢 A muffed fly ball. [10.13a]

🟢 A failure by a fielder to touch the bag or runner after catching a thrown or ground ball in time to put out the batter-runner or another runner on a force play. [10.13b and 10.13c]

🟢 A wild throw that allows a runner to reach a base safely or to advance a base when a good throw would have caused the runner to be out. Only one error is charged, regardless of how many bases are advanced. [10.13d]

🟢 A muffed catch of a throw that allows a runner to advance. [10.13e]

◌ The awarding of one or more bases due to defensive interference or obstruction. [10.13f]

No error is charged in the following situations:

◌ When the catcher makes a wild throw in an attempt to catch a base runner trying to steal, unless the base runner (or another base runner) advances an extra base. [10.14a]

◌ When on a wild throw the official scorer judges that even a good throw would not have put out the runner, unless the runner advances an extra base. [10.14b]

◌ When in attempting to complete a double or triple play a fielder makes a wild throw (unless, once again, a runner advances an extra base on the play). [10.14c]

◌ When a fielder who drops a ball, whether on the fly or on the ground, recovers in time to force out any runner at any base. [10.14d]

◌ When a fielder fails to catch a fly ball with a runner on third before two are out, because, in the official scorer's judgment, he was preventing the runner on third from scoring on the catch. [10.14e]

◌ The pitcher is not charged with an error when a batter reaches first on a walk, wild pitch, or passed ball, or when he's hit by a pitch. A strikeout is credited to the pitcher on a third strike that gets away from the catcher, along with a wild pitch or a passed ball, depending upon the official scorer's judgment. In the same way, no error is charged when runners advance on a wild pitch or passed ball. [10.14f]

Fielding Championships

The sum total of errors, putouts, and assists are factored into one average that distinguishes a player's defensive prowess. The fielding average is computed by dividing the sum of the putouts and assists made by the player by the number of putouts, assists, and errors committed. [10.22d]

The highest average wins the fielding championship, but in order to qualify, a catcher must have played in at least half his team's games, an infielder or outfielder must have played in two-thirds,

Team Error

Lots of people have suggested over the last twenty years that baseball's statistics include "team error." One of the most persistent proponents was long-time *New York Daily News* sportswriter Dick Young, a past member of the Scoring Rules Committee.

As the name suggests, the "team error" would be assigned to a team rather than an individual player. It would be used in situations in which an error must be charged (out of fairness to the pitcher and his ERA) but in which there is no individual culprit on whom to lay the blame.

One situation in which "team error" would be applicable is the case in which two defensive players collide on a fly ball and, as a result, the ball drops. Another is the case in which the paths of an accurately thrown ball from the outfield and a base runner intersect—and the ball bounces away and the base runners advance a base.

A third application is a play in which a fielder attempting to catch a bad throw interferes with a base runner. Today, the official scorer is obliged to charge the fielder trying to catch the ball with an error because of the interference call, although the fault is not truly his. The team error call would relieve that player's fielding percentage of the burden of carrying that error.

Although the idea has been much discussed for the last twenty years, it has not yet been adopted.

and a pitcher is required to have pitched as many innings as his team has scheduled games. The lone exception is that pitcher who, though having pitched a lesser number of innings, has handled more total fielding chances with a higher fielding average than the other pitchers with the requisite number of innings. [10.23c]

Pitching Statistics

As with the batter, the actions of the pitcher are measured by a wide variety of statistical categories, all calculated to compute his effectiveness (or lack thereof). Probably the most crucial statistic is the won-lost record.

Winning and Losing Pitcher. In order to be credited with a victory, a starting pitcher must pitch at least five complete innings, his team must be in the lead when he departs, and his team must retain that lead for the rest of the game. [10.19a]

If a game is shortened to five innings, the starting pitcher gets the win if he pitched four complete innings. [10.19b]

A relief pitcher is credited with a win when he is the pitcher of record at the time his team takes the lead if they hold it to the end of the game. The exception is in cases in which a pitcher was ineffective but his successor was effective. In such instances the official scorer may award the win to the second reliever. [10.18c]

If the pitcher is taken out of the game for a pinch hitter or pinch runner, he remains the pitcher of record until his relief takes the mound in the next half-inning. Therefore, he is the beneficiary of any runs scored during his team's at-bats in the inning he is substituted for. [10.19d]

A pitcher is charged with a loss when runs for which he is responsible give the opposition a lead that they never relinquish, regardless of the number of innings pitched. [10.19e]

A pitcher shall not be credited with a shutout unless he pitches a complete game. The lone exception is a situation in which a relief pitcher comes in with no one out in the first inning and no runs in. When two pitchers combine for a shutout, that shall be noted in the league's official pitching records. [10.19f]

In All-Star competition, the winning pitcher is not required to pitch five complete innings. Rather, the winning pitcher is customarily the one who is the pitcher of record when the winning team takes a lead that it holds to the game's conclusion. Should that pitcher of record be knocked out after the winning team has a "commanding lead," the decision is left to the scorer to credit that pitcher or a later one with the win. [10.19g]

Saves. Now we come to relief pitchers and the touchstone of their success, the save. The save is a relatively new concept. In baseball's early days, the starting pitcher was expected to stay in there until the bitter end; in fact, the term "save" wasn't even coined until the the 1950s, when Allan Roth first used it to describe the accomplishments of Joe Black and Clem Labine out of the Brooklyn Dodgers' bullpen.

Baseball did not officially recognize the save in its statistics until 1969, although for years *The Sporting News* had awarded its Fireman of the Year Award to the best reliever in each league (determined

The Incompleat Game

During warm-ups before the first game of a doubleheader on September 14, 1971, Expos pitcher John Strohmayer pulled a back muscle. Manager Gene Mauch sent Bill Stoneman to the mound instead.

The game was at Shea Stadium, and Stoneman pitched well, throwing every pitch of the game for his team and beating the Mets 12–1. But did he pitch a complete game? Yes and no.

Yes, because the official scorer ruled that he did. No, because his name wasn't on the lineup card. The Book does not address this situation, so the scorer made a judgment call.

by adding wins in relief and saves). And in 1973, 1974, and 1975 the requirements for a save were amended slightly. But today, in order to be credited with a save, a relief pitcher must meet all of the following conditions:

⚾ He must finish the game.

⚾ His team must win the game.

⚾ He may not be the winning pitcher.

In addition, to qualify for a save the reliever must meet *one* of the following three conditions:

⚾ When he entered the game, his team must have been leading by no more than three runs, and he pitched effectively; or

⚾ When he entered the game, the tying run must have been on base, on deck, or at bat; or

⚾ He pitched three or more innings effectively. [10.20]

Wild Pitches and Passed Balls. A wild pitch is scored when a pitched ball gets past the catcher because it was beyond his reach (given the exertion of "ordinary effort" by the catcher) or if the ball bounces before reaching the plate. It is a passed ball if the ball gets by the catcher when, again with "ordinary effort," he should have been able to catch it. [10.15]

Bases on Balls. It is a base on balls when a batter is awarded first base after not having swung at four pitches adjudged by the umpire to have been thrown outside the strike zone; it is an intentional base on balls when the pitcher purposely throws his pitches outside the strike zone in order to send the batter to first. [10.16]

Strikeouts. A strikeout is recorded whenever a batter is put out by a third strike, whether it is caught by the catcher or not. A foul bunt on a two-strike count is also a strikeout, except when the bunt is popped up and caught by a fielder. In that event, it is a putout.

For scoring purposes, in the event a substitution is made for a batter with two strikes on him and the substitute strikes out, the original batter is charged with the strikeout. Any other result of the plate appearance, however, is credited or charged to the substitute. [10.17]

Earned and Unearned Runs. Earned runs are those for which the pitcher is responsible. They must score without benefit of errors. [10.18a] Unearned runs are those that are scored by a batter who reaches base on a muffed fly, interference, obstruction, or any fielding error, or by a runner whose "life" has been prolonged by an error, or who advances on an error, passed ball, or defensive interference or obstruction when he would not have scored without the misplay. [10.18b, 10.18c, and 10.18d]

The pitcher's own contributions to an inning are significant factors in determining earned or unearned runs. Some key distinctions are as follows:

⚾ Intentional walks or wild pitches, being the pitcher's own fault, do not render any subsequent runs unearned. [10.18a]

⚾ Pitcher's errors are to be treated the same way as fielders' errors; they therefore can render runs unearned. [10.18e]

⚾ When an error occurs, The Book instructs that the pitcher is to be "given the benefit of the doubt" in establishing how the runners would have advanced if the error had not occurred. [10.18f]

"K" As in Strikeout: Two Theories

Why is the letter "K" used as the universal scoring symbol for a strikeout? Pick one of the following:

(a) Henry Chadwick, who referred to a strikeout victim as "being struck," adopted the last letter in "struck" as a convenient symbol.

(b) One of the game's earliest scorekeepers was named Kelly. He appropriated his own initial.

Earned Run Average. The ERA is calculated by multiplying by nine the number of earned runs charged against a pitcher and then dividing by the total innings pitched. [10.22e] The ERA champion is the pitcher with the lowest ERA who has pitched at least as many innings as his team had scheduled games. [10.23b]

The accountability of a pitcher who is being relieved is determined as follows:

◯ He is charged with any run scored by the runner(s) he left on base. In the event one of the runners he left on base is put out in a fielder's choice, the departed pitcher assumes responsibility for the runner who reached base on the play. [10.18g]

◯ He is charged with the base on balls if he leaves the game with a 2–0, 2–1, 3–0, 3–0, 3–1, or 3–2 count. Otherwise that batter shall be the responsibility of the relief pitcher. [10.18h]

The relief pitcher does not benefit from "previous chances for outs." That is, if runs score on the reliever that would have been unearned had the departed pitcher remained in the game (for example, because they reached base or advanced on an error), the runs that are the responsibility of the reliever are charged to him as earned runs. [10.18i]

The Scorecard

Henry Chadwick is the man we have to thank for baseball's scoring system. A writer for *The Brooklyn Eagle*, he dedicated his life to getting the word out about the game. He—and his scoring system—played no small part in making baseball our national pastime. For his trouble, he was in his own time widely referred to as "the Father of Baseball."

Chadwick's "Rules of Scoring" were adopted in 1880, and much of his system remains in use to this day. That doesn't mean, however, that keeping score is a matter of following Chadwick's exacting standards. It isn't. As Thomas Boswell has written, "Any person claiming to be a baseball fan who does not claim to have invented the quickest, simplest, and most complete method of keeping score is probably a fraud."

Examining another person's scorecards can be a lot more revealing than a handwriting analysis. Admittedly, the desire to keep score in the first place suggests that the person has a penchant for organization, a fondness for order, and an instinct for control. But there's more, too.

Some people take the KISS approach ("Keep It Simple, Stupid"). Red Barber once reported that he knew a broadcaster who would simply jot down an "0" for an out, an "X" for a hit, a "W" for a walk, and an "E" when a hitter got on base on an error, and leave it at that. At the other extreme, there are many who record every pitch, the umpires' names, and the paid and actual attendance. Next time you're at the ballpark, look over the shoulder of a few of the people nearby who are keeping score. Chances are it'll be more revealing than a long look inside their medicine cabinets.

Even if you've never kept score—and even if you have always thought people who do so are a little bit loony—you owe it to yourself as a baseball fan to try it at least once.

Whatever sort of scorer you are, you'll need to start with a blank scorecard. Usually they are to be found in the center of programs sold at major league games, but you can also buy large and more official-looking blanks at sporting goods stores.

The scorecard is a blank grid. The spaces running down the left-hand side of the sheet are for the players' names. There is usually space for their positions and uniform numbers, too. The smaller spaces that march across the page from left to right are for each of the innings played: you record what each batter up in an inning accomplishes in his plate appearance. Two blank sheets will be required, one for each team.

Next, you need the starting lineups. If you're working from a game on TV, you can write fast when the lineups are given before the game, or you can get the batsmen's names as they come to the plate. When you go to the ballpark, the electronic scoreboards usually list the lineups prior to the start of a game, and the public address announcer also announces each player, his number, his fielding position, and his spot in the batting order before the playing of the national anthem. Enter the names of the players on the scorecard in the order in which they are to hit, home team and away.

Position Numbers. Our friend Henry Chadwick was responsible for devising the numerical system for identifying players by position. He assigned each defensive position a number, and his system has become universal.

It runs as follows:

1–Pitcher (p)

2–Catcher (c)

3–First Baseman (1b)

4–Second Baseman (2b)

5–Third Baseman (3b)

6–Shortstop (ss)

7–Left fielder (lf)

8–Center fielder (cf)

9–Right fielder (rf)

Scoring Symbols. Most of the abbreviations used to record the results of a plate appearance are quite straightforward: a base on balls (or walk) is logically represented by the letters "BB," a passed ball by "PB," and so on. Not everyone uses exactly the same system (some use "W" for walk, for example), but generally common sense prevails. The usual symbols are as follows:

BB–Base on Balls

BK–Balk

CS–Caught Stealing

E–Error

FC–Fielder's Choice

HB–Hit Batsman

K–Strikeout

PB–Passed Ball

SB–Stolen Base

SH–Sacrifice Bunt

SF–Sacrifice Fly

WP–Wild Pitch

There's room for a little creativity, too. If something happens that you don't have a symbol for, make one up.

Henry McLemore, a baseball columnist in the 1940s, once told a story about his wife's innovative scoring. She developed her own score sheets and, apparently, also evolved some of her own nomenclature. One day McLemore looked over and noticed that following

KNICKERBOCKER BALL CLUB.

FINES	NAMES	HANDS OUT						RUNS	REMARKS
	Wheaton	–	3					ⅢⅡⅠ	
	Tucker							ⅢⅡ	
	Stroncrief	3	1	1				11	
16fa	*Morgan*	1	2					111	
	Burke	2						111	
	Surney	2	2					111	
16fa	*Vanageand*	3						1	
	Waldhead	1	3					11 — 25	*Winner by 2 aces*

NEW-YORK, *October 17ᵗʰ 1845.*   *Dan'l Drake Smith*   UMPIRE.

The First Scorecard

Well, maybe it's not the first scorecard, but it is the earliest surviving scorecard—from October 17, 1845—and it does suggest how far we have come.

Of course, it was a different game they played that day. It lasted only four innings, and the winner was determined by the first team to reach twenty-one runs.

You might also note that the first column is set aside for fines. Messieurs Morgan and Vanageand were fined sixteen cents apiece for swearing.

an intentional pass, his wife carefully wrote "HDWH" next to the batter's name. He asked her about it, and she explained, "It means 'He deliberately walked him.'"

You'll also need to establish some general rules for yourself for the codification of outs, strikeouts, hits, and runners.

Outs: There is some difference of opinion as to how to deal with ground-outs and pop-ups. As a general rule, outs are recorded using the defensive players' position numbers: a ground-out on which the shortstop fielded the ball and threw to the first baseman for the out would be scored "6–3." The entry for a fly to the center fielder would be simply an "8."

Some scorers go further, however, and add an "L" for a line drive, a "D" for a deep drive, a "P" for an infield pop-up, or an "F" for a fly ball. To start with, you are probably better off using just the numbers for ground-outs, an "L" for liners, and an "F" for balls hit high in the air.

Strikeouts: These are represented in the scorecard with a "K." A backward K is favored by many scorers when the batter strikes out on a called third strike, though some scorers use a Kc.

Runners on Base: When a hitter does not reach first or any other base, you can fill the box with your "6–3" or "F9" or "K." However, when a batter becomes a runner—whether by a hit or an error or a walk or any other means—it is necessary to leave yourself some space in which to record what happens to him, whether he is erased on the next pitch in a double play or he makes his way 'round the bases to score.

The traditional means of entering a base runner on a scorecard is by drawing a little diamond within the appropriate box. Then the quadrant that corresponds to the base reached is marked. Thus, taking the vantage of official scorer in the press box looking down on the action from behind home plate, you indicate a runner at first base with a notation outside the diamond in the lower right-hand corner of the box; his progress around the bases is recorded counterclockwise.

Some people locate the runner at first base in the upper left-hand corner of the box; some people don't use diamonds but a series of dashes to indicate the number of bases gained on a hit-with "-" for a single, "=" for a double, and so on. But for our money, the tried-and-true diamond is a scorer's best friend.

Hits: When a batter hits his way on, mark the relevant quadrant with a "1B," "2B," "3B," or "HR," depending upon whether the hitter strokes a single, double, triple, or homer. As the players move around the bases or are put out, the advances are indicated in the appropriate quadrant. When someone scores, the diamond is then filled in for easy visual reference. Now you're a master of the art.

The Box Score

The box score has been called "the DNA of baseball," and the description fits. In a few inches of agate type is encoded the rich experience of a baseball game. To the uninitiated, it's so much grey printer's ink, but to the baseball aficionado, the box score tells all.

How to Read a Box Score

Final Score

How the Runs Scored:

Batting Symbols:

ab: at-bats

r: runs

bi: runs batted in

bb: walks

so: strikeouts

lo: runners left on base

   or not advanced

avg: postgame average

Note: Substitutes are indented.

More Batting Info:

Player season totals for doubles (2B), triples (3B), and home runs (HR), along with name of pitcher who allowed extra base hit

Season total, plus inning, runners on and number of for home runs

GDHP: grounded into double plays

LO: team total left on base

Base running:

SB: stolen bases, with season total, against which pitcher/catcher

CS: caught stealing, with season total, against which pitcher/catcher

Fielding:

E: error, with season totals, type of error

Outfield assists

DP: double plays, with fielders involved

PB: passed ball

Pitching:

ip: innings pitched

era: postgame ERA

bf: batters faced

BS: blown save, with season totals

H: hold (relief pitcher holds lead, does not qualify for save, with season totals)

S: save, with season total

IBB: intentional walk

Pitchers' total number of pitches, number of strikes

Game Data:

T: time of game

Att: attendance

Temperature, wind speed and direction in relation to field

ROYALS 10, TIGERS 1

Royals 3rd: Beltran doubled. Damon doubled, Beltran scored. Sweeney singled, Damon scored. **Royals 2-0.**

Royals 4th: Giambi singled. Kreuter safe at first on fielding error, Giambi to third. Febles grounded into fielder's choice, Giambi scored. **Royals 3-0.**

Royals 5th: Damon singled. Sweeney doubled, Damon to third. Dye intentionally walked. Giambi singled Damon scored, Sweeney to third, Dye to second. Kreuter singled, Sweeney and Dye scored. **Royals 6-0.**

Royals 6th: Beltran tripled. Randa hit sacrifice fly, Beltran scored. **Royals 7-0.**

Tigers 8th: Kapler homered. **Royals 7-1.**

Royals 8th: Damon walked. Sweeney singled, Damon to second. Pose safe at first on throwing error, Damon to third, Sweeney to second. Giambi safe at first on fielding error, Damon and Sweeney scored, Pose to third. Pose scored on wild pitch. **Royals 10-1.**

Detroit	000	000	010 - 1
Kansas City	002	131	03X - 10

DETROIT	ab	r	h	bi	bb	so	lo	avg
Polonia dh	4	0	2	0	0	1	1	.419
Higginson rf	3	0	0	0	1	1	3	.246
Encarnacion lf	4	0	0	0	0	1	1	.274
Palmer 3b	4	0	0	0	0	2	1	.278
Clark 1b	4	0	0	0	0	1	1	.240
Easley 2b	2	0	0	0	0	0	0	.263
Kapler cf	3	1	2	1	0	0	1	.246
Haselman c	3	0	1	0	0	0	1	.310
D.Cruz ss	2	0	0	0	0	0	1	.249
Totals	**29**	**1**	**5**	**1**	**1**	**6**	**10**	

▶ **BATTING — HR:** Kapler (11, 8th inning off Witasick 0 on, 0 out). **S:** D.Cruz. **RBI:** Kapler (27). **Runners left in scoring position, 2 out:** Higginson 1. **GIDP:** Higginson. **Team LOB:** 4.
▶ **BASERUNNING — CS:** Polonia (2, 2nd base by Witasick/Kreuter).
▶ **FIELDING — E:** Palmer (11, catch); D.Cruz 2 (6, throw, bobble). **DP:** 1 (D.Cruz-Easley-Clark).

KANSAS CITY	ab	r	h	bi	bb	so	lo	avg
Beltran rf	5	2	2	0	0	1	4	.297
Randa 3b	3	0	0	1	0	1	1	.285
a-Leius ph-3b	1	0	0	0	0	0	0	.206
Damon lf	4	3	3	1	1	0	0	.304
Sweeney 1b	5	2	3	1	0	0	1	.311
Dye rf	3	1	2	0	1	0	1	.298
b-Pose ph-rf	1	1	0	0	0	0	0	.328
Giambi dh	5	1	2	2	0	0	1	.265
Kreuter c	4	0	2	2	1	1	1	.268
Febles 2b	5	0	1	1	0	1	6	.287
Scarsone 2b	0	0	0	0	0	0	0	.167
Sanchez ss	4	0	0	0	0	0	4	.253
Totals	**40**	**10**	**15**	**8**	**3**	**4**	**19**	

a-grounded to shortstop for Randa in the 8th; b-reached on error for Dye in the 8th.

▶ **BATTING — 2B:** Beltran (16, Thompson); Damon 2 (20, Thompson 2); Sweeney (18, Thompson). **3B:** Beltran (2, Thompson). **SF:** Randa. **RBI:** Damon (36), Sweeney (37), Febles (31), Giambi 2 (9), Kreuter 2 (26), Randa (31). **2-out RBI:** Damon, Sweeney. **Runners left in scoring position, 2 out:** Febles 2, Dye 1, Sweeney 1, Beltran 2. **GIDP:** Febles. **Team LOB:** 10.
▶ **FIELDING — DP:** 1 (Febles-Sanchez-Sweeney).

PITCHING	ip	h	r	er	bb	so	bf	era
DETROIT								
Thompson L,6-7	6	11	7	6	2	2	31	4.52
Blair	2	4	3	0	1	2	13	7.99
KANSAS CITY								
Witasick W,3-5	8	5	1	1	0	6	28	6.35
Pisciotta	1	0	0	0	1	0	4	10.80

WP: Thompson, Blair. **IBB:** Dye (by Thompson). **HBP:** Easley (by Witasick). **Pitches-strikes:** Witasick 90-57; Pisciotta 15-7; Thompson 116-69; Blair 27-20.
▶ **UMPIRES — HP:** Morrison. **1B:** Hickox. **2B:** Barnett. **3B:** Kosc.
▶ **GAME DATA — T:** 2:31. **Att:** 19,021. **Weather:** 76 degrees, rain. **Wind:** 6 mph, in from left.

Managers, players, and fans alike open the morning paper seeking the unique thumbnail theater that is the box score. You can learn the simple stuff like who homered or who got the win. For Rotisserie League baseball fans, box scores are a means of gauging their imaginary teams' progress. Managers like Tony La Russa use them to get a competitive edge over other managers by analyzing their key decisions. Even in the early morning, when you're seated quietly at the breakfast table with only *USA Today* for company, strategies and tendencies can be discerned.

If the box score is the engine of baseball's statistical analysis—and it is—then the compilations of data based on box scores help make baseball the timeless wonder that it is.

Can You Make the Call?

You may not want to quit here; on the pages that follow, there's a chronological listing of the changes made in scoring practice since the game's inception, and then a glossary and a list of all the significant major league rule changes. The fact is, though, as far as today's edition of The Book is concerned, you now know it all.

However, chances are that as you apply what you learned to today's game or next year's World Series, you'll discover that the game is forever offering up new and unfamiliar situations. No game is just like any other, and in the course of most contests, unique situations occur. So wear your newfound expertise proudly—but don't be surprised if now and again the game of baseball throws you a curve.

Scoring Rule Changes: The Highlights

1865 The first sliding steal of a base is perpetrated, by Eddie Cuthbert of the Philadelphia Keystones. Official averages are computed.

1877 A hitter is no longer charged with an at-bat for a base on balls.

1883 An error is charged to the pitcher for a base on balls, wild pitch, hit batter, and balk.

1885 The pitcher is credited with an assist on a strikeout.

1886 A hit batsman is not to be charged with a time at-bat. No stolen base is to be credited to a runner for bases advanced by his own volition (as when a base runner goes to third on a single).

1887 A base on balls is scored as a hit (for this season only). No error is charged to the pitcher for a base on balls, wild pitch, hit batter, and balk.

1888 A hit batsman is credited with a hit. The walk no longer is scored as a hit or counted as a time at bat. An error is charged to the pitcher for a base on balls, wild pitch, hit batsman, and balk.

1889 The sacrifice is first recognized in the statistics of the game; the batter is still charged with an at-bat. No error is charged to the pitcher for a base on balls, wild pitch, hit batter, and balk. A pitcher is not credited with an assist on a strikeout.

1893 The batter credited with a sacrifice is not charged with a time at bat.

1898 A stolen base is credited when a runner reaches a base he attempts to steal without the aid of batting or fielding errors or a hit by the batter.

1900 A pitcher must win at least fifteen games to qualify as the league leader in the category of Winning Percentage. (The earlier rule stated that a pitcher must appear in twenty-five games.)

1908 A batter is excused on a sacrifice fly from an at-bat when a run scores after the catch of his fly.

1909 If a runner is thrown out on an attempted double steal, neither runner is credited with a stolen base. A bunt on a third strike is a strikeout, and the catcher is credited with the putout. The pitcher or catcher is charged with an error if a batter reaches first base on a wild pitch or passed ball.

1912 Earned runs are charged to a pitcher when a player scores by means of safe hits, sacrifice hits, base on balls, hit batsmen, wild pitches, and balks.

1917 Official records include earned runs for the first time. Earned runs are also charged to a pitcher when a player scores by means of a stolen base.

1920 No stolen base is credited when the defense makes no attempt to get the runner out. The RBI is added to scoring. A player must appear in at least one hundred games to qualify as the league leader in Batting Average and Slugging Average. Before this there was no official rule, but it was generally accepted that a man had to play in sixty percent of the scheduled games to qualify.

1926 The sacrifice fly rule is amended so that a batter is charged with no at-bat when any base runner advances a base on a fly ball. Pitchers are not credited with a strikeout if a batter reaches first base because of a wild pitch on the third strike.

1931 The generosity of the 1926 change in the sacrifice fly rule apparently was too much. This year the sacrifice is declared extinct; there were no more sacrifice flies until 1939.

1939 A cameo appearance for the sacrifice fly rule. It was banished again after this season.

1945 A player must have at least four hundred at-bats to qualify as the league leader in Batting Average or Slugging Average.

1950 A player must play in at least two-thirds of his team's scheduled games to qualify as the league leader in Batting Average or Slugging Average.

1951 A player must have at least four hundred at-bats to qualify as the league leader in Batting Average or Slugging Average. However, if there is any player with fewer than the required number of times at bat whose average would be the highest if he were charged with this required at-bat total, then he shall be recognized as the league leader. A pitcher must pitch a total of at least one inning for every scheduled game to qualify as the league leader in the categories of Earned Run Average or Fielding Average. (Before this, he had to pitch at least ten complete games and at least one hundred innings.)

1954 The return of the sacrifice fly, this time as it exists today; the batter is credited with one when a runner scores on a caught fly.

1955 The 1951 rule is repealed. A player must have at least four hundred at-bats, period, to qualify as the league leader in Batting Average or Slugging Average.

1957 A player must have a total of at least 3.1 plate appearances for every scheduled game to qualify as the league leader in Batting Average or Slugging Average.

1967 A player must have a total of at least 3.1 plate appearances for every scheduled game to qualify as the league leader in Batting Average or Slugging Average. However, if there is any player with fewer than the required number of plate appearances whose average for a season will not have changed with this required number of appearances, then the player shall be recognized as the league leader in Batting Average or Slugging Average.

1969 Relief pitchers are acknowledged as fundamental to the modern game of baseball, and a statistic reflecting their importance becomes a formal part of baseball's paper trail. The save is added to baseball's official statistics. Runs are earned by a relief pitcher who enters the game in the middle of an inning as if he entered the game at the beginning of the inning.

1973 A reliever is credited with a save for "protecting" a lead (even if it was a 10–1 rout).

1974 The save rule is again amended. No save is to be credited to a pitcher unless the tying run is on base or at the plate or unless he pitches three effective innings.

1975 The save is changed yet again. Now if the tying run is on deck when the reliever arrives, he may still earn a save.

1978 A pitcher who pitches only a third of an inning in a season will not have his ERA rounded off. His total for innings pitched will be carried as one-third.

1983 A pitcher's ERA is to be calculated henceforth with fractions of innings pitched rather than only with full innings.

1989 The "game-winning RBI" (previously credited to a batter who gave his club "the lead it never relinquished") is eliminated as an official statistic.

Definition of Terms
Glossary

Chapter 2 of The Book—called Definition of Terms—devotes several pages to setting down exactly what is meant by some of the most commonly used terms in the game. A few of the definitions are useful to the reader who is not an absolute novice, but many state the obvious, to put it mildly. Even more disconcerting is the fact that the list is not even remotely comprehensive (it includes "**Safe**" but not "**Out**" and "**Wild Pitch**" but not "**Passed Ball**," to give just two examples).

As you've already seen, in our version of Chapter 2 we found it more helpful to expand upon some of the most important terms, especially those not discussed at length in other parts of The Book. But lest you feel shortchanged, here's the full list of The Book's terms:

Adjudged. We don't rely much on the word in this book, but it appears often in The Book, where it means "decided by the umpire."

Appeal. An appeal is the act of a defensive player who claims that an offensive player has violated the rules. (See Chapters 4 and 7.)

Balk. Volumes could be written about this rule violation, but suffice it to say here that a balk is an illegal act by a pitcher with a runner or runners on base. (See Chapter 8.)

Ball. A pitch that is not in the strike zone and is not struck by the batter. Ever since 1889, it has taken four of them to earn a walk, or Base on Balls.

Base. One of four points—canvas bags for first, second, and third and a rubber plate for home—that must be touched by a runner in order to score a run. (See Chapter 1.)

Base Coach. A team member stationed at first or third base whose job it is to direct the batter and the base runners. (See Chapter 4.)

Base on Balls. A free pass to first base, awarded to a batter who receives four pitches outside the strike zone and has the good sense (and good reflexes) not to swing at them.

Batter. The fellow in the batter's box. (See Chapter 6.)

Batter-Runner. This term describes the condition of the batter who has managed to get on base.

Batter's Box. Its boundary lines are usually invisible by the second inning, but they're there nonetheless. The batter's box is where the batter must stand during his time at bat. (See Chapter 1 for a description of the playing field.)

Battery. The pitcher-and-catcher combination.

Bench. Also called the dugout, this is where players, substitutes, and other uniformed members of the team sit when they're not busy on the playing field. (See Chapter 1.)

Bunt. A ball that is intentionally tapped slowly within the infield.

Called Game. A generic term for any game that is terminated by the umpire-in-chief, including rainouts, suspended games, and forfeits. (See Chapter 4.)

Catch. When he gets secure possession of a ball in his hand or glove, a fielder makes a catch (no fair using his cap or any other props). He must also hold onto the ball long enough to prove that he has control of it.

Catcher. The fielder behind the plate. Roger Angell said it better: "The catcher is the physical and emotional focus of every baseball game; he faces outward, surveying and guiding it all, and everyone else on the team looks in at him. The rock-hard catcher is the jewel of the movement."

Catcher's Box. The area where the "jewel of the movement" (see Catcher) must stand until the pitcher delivers the ball.

Club. A management term that refers to the people who assemble the team personnel, provide the playing field and associated facilities, and represent the team in their relations with the league.

Coach. A uniformed team member who works for the manager. Some are base coaches; others supervise batting, pitching, and other skills.

Dead Ball. A ball is dead (and out of play) when play has been suspended for any reason.

Defense. The team in the field. Some pundit has pointed out that baseball is the only game in which the defensive team controls the ball.

Doubleheader. Two games played in immediate succession, with a twenty-minute intermission. (See Chapter 4.)

Double Play. A play by the defense in which two offensive players are put out as a result of continuous action, with no errors between putouts.

Dugout. See Bench.

Fair Ball. A batted ball that lands in fair territory; or one that flies over fair territory on its way to the outfield or out of the park; or one that touches first, second, or third base; or one that hits a player or an umpire in fair territory. (See Chapter 2.)

Fair Territory. The area of the playing field from home plate within the first- and third-base lines to the bottom of the playing field fence and perpendicularly upward. Foul lines are in fair territory.

Fielder. Any defensive player.

Fielder's Choice. Considerably easier than Sophie's, this is the act of a fielder who, in handling a ground ball, throws to a base other than first in order to put out a base runner who is closer to scoring than the batter-runner. (See Chapter 10.)

Fly Ball. A batted ball that goes high in the air.

Force Play. This is a play in which a runner loses his right to occupy a base because the batter has become a runner. (See Chapter 6.)

Forfeited Game. For any one of several rule infractions (they're listed in Chapter 4) the umpire-in-chief may declare that a game is over and the "offended" team is automatically the winner. In case of a forfeit the score is Offended Team 9, Bad Guys 0.

Foul Ball. A batted ball that lands on foul territory between home and first or home and third; or one that passes over foul territory on its way into the outfield or out of the park; or one that hits a player, an umpire, or any "foreign object" in foul territory. (See Chapter 2.)

Foul Territory. The part of the playing field outside the first- and third-base lines extended to the fence and perpendicularly upward. (See Chapter 2.)

Foul Tip. A batted ball that goes directly from the bat to the catcher's hands and is legally caught (no rebounds allowed unless the catcher's glove or hand touches the ball first). A foul tip that's caught is a strike, and the ball is in play. (See Chapter 6.)

Ground Ball. A batted ball that rolls along or bounces close to guess-what.

Home Team. The players on whose grounds the game is played. If they don't win it's a shame. If a game is played on neutral territory, a home team is mutually agreed upon.

Illegal. Not according to the rules in The Book.

Illegal Pitch. A pitch is illegal if it's delivered incorrectly—that is, not according to the many specifications enumerated in Chapter 8.

Infielder. It usually means one of the following defensive players: first baseman, second baseman, third baseman, or shortstop.

Infield Fly. A fair fly ball (not a line drive or bunt) that can be caught by an infielder with ordinary effort when first and second or first, second, and third are occupied before two are out. Despite the definition of Infielder above, the pitcher and catcher are considered infielders for the purposes of this rule, and so are any outfielders stationed in the infield. (See Chapter 2.)

In Flight. A ball that has not yet touched the ground or any object other than a fielder or an umpire.

In Jeopardy. When the ball is in play and an offensive player is liable to be put out, he is considered "in jeopardy."

Inning. Six outs, three per side.

Interference. The act of hindering play. Interference may be charged to any of several participants in the game: offensive players, defensive players, umpires, even spectators. (See Chapters 5 and 7.)

League. A group of clubs who play one another for the championship. In the majors there are two leagues, and only one of them has the DH. (See Chapter 10.)

League President. The enforcer of the official rules, he resolves disputes, mediates protests, and fines or suspends players, coaches, managers, and umpires at his discretion. His decision is final. (See Chapter 10.)

Legal. According to the rules in The Book.

Line Drive. A batted ball that goes sharply and directly to a fielder without touching the ground.

Live Ball. It's still in play.

Manager. He's responsible for the team's actions on the field, and he represents the team to the umpire and the opposition. He must be appointed at least a half-hour before game time, and if he is unable to carry out his duties, he must appoint someone to take his place.

Obstruction. The act of a fielder—one who's not in possession of the ball and not in the act of fielding the ball—that impedes the progress of a base runner. (See Chapter 7.)

Offense. The team at bat.

Official Scorer. He sits in the press box and makes decisions involving judgment, such as whether a batter has reached base on a hit or an error. (See Chapter 10.)

Out. There are three of them in a team's time at bat.

Outfielder. Left, right, and center.

Overslide. What a base runner does when he slides so vigorously into a base (not first base) that he loses contact with it.

Penalty. The punishment for a violation of the rules.

Person. A euphemism for the body, the clothes, or the equipment of a player or umpire. Typically used as in, "If the ball touches his person . . ."

Pitch. A ball delivered to the batter by the pitcher. This is not to be confused with Throw (no matter how badly the pitcher does it).

Pitcher. The player who delivers the pitch to the batter.

Pivot Foot. The one that's in contact with the rubber as the pitcher makes his delivery.

"Play". What the umpire says to get a game started or to resume play.

Quick Return. An illegal pitch, made with obvious intent to catch off-guard a batter who isn't ready. (See Chapter 8.)

Regulation Game. Usually it's nine full innings, but there are many exceptions, all of which are described in Chapter 4.

Retouch. The act of a base runner returning to a base. (See Chapter 7.)

Run. One of these is scored when a batter becomes a runner and touches first base, second base, third base, and home—in that order.

Rundown. One of the fundamentals of the game—the act of a defensive player attempting to put out a base runner between bases. (It's what the Red Sox forgot how to do in Game 3 of the 1986 World Series.)

Runner. An offensive player who is somewhere on the base paths.

"Safe". What the umpire calls to indicate that the base runner gets to keep his base.

Set Position. One of the two legal positions from which a pitcher may make his delivery; the other is the Windup Position. (See Chapter 8.)

Squeeze Play. An attempt by a runner on third to score on a bunt.

Strike. A legal pitch that: is swung at and missed; is not swung at but is in the strike zone; is fouled by the batter with fewer than two strikes in the count; is bunted foul; hits the batter as he swings; is in the strike zone when it hits the batter; is a foul tip.

Strike Zone. That area over home plate the upper limit of which is a horizontal line at the midpoint between the top of the shoulders and the top of the uniform pants (roughly his armpits), and the lower level is a line at the hollow beneath the kneecap.(See Chapter 2.)

Suspended Game. A called game that must be completed later.

Tag. A fielder may tag either a base runner or a base, but in both cases he must have the ball securely in his hand or glove. He may tag a base with any part of his body, but he has to tag the runner with the ball or the glove with the ball in it.

Throw. The act of propelling the ball with the hand and arm. Not to be confused with Pitch.

Tie Game. A regulation game that's called when both teams have the same number of runs. (See Chapter 4.)

"Time". The legal interruption of play, during which the ball is dead. Only the umpire may call "Time." (See Chapter 4.)

Touch. To come into contact with. For these purposes touching a player or an umpire means coming into contact with his clothes, his equipment, or any part of his body.

Triple Play. A defensive action in which three players are put out as a result of continuous action—with no errors between putouts.

Wild Pitch. A pitch so high, low, or wide of the plate that it can't be handled with ordinary effort by the catcher. The official scorer is the one who decides what "ordinary effort" is.

Windup Position. One of the two legal positions from which a pitcher may make his delivery; the other is Set Position. (See Chapter 8.)

1845 to 1999
Major League Rule Changes

A chronology of rule change highlights appears at the end of many of the chapters in this book. For example, rule changes that have affected the batter are at the end of Chapter 6, and those having to do with the pitcher are at the close of Chapter 8. The following is a compilation of all the important major-league rule changes that have been made since 1845. In assembling the research for this book, we found a number of small disagreements on dates; virtually all, however, occurred in the nineteenth century, and most discrepancies were of but one year.

The bracketed reference that follows some of these rules refers to the rule number in today's *Official Rules of Baseball*. In some cases, the rule as it reads today is considerably different from the way it was written then.

~ 1845 ~

— Although some sources say that the first written "baseball rules" date from 1834 or 1842, a more commonly cited year of origin is 1845, when the New York Knickerbockers created a formal code of playing rules. The rules limited each team to nine players, laid out the field in what designer Alexander Cartwright termed his "baseball square" (with ninety-foot sides), and established that the winner was the team who scored twenty-one aces, given that each team had an equal number of turns at bat.

— There are no restrictions on bat size or shape. [1.10]

— The ball weighs three ounces. [1.09]

— The pitching distance is forty-five feet. [1.07]

— Provisions are made for an umpire. [9.01a]

~ 1846 ~

— The first recorded argument between a player and an umpire. The umpire wins.

~ **1848** ~

— A rule is introduced requiring that a baseman must hold the ball in order to put out a runner. (Before this the base runner was out if the ball hit him.) [7.08]

— Only the batter-runner making for first may be retired on a force. (Before this any runner could be retired on a force.) [7.08]

~ **1849** ~

— The New York Knickerbockers introduced the first uniforms, blue and white cricket outfits. [1.17]

~ **1854** ~

— The ball weighs from 5 1/2 to 6 1/2 ounces and is from 2 3/4 to 3 1/2 inches in diameter. [1.09]

~ **1857** ~

— The nine-inning game is introduced. [4.10]

~ **1858** ~

— Balls caught on one hop are no longer outs. [6.05]
— The called strike is introduced. [6.05]
— One umpire, chosen by the home team, is in charge of a game. [9.03a]
— The pitcher is allowed to make a short run in his delivery. [8.01]

~ **1859** ~

— The bat is limited to 2 1/2 inches in diameter (before this a bat like that used in cricket with a 4-inch-wide flat face had been commonplace). [1.10]

~ **1860** ~

— Whitewash is used to mark the foul lines. [1.04]
— The umpire of a game is selected by the captain of each team. He is given the authority to suspend play, and he must make a call when a ball is foul. [9.04]

~ 1861 ~

— At the end of a game an umpire must declare the winning club and record his decision in the scorebook of each team before he leaves the field. [9.04]

~ 1863 ~

— The pitcher is not permitted to take even a step in his delivery. Both feet must be on the ground when he releases the ball. [8.01]

— The bat must be round and of wood. Its width is still limited to 2 1/2 inches, but its length is not restricted. [1.10]

~ 1864 ~

— When a runner circles the bases, he must touch each one. [7.02]

~ 1865 ~

— The first sliding steal of a base, by Eddie Cuthbert of the Philadelphia Keystones. [10.08]

— The first batting averages are computed. [10.22]

— The pitcher's box—twelve feet by three feet—replaces the twelve-foot line. [1.07]

— The umpire must also record the results of a game in the scorer's book. [9.04]

~ 1866 ~

— The pitcher's box is enlarged to a four-by-twelve-foot rectangle. [1.07]

~ 1867 ~

— The pitcher's box is six feet by six feet. [1.07]

— Pitchers are allowed to take as many steps as they like in their delivery. [8.01]

~ 1868 ~

— The pitcher's box shrinks to a four-by-six-foot box. [1.07]

— The Cincinnati Red Stockings introduce knickerbocker trousers. [1.17]

— The bat is to be no more than forty-two inches long. [1.10]

~ 1869 ~

— The pitcher's box is a six-foot square. [1.07]

~ 1870 ~

— A runner is allowed to overrun first base. [7.08]
— The batter is given the right to call for a high or a low ball.

~ 1872 ~

— The pitcher is allowed to snap the ball during delivery, but he's restricted to a below-the-waist motion. [8.01]
— The ball is required to weigh not less than 5 and not more than 5 1/4 ounces, with a circumference of not less than 9 and not more than 9 1/4 inches. [1.09]
— An "injured" ball is to be changed only in even innings upon request of the captain of either team. [3.01]

~ 1875 ~

— The (unpadded) catcher's glove is introduced, by Charles G. Waite. [1.12]

~ 1876 ~

— The National League is established.
— The umpire says, "Play" for the first time. [4.15a]
— If an umpire is unable to see whether a catch has been fairly made, he may confer with spectators and players.

~ 1877 ~

— To choose an umpire the league selects "three gentlemen of repute" in each city where there is a team. At least three hours before a game the visiting team chooses the umpire from among them. [9.01]
— A time at bat is not charged to a batter who walks. [10.16]
— Canvas-covered bases are required. They are fifteen inches square, the same as today. [1.06]
— Home plate is relocated to its present spot. [1.05]

~ 1878 ~

— Umpires get paid, by the home team: five dollars a game.

~ **1879** ~

— The National League names twenty men living in or near cities where the league has teams as "fit" to be umpires, and each game is run by someone from the list. This rule remained in force until 1883. [9.01]

— An umpire's fees and expenses are paid by the visiting club.

— An umpire is given the power to impose fines—of not less than ten dollars and not more than twenty dollars—when he thinks it's necessary.

— An umpire may terminate a game after a rain delay of thirty minutes. [4.12]

— The pitcher is required to face the batter when he pitches. [8.01]

— All pitched balls must be called strikes, balls, or fouls.

— The number of strikes in an out is officially three. [6.05]

— There are nine balls in a walk. [6.08a]

~ **1880** ~

— The runner hit by a batted ball is out. [7.08]

— The catcher is required to catch a third strike on the fly. [6.05]

— The base on balls decreases to eight. [6.08a]

— The limits of the fines an umpire may impose change. Now it's not less than five dollars and not more than fifty dollars.

~ **1881** ~

— The base on balls is seven. [6.08a]

— The pitching distance is lengthened to fifty feet. [1.07]

— The pitcher is fined for deliberately hitting a batter with the ball.

— A spectator who "hisses or hoots" at or insults the umpire may be ejected from the grounds. [9.01e]

— The base runner may no longer be put out when he is returning to his base on a foul ball. [5.09]

~ **1882** ~

— The three-foot-long base line is adopted. [1.04]

— Umpires may not reverse decisions on matters of judgment. [9.02]

— Umpires may not confer with spectators or players. [*General Instructions to Umpires*]

— If an umpire imposes a fine or declares a forfeit, he must report it to the league secretary within twenty-four hours. [4.18]

— Umpire corruption rears its ugly head for the first and only time: a National League umpire, Richard Higham, is expelled from the league for collusion with gamblers.

— The American League is formed.

~ 1883 ~

— A foul ball caught on the bounce ceases to be an out. It must be caught before it touches the ground. [6.05a]

— The first system of salaried umpires is introduced, under the same system that is in use today. The four men hired came from cities not represented in the league. [9.01]

— An error is charged to the pitcher for a base on balls, wild pitch, hit batter, and balk. [10.13]

— Pitching is allowed from anywhere up to shoulder height. [8.01]

~ 1884 ~

— Almost all restrictions on a pitcher's motion are lifted. He may throw the ball with virtually any motion he chooses, provided that his delivery is not higher than his shoulders and he is facing the batter at the moment of windup. He is allowed only one step before delivery. [8.01]

— A base on balls is six. [6.08a]

~ 1885 ~

— Home base may be made of marble or whitened rubber. [1.05]

— The bat may have one flattened side. (This rule lasted only one year.) [1.10]

— The pitcher is credited with an assist on a strikeout. [10.11]

~ 1886 ~

— A base on balls is five. [6.08a]

— The pitcher's box becomes four feet by seven feet. [1.07]

— An umpire may introduce a new ball at any time. Before this year, when a ball was lost, the umpire gave the team five minutes to find it before he threw in a new one. An umpire must have two baseballs at his disposal at all times. [3.01]

— First and third base are moved within the foul lines.

— A hit batsman is not charged with a time at bat. [10.02]

— No stolen base is credited to a runner for bases advanced by his own volition. [10.08]

~ 1887 ~

— The pitcher's box is 4 feet by 5 1/2 feet. [1.07]

— A pitcher must keep one foot on the rear line of the box and may not take more than one step in delivering the ball. Before delivery he must hold the ball in front of him so that it is visible to the umpire. [8.01]

— No error is charged to the pitcher for a base on balls, wild pitch, hit batter, and balk. [10.13]

— The umpire may call a game if the spectators are disorderly. The maximum fine for arguing with an ump or protesting a call is ten dollars.

— The batter is no longer allowed to request a high or low pitch.

— A batter hit by a pitched ball is entitled to first base and not charged with a time at bat. [6.08b]

— A strikeout is called on four strikes. (This rule lasted only one season.) [6.05]

— Home plate is to be made of rubber and is to be twelve inches square. [1.05]

— A base on balls is scored as a hit and counted as a time at bat. This rule lasted one season only. [10.16]

~ 1888 ~

— A base on balls is not counted as a hit and not charged as a time at bat. [10.16]

— If a runner is hit by a batted ball, the batter is credited with a hit. [10.05]

— The strikeout is back to three strikes. [6.05]

— It is a ground-rule double instead of a home run if the ball is batted over the fence in fair territory where the fence is less than 210 feet from home plate. [6.09]

— The mandatory fine for a coach who leaves the coach's box to protest a call is five dollars.

— An error is charged to the pitcher for a base on balls, wild pitch, hit batter, and balk. [10.13]

— A hit batsman is awarded first base and credited with a hit. [6.08]

— A batter is credited with a hit when his batted ball hits a base runner. [10.05]

~ 1889 ~

— No error is charged to the pitcher for a base on balls, wild pitch, hit batter, and balk. A pitcher is not credited with an assist on a strikeout. [10.13]

— The sacrifice bunt is statistically recognized, but the batter is charged with a time at bat. [10.09]

— A base on balls is four, and there it remains. [6.08a]

~ 1890 ~

— The ump is called "Mr. Umpire" for the first time.

~ 1891 ~

— Substitutions are allowed at any time during a game, but once he has been substituted for, a player may not return. [3.03]

~ 1892 ~

— It's a ground-rule double instead of a home run if the ball is hit over the fence in fair territory if the fence is less than 235 feet from home plate. [6.09]

~ 1893 ~

— A batter credited with a sacrifice is not charged with a time at bat. [10.09]

— The pitching distance is increased to sixty feet, six inches, where it remains today. [1.07]

— The pitcher's box disappears (never to be seen again) and is replaced by the rubber—a slab twelve inches long and four inches wide. [1.07]

— The pitcher is required to place his rear foot against the slab. [8.01]

~ 1894 ~

— The batter is charged with a strike for hitting a foul bunt. [6.05d]

~ 1895 ~

— The pitcher's rubber is enlarged to its present size of twenty-four by six inches. [1.07]

— The maximum diameter of the bat is increased to 2 3/4 inches, where it remains today. [1.10]

— The infield fly rule is adopted: The umpire may call an infield fly when there is one out and first and second or first, second, and third base are occupied. [6.05e]

— A strike is charged to a batter for a foul tip. [6.05a]

— The limits on fines change again—to not less than twenty-five dollars and not more than one hundred dollars.

— If the crowd becomes so unruly that the game is stopped for more than fifteen minutes, the umpire may declare a forfeit. (If that happens, the visitors win, 9–0.) [4.17]

~ 1896 ~

— A twenty-five dollar fine is imposed on a coach or a player who uses vulgar language. It costs players five to ten dollars for any other first offense, twenty-five dollars and possibly ejection for a second offense, and mandatory ejection for a third offense.

~ 1897 ~

— Intentionally discoloring or injuring the ball is punishable by a five-dollar fine. The ball is replaced. [3.02]

— The umpire has twelve hours to report a fine or an ejection to the league president, four hours for a "flagrant offense." [9.05a and 9.05b]

~ 1898 ~

— A stolen base is credited to the base runner when he reaches a base he attempts to steal without the aid of batting or fielding errors or a hit by the batter. [10.08]

— The first official balk rule: A pitcher is compelled to throw to a base if he makes a motion in that direction. [8.05]

~ 1899 ~

— The balk rule is refined: A pickoff throw may not be faked; a pitcher must complete his motion. [8.05]

~ 1900 ~

— A pitcher must win at least fifteen games to qualify as the league leader in the category of Winning Percentage. (The earlier rule stated that a pitcher must appear in twenty-five games.) [10.23]

— The shape of home plate is changed, from a twelve-inch square to a five-sided figure seventeen inches wide. [1.05]

~ 1901 ~

— The first two fouls are termed strikes (in the National League). [6.05b]
— The catcher is no longer allowed to catch two strikes on a bounce. [4.03]
— The infield fly rule is in effect when there are no outs as well as one out. [6.05e]
— The American League joins the majors (the National League got started in 1876), and the rule discrepancies begin. For instance, the National League declares that any foul ball not caught on the fly is a strike unless the batter has two strikes on him. The AL does not agree—at least not right away. [6.05]
— If an offense is "flagrant" enough, the league president may suspend a player or coach who has been fined and/or ejected by an umpire. [9.05c]

~ 1903 ~

— If there is only one umpire in a game, he may stand anywhere on the field he likes. [9.03a]
— The American League agrees that any foul ball not caught on the fly is a strike unless the batter has two strikes on him. [6.05]

~ 1904 ~

— The height of the pitcher's mound is established. It may not be higher than fifteen inches above the base lines and home plate. [1.07]

~ 1906 ~

— The umpire gets authority over the groundskeeper. [9.01e]

~ 1908 ~

— Pitchers are forbidden to scuff or soil a new ball. [8.02]
— Four umpires are assigned to the World Series for the first time. Only two work in a game at a given time.
— The sacrifice fly rule is adopted, exempting the batter from an at-bat when a run scores after a catch. [10.09]

~ 1909 ~

— All four umpires assigned to the World Series work in each game.

— The pitcher or catcher is charged with an error if a batter reaches first base on a wild pitch or passed ball. [10.13]

— A bunt on a third strike is a strikeout. The catcher is credited with the putout. [10.17]

— If a runner is thrown out on an attempted double-steal, neither runner shall be credited with a stolen base. [10.08]

~ 1910 ~

— The umpire organization chart is established. The plate umpire—the one who judges balls and strikes—is appointed the umpire-in-chief, and the others are field umpires. An umpire may not interfere with or criticize his colleagues' decisions. Only the umpire-in-chief may declare the game a forfeit. [9.04]

— The captain of a team must notify the umpire-in-chief of any substitution. [3.03]

— An umpire must warn players on the bench for excessive yelling before he can fine or otherwise punish them for it. [9.01d]

— Before a game begins, the umpire must announce any special ground rules. [9.04]

— The cork-center ball is adopted for regular use (it had been used in the previous year for occasional play). [1.09]

~ 1912 ~

— Earned runs are charged to a pitcher when a player scores by means of safe hits, sacrifice hits, bases on balls, hit batters, wild pitches, and balks. [10.18]

~ 1914 ~

— In the case of fire, panic, or storm, the umpire does not have to wait until the pitcher has the ball on the mound to call a time-out. [9.04]

~ 1917 ~

— Earned runs are also charged to a pitcher when a player scores by means of a stolen base. [10.18]

~ 1920 ~

— The abolition of the spitball, with a "grandfather clause": Each team is allowed to appoint two spitball pitchers for the 1920 season. [8.02]

— A ball that hits an umpire is in play. [5.08]

— The umpire may suspend play at any time for an injury to a player or an umpire. [4.12]

— After a thirty-minute rain delay an umpire may terminate a game. [4 12]

— A player must appear in at least one hundred games to qualify as the league leader in Batting Average and Slugging Average. Before this there was no official rule, but it was generally accepted that a man had to play in sixty percent of the scheduled games to qualify. [10.23]

— The category of RBI is added to scoring. [10.04]

— A runner may not run the bases in reverse order "for the purpose of confusing the fielders or making a travesty of the game." [7.08i]

— The ball has its gloss removed before a game by the umpire. [3.01]

— Enter the "lively ball." Australian yarn, said to be stronger than its American equivalent, may be wound tighter, so the ball's bounce and hardness increase. [1.09]

— No stolen base is to be credited when the defense makes no attempt to get the runner out. [10.08]

~ 1921 ~

— Another grandfather clause in the spitball rule: Eight National League and nine American League pitchers are officially designated as spitball pitchers and allowed to use the spitter for the rest of their careers. [8.02]

~ 1925 ~

— Pitchers are allowed to use a rosin bag. [8.02e]

~ 1926 ~

— Pitchers are not credited with a strikeout if a batter reaches first base because of a wild pitch on the third strike. [10.17]

— It is a ground-rule double instead of a home run if the ball is hit over the fence in fair territory if the fence is less than 250 feet from home plate. [6.09]

— The cushioned cork-center baseball is introduced. [1.09]

— The sacrifice fly rule is amended to exempt a batter from an at-bat when a runner advances from first to second or second to third as well as on scoring. [10.09]

~ 1931 ~

— A fair ball that bounces through or over a fence or into the stands is considered a ground-rule double instead of a home run. [6.09]

— The sacrifice fly is eliminated. [10.09]

~ 1933 ~

— Three umpires to a daily game come into regular use.

~ 1934 ~

— Both major leagues are required to adopt the same brand of baseball. [1.09]

~ 1935 ~

— The first umpire school opens, in Hot Springs, Arkansas.

— The first major league night baseball game is played, in Cincinnati on May 24.

~ 1939 ~

— Six umpires are appointed to the World Series, two of whom work as alternates.

— The pitcher is allowed to have his free foot in front of or behind the rubber, with his pivot foot in front of or on the rubber (but always in contact with it). [8.01]

— A batter is credited with a sacrifice fly and not charged with a time at bat if he hits a fly ball that is caught and a runner scores on the catch. This rule lasted only a year. [10.09]

~ 1940 ~

— A batter is no longer credited with a sacrifice fly. [10.09]

— The pitcher is permitted to take two steps—one forward, one backward—as long as his pivot foot remains in contact with the rubber at all times. [8.01]

— It is a balk if a pitcher throws or fakes a throw to an unoccupied base. [8.02]

— The umpire assumes authority over trainers. [9.01e]

~ 1945 ~

— A player must have at least four hundred at-bats to qualify as the league leader in Batting Average or Slugging Average. [10.23]

~ 1947 ~

— Six umpires are hired to work in the World Series, all of them on the field.

~ 1949 ~

— On December 21 the "new" rules are issued. There are no major changes, but many ambiguities are eliminated, and they are recodified into the ten sections we have today.

~ 1950 ~

— An umpire may no longer levy fines. That job is reserved for the league president.

— The pitcher's mound must be fifteen inches above the level of the base lines. [1.07]

— A player must play in at least two-thirds of his team's scheduled games to qualify as the league leader in Batting Average or Slugging Average. [10.23]

~ 1951 ~

— A pitcher must pitch a total of at least one inning for every scheduled game to qualify as the league leader in the categories of Earned Run Average or Fielding Average. (Before this, he had to pitch at least ten complete games and at least one hundred innings.) [10.23]

— A player must have at least four hundred at-bats to qualify as the league leader in Batting Average or Slugging Average. However, if there is any player with fewer than the required number of times at bat whose average would be the highest if he were charged with this required at-bat total, then he shall be recognized as the league leader. [10.23]

~ 1952 ~

— Four umpires to a regular game becomes standard practice.

~ 1954 ~

— A batter is credited with a sacrifice fly and not charged with a time at bat if he hits a fly ball and the runner scores on the catch. [10.09]
— Offensive players are required to "carry all gloves and other equipment off the field . . . while their team is at bat." [3.14]
— The bat may be made of two or more pieces of wood laminated together. [1.10]

~ 1955 ~

— The 1951 rule is repealed. A player must have at least four hundred at-bats, period, to qualify as the league leader in Batting Average or Slugging Average. [10.23]
— When a base is occupied, a pitcher must deliver the pitch within twenty seconds of receiving it from the catcher. If he fails to do so, the umpire may call a ball. [8.04]

~ 1956 ~

— A base runner who interferes with a batted ball in order to break up a double play is to be declared out, as is the batter. [7.08h]

~ 1957 ~

— A player must have a total of at least 3.1 plate appearances for every scheduled game to qualify as the league leader in Batting Average or Slugging Average. [10.23]

~ 1959 ~

— Minimum fence distances are established for new ballpark construction. [1.04]

~ 1962 ~

— Oversized gloves are banned for use by pitchers, infielders, and outfielders. [1.14 and 1.15]

— Batters may apply a grip-improving substance to the bat, though not beyond eighteen inches of its length beginning at the handle. [1.10]

~ 1967 ~

— A player must have a total of at least 3.1 plate appearances for every scheduled game to qualify as the league leader in Batting Average or Slugging Average. However, if there is any player with fewer than the required number of plate appearances whose average would be highest if he were charged with this required number of appearances, then the player shall be recognized as the league leader in Batting or Slugging Average. [10.23]

~ 1968 ~

— The pitcher's mound is lowered to ten inches above home plate and the base lines, where it remains today. [1.07]
— If a pitcher "goes to his mouth" with men on base, a balk is declared. If the bases are empty, a ball is called. [8.02]

~ 1969 ~

— Runs are earned by a relief pitcher who enters the game in the middle of an inning as if he entered the game at the beginning of the inning. [10.18]
— The category of Saves is added to baseball statistics. [10.20]

~ 1971 ~

— All major league players must wear protective helmets at bat. [1.16]

~ 1973 ~

— The year of the DH. The American League votes to accept the designated hitter rule on a three-year experimental basis. The National League votes against it. [6.10]
— A reliever is credited with a save for "protecting" a lead. [10.20]

~ 1974 ~

— The save rule is amended slightly; no save is to be credited to a pitcher unless the tying run was on base or at the plate or unless he pitched three effective innings. (Before this a reliever was given a save if he maintained the lead, no matter what the score when he arrived.) [10.20]

— Umpires may declare illegal pitches without any physical evidence. If they think that the motion of the ball indicates that the pitcher is throwing a spitter or a defaced ball, they may issue a warning and, if it happens a second time, eject a pitcher from the game. [8.02]

~ 1975 ~

— The ball may be covered with cowhide as well as horsehide. [1.09]
— Cupped bats are allowed. [1.10]
— The save is refined once more; if the tying run is on deck, a pitcher is credited with a save. [10 20]

~ 1976 ~

— The American League accepts the DH as a permanent part of the rules. The National League reaffirms its opposition. [6.10]

~ 1978 ~

— A pitcher's ERA is to be calculated henceforth with fractions of innings pitched rather than with full innings. [10.22]

~ 1983 ~

— A pitcher who pitches only a third of an inning in a season will not have his ERA rounded off. His total for innings pitched will be carried as one third. [10.22]

~ 1988 ~

— Protective helmets are mandatory for catchers. [1.16d]

~ 1989 ~

— The "game-winning RBI" (previously credited to a batter who gave his club "the lead it never relinquished") is eliminated as an official statistic. [10.04e]

INDEX

About the Authors

Hugh Howard is the author of *The Preservationist's Progress*, the forthcoming *Wright for Wright*, and numerous other books.

Kathleen Moloney, a freelance writer living in Manhattan, has written books about business, etiquette, and ventriloquism, among other topics. Her latest book is *It's Nobody's Fault: New Help for Troubled Children*.

Glen Waggoner, baseball editor of *ESPN: The Magazine*, is the coauthor of Jim Flick's *On Golf*, among other books. He lives in New York City.